New North Church:
From Birth to Death in Early Boston

by

Charles Chauncey Wells

Steven Fanning

Chauncey Park Press

Oak Park, Illinois

New North Church:

From Birth to Death in Early Boston

Charles Chauney Wells and Steven Fanning, Ph.D.

©2014 Chauncey Park Press - 2nd Edition

Designed by Suzanne Austin Wells
Chauncey Park Press
735 N. Grove Avenue
Oak Park, Illinois 60302
chauncey@wells1.com

Cover photo by Erin Ryan Lordan, Oak Park, Illinois

Printed in the United States of America
Library of Congress Control Number: 2014910897
ISBN: 9780966780888

New North Church — Puritan — Congregational — Unitarian
Boston History 1712-1870

MINISTERS OF NEW NORTH CHURCH

John Webb, settled 20 Oct. 1714,
died 16 April 1750

Peter Thacher, settled 28 Jan 1720, died 1738 (1738/9), age 61.

Andrew Eliot, settled 14 April 1742, died 13 Sept 1772, age 59.

John Eliot, settled 3 Nov. 1779,
died 14 Feb 1813, age 59.

Francis Parkman, settled 8 Dec. 1813,
resigned 1849, died 11 Nov. 1852

Amos Smith, settled as colleague, 7 Dec., 1842, resigned 1848.

Joshua Young, settled in 1849, resigned in 1852.

Arthur Buckminster Fuller,
settled in 1853, resigned in 1859.

William Rounseville Alger, 1857,
Bulfinch St. Church: resigned in 1868.

TABLE OF CONTENTS

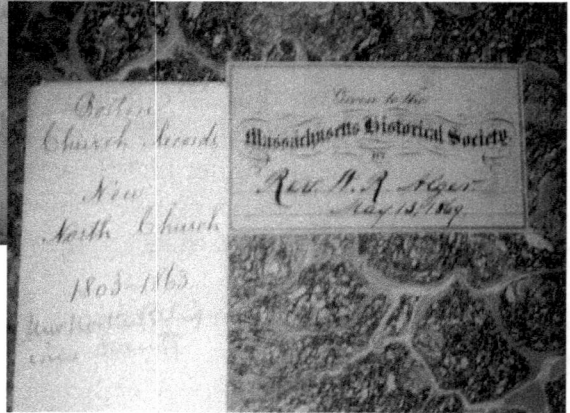

INTRODUCTION

After 300 years, why this book?

New North Church offers us a perfect window into the evolution in social and religious thought in Boston and those who sprang from it. It takes us from about 60 years before the American Revolution to just before the Civil War.

Today we would view early Puritanism as a religious cult, people totally devoted to religion. Indeed the "city upon a hill" that John Winthrop preached was a theocracy, although a somewhat democratic one. Nearly everything revolved around religion and worship.

This then evolves into Congregationalism, much more moderate, easier to practice, and perhaps more to what Christ himself might like to see in his followers. Then in Boston Congregationalism evolves into Unitarianism with its ultimate freedom to interpret God and Christ as one's conscience dictated. Later offshoots from this are Christian Science and the Transcendental Movement.

This is also a time when nearly all of the people were English-Americans and that is why they called the place "New England." Then come the French Protestant Huguenots who gave us citizens like Paul Revere, the African Americans, some free, but mostly originally slave, and then the onslaughts of the Irish, the dispossessed Jews, and the Italians. Out of this salad bowl comes what we today know as Boston. No longer does Boston send people out to populate America, but many more are now flowing back for better economic, social, and educational opportunities. We see this especially in today's colleges and universities, music education, high tech development, and a huge medical industry--all making the new New England.

The period from 1713 – 1864 is the perfect time to picture the beginning of these important changes in society. While we may decry the excesses of Puritanism and its intolerance, we do have to admire the fact that its intolerance was the seed of the abolitionist movement to stamp out the curse of slavery in America.

Samuel Adams, whom some call "the last Puritan," said "a slave cannot live in my house," when someone wanted to give him a black woman for a servant. He did accept her as someone to live and work in his house, but as a free person, not as a slave. Most New North Church members began to see the logic in his thinking even though they still thought African Americans should sit up in the balcony.

Strangely, we see Prince Hall, black abolitionist and founder of Prince Hall Freemasonry, continue his membership when he could have joined other African American churches. We see both white Boston leaders along with trades people and artisans all worshiping together until the North End became a slum and they moved to other churches and neighborhoods. We see then the end of Near North Church as a congregation.

Enjoy this important bit of history and be thankful that you can be on this side of history and did not have to live it then.

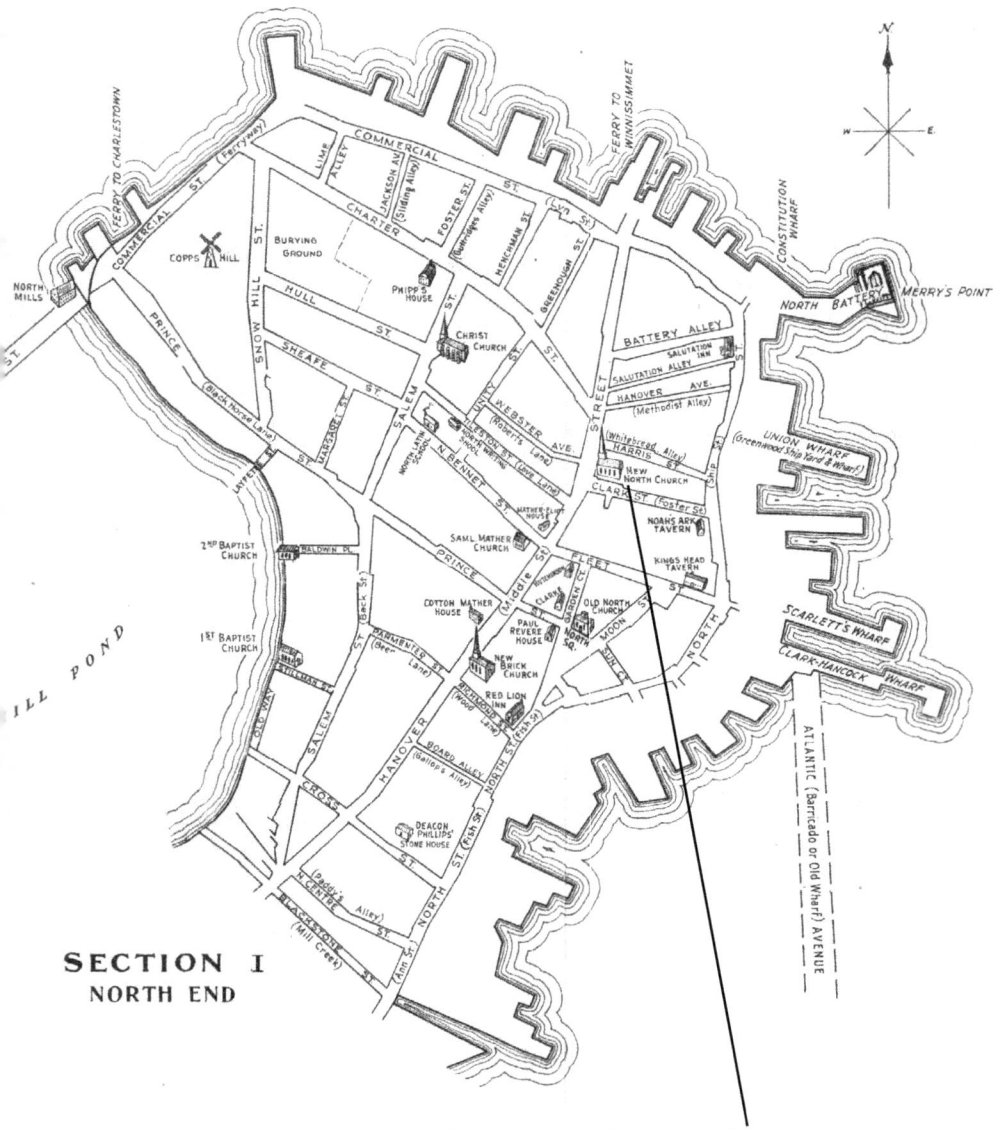

SECTION I
NORTH END

New North Church, located at Hanover and Clark.
This map is taken from *Crooked and Narrow Streets of
Boston* and shows all the churches of the North End in
1810. The church building still stands today.

CHAPTER 1

NEW NORTH BEGINS AS A PURITAN CHURCH

During its 150-year history, New North or 5th Church became one of Boston's largest and had one of the most interesting histories of any church in the city. This is because of how it was founded and the many interesting people that attended its services from 1713 to its closing in 1863.

New North began as a Puritan church, the movement that sought to purify and simplify the Church of England, and was the same as nearly every other church in early Boston since the town's founding in 1630. The church evolved into a Congregational congregation, which still accepted the Trinity (Father, Son and Holy Spirit as distinctly separate, but united in one Godhead), but whose rules made church membership much easier. Then its members embraced Unitarianism with its even more simplified doctrines.

It was always located in the Boston's North End, that bustling part of Boston dominated by wharves, shipyards, ship suppliers, warehouses, and farther up the hill the homes of the owners and workers in these businesses. At that time, it was a cosmopolitan place, where all economic groups lived together, some with larger and better houses and some with more modest dwellings. Some had slaves, who lived with them in their homes, but owning slaves was limited to the wealthy and some Puritans even at that time would have no part of slavery. Most families were British-American with a few French Huguenots like the Reveres and Juliens living there. It was only later that the Irish, Jews, and the Italians would come to live here as the more successful original inhabitants left for better Boston neighborhoods.

In Boston of that day, a person was valued for what he contributed to society. Good works and Puritanism worked hand in hand. While you could never earn your way into heaven by doing good works as the Catholics believed, it was certain you could never make it in without doing them. Puritans believed in the damnation of hell and they were always aware of that, but most also believed they could be saved by the Grace of God. So all men were expected to support the church, help the poor, and be active churchmen. Women ran a Godly and tidy household, reared many children, and helped their families and neighbors. This carried over into civic duty being a virtue where nearly every man served in some job or post in the town government and made it function.

New North Branches Off

In 1712, 17 "substantial mechanics" or craftsmen petitioned their pastor, The Rev. Cotton Mather, and the ruling elders of Old North Church to form another congregation. This does not seem to stem from problems within the congregation or with the Rev. Mather, but rather the desire to form another neighborhood church and expand the faith.

Cotton Mather

Bostonians liked to attend church within walking distance of their homes. They spent most of the day on Sunday in church. They would go to Sunday morning services, which had long prayers and long sermons, then go home for lunch and return at 2 for more services the rest of the day. For many, there was also the Thursday afternoon lecture, which merchants and craftsman left their work to attend. Indeed church attendance was mandatory and you were fined if you were missing. Children attended with adults and were made to behave and not be disruptive. Boys especially were singled out, sat together, and were disciplined often. For many like Benjamin Franklin, who could not remember when he could not read, the Bible was their first reading material.

The Old North Church (2ⁿᵈ Church) from which the New North grew is not to be confused with what today we call the "Old North Church," which is actually Christ Episcopal Church on Salem Street. The original Old North Church at North Square was Puritan and is known for its famous pastors: Increase, Cotton and Samuel Mather, who served 1664-1741. With Paul Revere as a member, it was considered a hotbed of Revolutionary fervor and was torn down for firewood by the British. Others churches like New North at North and Clark Streets supplanted it.

The fact that the New North Church was formed by North End craftsmen is significant and shows the growing power of the working classes of Boston over the upper classes of government officials and those in high church positions. Some of those forming the church included Matthew Butler and John Goldwaith, both brick masons; John Dixwell, goldsmith; Eramus Stevens, carpenter; Caleb Lyman, shopkeeper, civic leader and soldier and later deacon; Joshua Cheever, merchant and deacon in 1720 and elder in 1736; and Samuel Holden, the oldest man in Boston when he died in 1793.**

Boston craftsmen earned more and lived better than their English counterparts. They had better wages, charged more for their goods, and were respected and not looked down upon because they were shopkeepers or worked with their hands. This is described in an Ancient & Honorable Artillery Company biography of Lemuel Gardner, cooper or barrel maker:

"He lived at a time of prosperity among mechanics (craftsmen) in Boston, who earning their money easily, lived generously. He belonged to a set, very hospitable, whose sideboards were loaded with plate, and who brought up their families in expensive style. They were enterprising, ready to promote all public improvements, firm friends, carried a great sway in public, sang good songs and seldom had a heavy heart or felt want."

**Other craftsman forming the church included James Barnard, Ebenezer Clough, Samuel Gardner, John Goff, William Parkman, Isaac and Moses Pierce, Alexander Sears, and Solomon and Elias Townsend, all names of families that will become prominent in Boston history.

Bostonian craftsmen lived this way until Dec. 16, 1773, when the Destruction of the Tea, or Boston Tea Party, occurred. George III in retaliation closed the Port of Boston and this resulted in the decline of shipping and trade upon which the city heavily depended. Boston and the North End lost population and were much poorer after the American Revolution. However, for those earlier years, the New North Church prospered as its members prospered.

Some North End Occupations

Chandler: Candlemaker (Benjamin Franklin's father's occupation)
Ship Chandler: Merchant who sells ship supplies
Cooper: Barrel maker (goods were shipped in wooden barrels)
Coppersmith: Maker of cooking utensils and other copper items.
Cordwainer: Shoemaker (after cordovan leather from Cordova,
        Spain)
Docker: Stevedore or unloader of ships
Fuller: Cloth finisher
Mastmaker: Maker and installer of ship's masts
Pump & Block Maker: Pump maker & carver of block & tackles
        for lifting cargos
Ropemaker: Wove ropes and assembled them in ropewalks
Sailmaker: Maker of canvass sails to power the ships
Truckman: Horse & wagon deliveryman
Warfinger: Wharf owner
Vulcan: Blacksmith
Yeoman: Ship's clerk

There were eight shipyards in the North End in 1810.

New North Church officially began in the winter of 1712 when 17 mechanics gathered to discuss forming another church. On April 10, 1712, they petitioned the Rev. Cotton Mather and the Old North Church elders to form the new neighborhood church. Then they moved ahead and purchased land from Thomas Hutchinson and in 1713 built a small wooden meeting house with a flat roof at the corner of Hanover and Clarke Streets. As one historian said: they were "unassisted by the more wealthy part of the community except for their prayers and good wishes."

Old North still had considerable influence in the new church's establishment because the three deacons originally selected were objected to by Cotton Mather. He was not willing to lose them and so three others including Capt. Caleb Lyman, shopkeeper and prominent civic leader and militia officer, were selected to lead the congregation.

John Webb, First Pastor

On May 5, 1714, the elders and church members met and signed the Covenant establishing the New North Church. On Aug. 2, they met and elected the Rev. John Webb as pastor. A graduate of Harvard College, he was installed as New North's first minister on Oct. 20, 1714 and served 36 years until he died April 16, 1750, at age 62. Next they ordained Ruling Elders and Deacons as leaders and managers of church affairs.

Samuel Drake in his *The History & Antiquities of Boston (1630-1770)* gives us special insight into how intensely religious Puritans were. Up to the mid-1750s, Church discipline was extremely important and, after this time, it was gradually relaxed, he relates.

"Unfortunates, male or female, who had committed errors were obliged to confess them before the whole congregation, however peculiar those errors might be. Females, under certain accusations, were obligated to stand up with a white robe or sheet before them, while the Minister read aloud their confession.

Sex before marriage and sex outside of marriage held special outrage. One unfortunate couple (not New North members) had a child born at 8 months instead of 9. Some ridiculed couples in these situations, saying they had "sat down to meat before grace." They were forced to stand before the congregation and confess and be fined. Fortunately as time went on, fewer couples were subjected this insult and it was often ignored even though it is estimated that up to 17% of the couples were pregnant before marriage.

Church minutes of April 20, 1729, show Alice Potter, a sister of the church, being suspended for fornication. Later in 1730, Jeremy Barton, brother of the church, is cited for drunkenness and lying, but, making a public and penitent confession, is restored to the church. His alcohol problem continues and he is again cited and restored in January 1740. Alice Gilbert is suspended from Communion of the Lord's Supper for fornication, but is restored several months later upon public confession.

Numerous such examples populate the early records. The offenses are publicly presented and voted on by the members for suspension and then upon confession, readmitted to the church. Amendment of life is the goal of these early procedures and they were deeply felt by church members themselves and known by people outside the community. They were a social disgrace and public pressure forced the members to change their ways or be further ostracized.

Later, the church moves to identify and punish deviations from the established doctrines and beliefs. Aug. 9, 1742, Charles Coffin is suspended for profanely disturbing two religious meetings. "That Brother Elnathan Agery be suspended and publicly admonished for open apostasy (rejection of one's religion) after a noted profession of his religion. Brother William Warman and Sister Ruth Jempson each for said apostasy and Sister Sarah Norton of slanderously describing her husband."

After about 1750, such brethren and sisters who should fall into scandal were allowed to confess to the church members after the main body of the congregation had been dismissed.

There are a few more entries about conduct, but after 1770 the church does not concern itself officially with publicly shaming or publicly identifying sins of its individual members.

April 17, 1758: Church minutes: "There has been for a long time a separation between Israel Hearsey and his wife Tabitha Hearsey, both of them members of this church. The church, taking the same into consideration, voted to appoint a committee to enquire into the matters of difference between them and also into any other matter of complaint against them or either of them and to make report at the next meeting."

May 12, 1758: #1 Voted that Mrs. Tabitha Hearsey has not exposed herself to any censure for her separation from her husband.

#2 Voted that our Brother Israel Hearsey be suspended from our communion on account of his scandalous behavior.

Huge Split in Church

One significant event in New North Church history is still notable today for its rancor and divisiveness. To understand this, one must first understand the bonds between Puritan pastors and their congregations. Many Puritans in England left for Boston and New England when their pastors either decided to migrate or were forced to do by Archbishop William Laud and his repressive measures against them. Pastors served congregations until they were either dismissed or when they retired or died as Mr. Webb did.

New North Church grew so rapidly it needed another pastor. The Rev. Peter Thacher, a brilliant and eloquent preacher, was elected after an especially heated and rancorous meeting. He had been serving the church in Weymouth, MA, for eight years and it was highly unusual to pick a currently serving pastor from another church. Some saw it as a case of a wealthy church poaching upon a poorer church for talent.

"Many of the congregation began to manifest signs of

disapprobation, founded upon the conviction that it was not right for a wealthier society to entice away from a poorer their minister," wrote one church historian.

"Weymouth, in God's sight, is as precious as Boston, and the souls there are of as great a worth as the souls here.

"And to the common objection, that it is a pity that Mr. Thacher, being so bright a light, should smoke out his days in so much obscurity, we answer:

First, bright lights shine brightest in the darkest places; and,

Secondly, bright lights are the obscurer of burning in a room where there are more, and as bright," referring to the large number of brilliant preachers in Boston.

Where there was harmony and peace before, there was intense anger and rebellion now. At a meeting to decide the issue, Ephraim Eliot in his tract published in 1822 discloses:

"The house was nearly filled with a multitude, among whom was a number of aggrieved persons. They began to raise a clamor and sent for the posse (dissidents) at Squire Lee's; who in a tumultuous manner ran to the meeting house, fought their way into the galleries and in a menacing style forbade the proceedings.

"Some of the more unruly and indecent actually scattered their water from the galleries upon the people below." Some years later, a female member said that it was liquor that rained down and that it ruined her outfit.

Several members of the Weymouth church produced statements that Peter Thacher had broken his promise in leaving them. At a meeting of Boston ministers, including Increase and Cotton Mather, the group heard the statements, but nonetheless voted to allow Peter Thatcher to take his position on Jan. 27, 1723, as John Webb's associate. He was a grandson of Thomas Thacher, the first minister of South Church, Boston, and not to be confused with another Boston divine, also named Peter Thatcher. He continued here until he died Feb. 26, 1738, age 61.

But the rancor did not end there. The opposing members

walked out and immediately formed The New Brick Church, which they called unofficially "Revenge Church of Jesus Christ." When they erected their meeting house in May of 1721, its leaders placed a rooster or cock as a weather vane atop its steeple.

"NEW BRICK CHURCH
THE COCKEREL CHURCH"
1721 — 1844
ON THIS SITE STOOD THE MEETING HOUSE ERECTED IN 1721. THE SOCIETY UNITED WITH THAT OF THE SECOND CHURCH IN 1779 TAKING ITS NAME. THE NEW BUILDING ERECTED IN 1845 WAS SOLD TO THE METHODISTS IN 1849.

Samuel Drake in his Boston history relates:

"Yet their zeal was great indeed, and descended to puerility. They placed a figure of a *Cock* as vane upon the steeple, out of derision of Mr. Thacher, whose Christian name was *Peter.* Taking advantage of a wind which turned the head of the Cock towards the New North when it was placed upon the spindle, a merry fellow straddled over it and crowed three times to complete the ceremony. Remarks are unnecessary."

Others saw it as a symbol of Peter denying Christ. Shem Drowe carved the weathervane in his shop and it later was placed over 1st Church in Cambridge. He later made the grasshopper weathervane that graced Faneuil Hall.

New Brick settled the Rev. William Waldron as its pastor and developed as the third Puritan church on the North End and existed until 1779.

Leading Dissidents forming New Brick were William Arnold, Daniel Ballard, James Barnes, Ebenezer Bridge, Samuel Burnell, Thomas Dogget, Benjamin Edwards, James Halsey, Owen Harris, Nathaniel Jarvis, Pelatiah Kinsman, Thomas Lee, Ephraim Moore (Mower), Thaddeus Macarty, Jonathan Mountfort, Robert Oring, Peter Papillon, Francis Parnell, James Pecker, Edward or Wm. Pell, Alexander Sears, James Tileston, Solomon Townsend, and John Waldo. It is significant that a number of them were instrumental in forming New North in 1714.

"The (New North) Society suffered a very considerable loss in numbers and in property, but it was soon repaired, as Mr. Thacher and Mr. Webb were very popular preachers, and greatly beloved. This matter has been minutely narrated as it is one of the most singular transactions in the history of the New England churches," another history related.

On the night the Rev. Mr. Thacher died, there was a tremendous storm, with thunder and lightning.

The next morning, a church member saw one of his friends and asked him if he knew that Parson Thacher was dead "No, when did he die?"

"In the midst of the storm," he answered.

"Well," said his friend, "he went off with as much noise as he came."

CHAPTER 2

New North Becomes Congregational

In 1730, New North enlarged and improved its building. It performed the first Boston church baptism of an African-American infant in 1750. And in 1770, it began baptizing adopted children, another first for a Boston church.

In 1734, America's first "Great Religious Awakening" began with the Rev. Jonathan Edwards at his church in Northampton, MA. That died down and then sprang up and spread like wildfire as the Rev. George Whitefield, a Church of England then Methodist preacher in Georgia preached all along the Atlantic seaboard. Both of them in their preaching had strong emotional appeals and thousands turned out to hear first Edwards and then Whitefield in Boston churches. On Mon., Sept. 22, 1740, Mr. Webb invited Whitefield to New North Church where 6,000 packed the place, flowing out through the doorways. Most Boston pastors were pleased to have so many enthusiastic members packing their meeting houses.

Top picture, Jonathan Edwards,
Bottom: George Whitefield

New North used the Bay Psalm Book from its beginning in 1713 until 1755 and then used Tate and Brady's version of the Psalms. About this time, the practice of reading and singing the psalms, line by line, alternately, was abolished or discontinued. In 1747, portions of the Scriptures began to be read between the first prayer and the singing before the sermon. Music and a choral society were added.

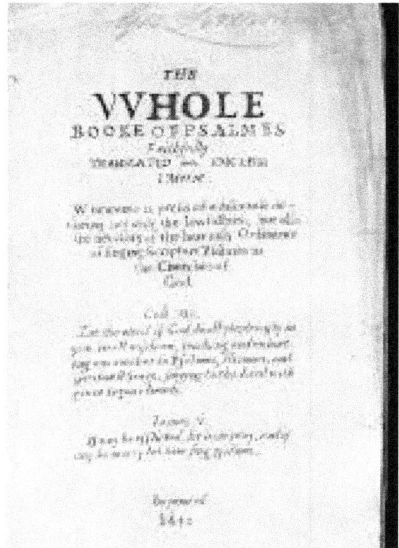

*Bay Psalm Book**

One of the difficulties in church growth was requiring a public confession that one had had a personal religious experience. To be a full member, the person had to stand up and tell about this before everyone. Church minutes of May 16, 1773, show a change in this:

"Whereas it hath been the practice of this church, when anyone hath been admitted to full communion to demand a Relation of Experiences. Which practice hath been sometimes attended with inconveniences and as there is no particular direction for this practice in the Word of God. . . .

"Voted that for the future, it be left to the choice of the person to be admitted, whether to make such a Relation or only to make a public profession of Christianity by assenting to the Covenant in use in this Church."

During difficult times, special days of "Fasting and Prayer" were celebrated. One such was Thur., July 14,1774, on "account of the difficulties of the present day." Following the Boston Tea Party on Dec. 16, 1773, King George III closed the port of Boston and dissolved the local government. This left many workers jobless and many merchants hurt because they could not get goods to sell, so this was a very difficult time for Boston economically.

**Bay Psalm Book was printed in Cambridge in 1640 and is considered to be the first book printed in America. It sold in Nov., 2014, for $14.2 million as one of two owned by Old South Church, Boston. New North replaced it in 1755 with a more poetic translation.

The Covenant at New North Church

This Covenant, used from about 1740 to about 1810, was given those admitted to the Sacrament of the Lord's Supper and to those who applied for Baptism for themselves or their children.

You do now, in the presence of the great God, his elect angels, and this Christian assembly, profess your belief in the Holy Scriptures; that they were given by the inspiration of God, and are the only sufficient rule of faith and practice.

You believe in Jesus Christ as the eternal Son of God, the only Mediator between God and man—the Lord and Head of his church. Sensible of your need of a Savior, your own proneness to sin and inability to that which is good, you look up to him, and receive him in all those characters and offices with which he is vested for the benefit of the children of men.

You believe the Holy Spirit to be the author of every good in the mind of man—the Leader, the Sanctifier and Comforter of his people.

You give yourself up to God in an everlasting covenant, never to be forgotten, to be for him and him only—to love, serve and obey him forever.

You submit yourself to the discipline which Christ has established in his Church, and as practiced by the people of God in this place.

You promise often to think of your obligations to come up to the table of the Lord, and that you will seek to have such difficulties removed as now prevent your approach to that holy ordinance.

Do you thus profess and promise?

Pew Rent Support

New North, like churches today, was supported by voluntary contributions. Members sat in *pews,* or long bench-like seats, and they paid monthly or yearly "pew rent" according to the pew's location. Congregants made their contributions in the following manner:

"At the stated time, Deacons stood up in their seats with boxes to receive the money and the congregation, or such of them as had anything to give, came out of their pews, passed around in an established order before the Deacons, and made their deposits for the Ministers. This mode of maintaining them was abolished in 1749, and that of assessments on pews adopted instead," Ephraim Eliot in his New North History in the *Eliot Family Papers* relates. In the early times, there was a "church tax," or portion of the real estate tax that went to support the church. That was discontinued here, but the practice continues to this day in England.

The beloved schoolmaster John Tileston (1735-1826) earned about 100 pounds per year, or about $ 21,000 in today's money. From his accounts, we learn his monthly contribution beginning in 1763 to be from 13 pence to 9 shillings or $ 11.35 to $ 94.00 monthly or from $136.00 to $1,128.00 yearly. Then he also paid yearly pew rent in the years 1768-1774 ranging from $ 95.00 in 1768 to $543.00 in 1774. He was a generous parishioner when you consider his income, but most Congregationalists tended to be generous in supporting their church and pastors.

New North Church continued to grow and by 1775, it had the largest congregation in Boston. It conducted services all through the Revolutionary War. Pastors from the other churches fled to the countryside or if they were Anglican fled to Canada.

Doctrinally, the 70-year period of father and son Andrew and John Eliot can be called New North's "Congregational Period," 1742 - 1813. This was a more liberal time with less church interference in people's lives and more emphasis on the "saving grace of God," rather than the "fiery pits of hell" concept of God's righteousness. This is not to say it was anything like today's liberal churches in its discipline and expectation of its parishioners. It was still extremely strict by modern standards.

Ephraim Eliot relates this liberalization under the Eliots:

"Until the settlement of the Rev. Eliot, Church discipline had been exercised with a pretty liberal hand. The crying sins were intemperance, fornication, scandal and contempt of the church with disturbances in the religious assemblies. Many were suspended, and many were again restored to charity and communion upon confession and repentance. In some cases, excommunication was resorted to," he wrote.

Then we see this public shaming suspended and the church community worries about other things. "Whereas several of our number have absented themselves from our communion and in particular Jonathan Dakin and Margaret Webber have gone over to the communion of the Church of England. John Gooding and Sarah Christie have renounced their infant baptism and joined themselves to the Baptists, voted that the church no longer look upon these persons as members, but regard themselves free from that," Church minutes June, 1747.

Because of their powerful preaching and their outreach into the North End community, the Eliots continued to build the church and its numbers increased. Bostonians especially admired that Andrew Eliot did not leave Boston as many ministers did during the Revolution and conducted regular services at the church.

Andrew Eliot Becomes Minister

Andrew Eliot (1718-1778), a Harvard College graduate in 1737, had become a colleague pastor with John Webb on April 14, 1742. He was popular and succeeded Dr. Webb when he died in 1750. He served faithfully and well until the Siege of Boston, which threw him into a deep depression.

In a letter to his son Andrew on April 23, 1775, he said:

"My Dear Son, I know not what to do, nor where to go. At present, I think to tarry in Boston. Whether ever I shall have the pleasure of seeing you, God only knows . . .most of the meeting houses shut up, the ministers gone, our congregations crowded with strangers. A town meeting in the forenoon agreed to give up their arms, in order to get leave to depart . . . This town a garrison: every face gathering paleness; all hurry and confusion; one going this way, another that; others not knowing where to go."

Ephraim Eliot describes the Rev. Eliot's condition as:

"The distress of his native town, the destruction of a considerable part of it, absence from his tender connections (his family went to the countryside), produced an evident alteration is his health and in his disposition.

"He became timid and despondent. He would sometimes console himself with the belief that the time of his confinement was the most useful part of his life. His countenance in the town certainly afforded great satisfaction and comfort to many who were confined with him and they spoke of it with the greatest gratefulness. A considerable number of them sat under his preaching so long as he lived," he concludes.

His last public appearance was in June 1778 and he died Sept. 13, 1778, age 60, after 36 years as chief pastor.

Dr. Ebenezer Wright served in the interim, but a number of candidates were called to preach to see who might be a likely choice. Although he did not actively solicit it, the Rev. John Eliot, Andrew's son, was finally selected to succeed his father.

"The ministry of the two Doctors Eliot comprised a term of 70 years. No root of bitterness sprang up, no discord prevailed. The affairs of the society went on like those of a well regulated family. The pastors were happy in the affections of their people and the people were contented under their ministrations. During the life of Dr. Andrew Eliot, very little alteration took place; son succeeded to father," a New North Church history relates.

"It was different during the life of Dr. John Eliot. When Rev. Mr. Gair was installed (1785) over the 2nd Baptist Church, which, until that time, had been a very small assembly, a sudden blaze was enkindled by him and Mr. Stillman, which seemed to enlighten great numbers of people, especially young girls and lads, many of whom left the New North."

Also in 1785 the Universal church began, followed shortly by John Murray and the Methodists opening their first chapel, where their doctrines were preached with zeal and enthusiasm, the history relates.

"These all had their places of worship in a close neighborhood with the New North, and drew off numbers from it, principally from the galleries, which have never been so well filled since. When the Rev. Peter Thacher (not Peter Thacher of the infamous 1723 controversy) was removed from Maiden to Brattle Street Church in Boston, some of the very friends who had been most influential in persuading Mr. John Eliot to take the place of his father, quitted his preaching and joined that society.

"This was the most unkind stroke of all," and he felt it as long as he lived. However, the seats were soon filled again, and it continued a very large congregation until his death.

New Bulfinch Designed Church

By 1800, the meeting house building had become old fashioned and, being made entirely of wood, was a fire hazard. A new building made of brick was in order. The old meeting house was demolished in 1802 and a new brick one, designed by Charles Bulfinch in the Early Republic style and seating 1,000, was built on the site. It was dedicated May 2, 1804, 90 years from the dedication of the first meeting house.

In 1805 a 1,300 lb. bell, cast by the Paul Revere Foundry and costing $800, was installed in the belfry. This building, moved back 12 feet and raised, then restored basically to its original form in 1965, continues to this day as St. Stephen's Roman Catholic Church. The only other church building surviving from that time on the North End is Christ Episcopal, which we now call the "Old North Church" on Salem Street just two blocks away.

As the years progressed, the North End was becoming less popular as a residential area. Ephraim Eliot says it in this way:

"The young gentlemen, who have married wives in other parts of the town, have found it difficult to persuade them to become so ungenteel as to attend worship at the North End; while the ladies of our church, as they have become wives, consider it a mark of taste to change their minister.

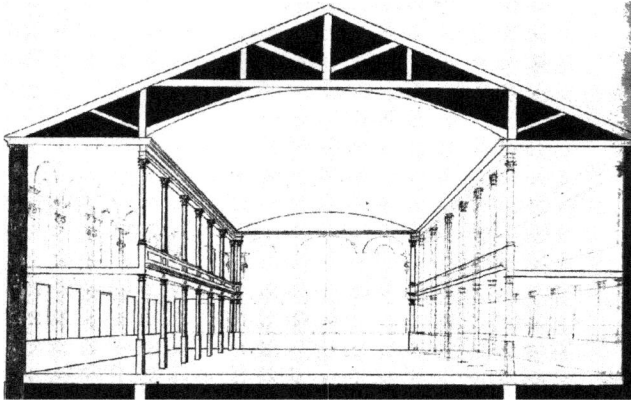

Original architectural drawing of New North Church

"Even the clergymen have abandoned that part of the town. There are six large congregations north of the canal which divides the town, and only one of their ministers resides there," he wrote.

Both Andrew and John Eliot retained their flock by living there, by entertaining both their parishioners and those outside the congregation on Sunday nights in their home, and by freely associating with their neighbors throughout the week. They did not just talk religion, they talked politics and the issues of the day in these social events.

"In some respects these men were very much alike. Methodical in their arrangement of time, they were both able to devote much to the interest of the societies to which they belonged, without interfering with the duties of their station as ministers of the gospel; and while respectively members of the corporation of Harvard University, they each devoted themselves to its concerns."

Ministry of John Eliot

"As a theologian, Dr. John Eliot took the Bible as his guide, in the light it was presented to his own mind. Good men he loved and associated with, although they differed from him in sentiment, and excluded none from his pulpit on that account.

"For this he has received severe reprimands from some of his brethren in the clerical profession: Once in particular, for inviting Mr. Hill, an amiable man, to preach for him, who belonged to the church called the church of New Jerusalem.

"He also gave offence by walking as a pall holder at the funeral of Mr. Jane, a Methodist minister in his neighborhood.

Rev. John Eliot, Oil on canvas by Samuel King, 1779, Massachusetts Historical Society, Boston. He was one of the founders of the Massachusetts Historical Society.

His friendship with Mr. John Murray, of the Universal church, was frowned upon. He was indeed a liberal Christian in the true sense of the word, no sense of bigotry or intolerance.

He supported the election of Mr. Hollis, professor of divinity at Harvard University, Ephraim Eliot wrote. He was convinced he was the best candidate and as Mr. Hollis, who founded the professorship of divinity and was both a Calvinist and a Baptist, did not require that the office should be confined to a belief of any particular dogma.

"He was a Trinitarian. The covenant of the New North church was a Trinitarian covenant, drawn up by his father. An assent to this was strictly required of all who were admitted into his church, or were baptized there; and also of those who applied to have the ordinance of baptism administered to their children.

"As he lived, so he died, calm and composed to the last; only concerned lest his patience should not hold out under the extreme pain which he suffered," and he told his friend Dr. Lathrop when asked if he was prepared to die, "I know where I have placed my hopes, and there I am contented to rest."

John Eliot died Feb. 14, 1813, age 60, greatly lamented, after 34 years as pastor.

Pew Diagram for 1813

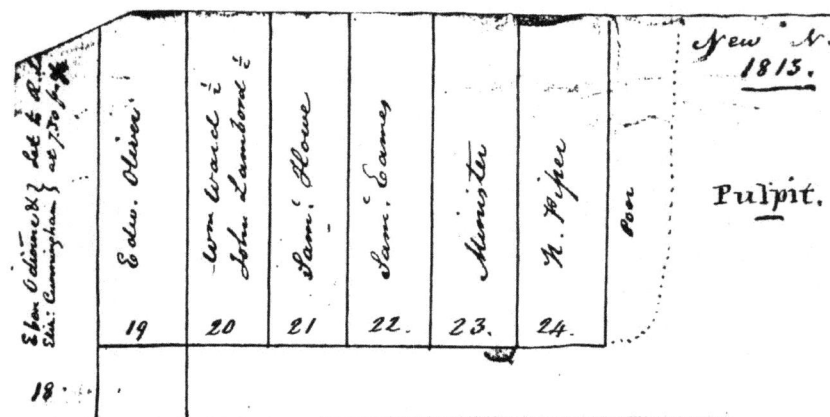

New N.
1813.

Pulpit.

Eben Odlinne & Stec Cunningham lot 6 R at 730 Ft	Edw. Oliver	Wm Ward & John Lambord	Saml Howe	Saml Eames	Minister	H. Piper	Poor
	19	20	21	22.	23.	24	

18

Left column	#			#	Center	Right	#
Jepson	17		97.	Simpkins	J. Emery	96
Webb	16		98.	Tho. Oliver	Kettell	95
Swift	15		99.	Simpkins	A. Stetson J. Edes	94
B. Lincoln	14		100.	McKean	H. Atkins	93
Barnard	13		101.	T. Rogers	Pico	92
B. Clark	12		102.	Wm Palfrey	T. Page	91
B. Varney — S. Norton tenant	11		103.	Jo. Lewis	D. Hastings	90
A. French	10		104.	Cruft & Burrows	Webber	89
Fracker	9		105.	Wm Howe	T. Williams	88
Danacott & Milk	8		106.	Eb. Tufts	Hill & Scott & Clark	87
L. Edes	7		107.	McCleary	J. Webster	86
Eliot { Rumney & Yates	6		108.	Capt. Richmond	A. Cutter	85
Mrs Hudson &c	5		109.	Brown.	Jo: { Dickman	84
Jo: { Chr Lincoln	4		110.	Jo: { Jo: Eustis	Jos { N. Lewis	83
that	3		111.	Socie...	Jos { E. Stearns	82
	2		112.	Soci.	Jo:	81

# of New North Church

Plot map (top) — lots numbered left to right:

25	26	27	28	29	30	31
B. Tilden	Henry Foule	John B. Hammatt	E. Eliot — Capt. Dark — to Satterlee many Capta.	B. Corney, L. Harris	Jos. Austin	J. Tuttle 17 — J. Bird — J. Raynor —

65. Silas Atkins	E. Eliot	64
66. Josiah Vose	Eliot	63
67. N. Goodwin	Dean & Rice	62
68. Tho. Hopkins	T. Tuttle	61
69. B. Barnes	Percival	60
70. N. Goodwin	J. Wells	59
71. Dr. Webster	Coombs	58
72. N. E. Symmes	N. Austin	57
73. E. Hart	D. Green & Oyler.	56
74. N. Faxon	Jo: Francis	55
75. Hutchinson	T. K. Emery	54
76. J. Bray	H. H. Williams	53
77. Knowlton	T. Lillie	52
78. So: { Leach & Parsons him Essty	Soci: { Let to Several	51
79. So. { R. Dawes	Soci:	50
80. So:	Soci: { Jno. Heath & T. Walsh	49

32	Goodwin Avis
33.	Ph: Adams
34.	Ch. Hammatt
35.	Grubb & Dean
36.	B. T. Wells
37.	Tho. Page
38.	U. & S. Welsh
39.	John Fenno
40.	Sam: Tuttle
41.	E. Chamberlin
42.	Jos. Grammar
43.	Curtis & Jones
44.	Tho. Leach
45.	Wm. Hutchins & J. Copen
46.	Tho. Lambord
47.	E. Tufts
48.	Soci: { Let to Sam. Barber

29

Pew Occupants for 1813

Begins on left Side Aisle from Back to Front

1. Missing data
2. Missing data
3. Obscured data
4. New North Pew: Lincoln
5. Mrs. Hudson, etc.
6. Eliot Pew: Rumney, Bates
7. L. Edes
8. Darracott & Milk
9. Fracker
10. A. French
11. B. Varney. S. Baxter, Tenant
12. B. Clark
13. Barnard
14. B. Lincoln
15. Swift
16. Webb
17. Jepson

Front of Church moving across to right

18. Eben. Odionne, Eliza Cunningham (obscured data)
19. Edward Oliver
20. Wm. Ward & John Lombard
21. Samuel Howe
22. Samuel Eames
23. Minister
24. N. Piper

Benches for Poor
Pulpit
Benches for Poor

25. B. Tilden
26. Henry Fowle

27. John B. Hammatt
28. B. Eliot Capt. Doan. Jn Ballister, Worthy Leightner
29. B. Comey, L. Harris
30. Jos. Austin
31. T. Tuttle Jr., J. Bird, J. Rayner

Right Row from Front to Back

32. Goodwin, Avis
33. Ph: Adams
34. Church, Hunnicutt
35. Grubb, Dean
36. Benj. Tuttle Wells
37. Thomas Page
38. W. & S. Welsh
39. John Fenno
40. Samuel Tuttle
41. E. Chamberlin
42. Jos. Graminor
43. Curtis & Long
44. Thomas Leach
45. Wm. Hutchins, let to J. Capen
46. Thomas Lombard
47. E. Tufts
48. Society: Let to Samuel Barber, undecipheralble

SIDE AISLE
Back of Church to Front

49. Society: Ms. Heath, Jn Wahave
50. Society:
51. Society: let to several
52. T. Lillie
53. H. H. Williams
54. T. K. Emery

55. Jn. Francis
56. D. Green & Tyler
57. N. Austin
58. Coombs
59. John Wells
60. Percival
61. Tyrell Tuttle
62. Dean Rice
63. Eliot
64. E. Eliot
65. Silas Atkins
66. Josiah Nose
67. N. Goodwin
68. Thomas Hopkins
69. B. Barnes
70. N. Goodwin
71. Dr. Webster
72. Abe. Symmes
73. E. Hart
74. N. Faxon
75. Hutchinson
76. J. Bray
77. Knowlton
78. Society: Lemuel Persons unintelligible
79. Society R. Dawes
80. Society

Back of Church
MAIN AISLE
Back to Front

81. Society
82. Soc. E. Steanes
83. Soc: N. Lewis
84. Soc: D. Tuckerman
85. A. Cutter
86. Dr. Webster
87. Hill (1/2) Scott, Clark (1/2)
88. T. Williams
89. Webber

90. D. Hastings
91. T. Page
92. Pico
93. H. Atkins
94. A. Stetson, S. Eades
95. Kettell
96. J. Emery

Front of Church to Back
97. Simpkins
98. Thomas Oliver
99. Simpkins
100. McKean
101. T. Rogers
102. Wm Palfrey
103. Jn. Lewis
104. Craft & Burrows
105. Wm Howe
106. Eb. Tufts
107. McCleary
108. Capt. Richmond
109. Brown
110. Soc: Jn. Eustis
111. Subscripton
112. Society

Back of Church

New North Church, now known as St. Stephen's Roman Catholic Church, 2014.

CHAPTER 3

UNITARIANISM AT NEW NORTH

One of the most significant developments in religion in America at the end of the 18th and the beginning of the 19th Century was the emergence of the Unitarian movement. Congregational churches in Eastern Massachusetts and in particular in Boston were the core of Unitarianism to such an extent that Unitarianism has been called "the Boston religion."

So Unitarianism, as practiced by the Rev. Francis Parkman, is the next doctrinal change at New North. It had gradually become distinct from the more conservative Congregationalism during the period covered by Vol. II of New North Church records and the New North Church was itself one of the early congregations to embrace a Unitarian theology.

Congregational churches as a whole were evolving during the 18th Century, largely as a result of the Great Awakening in the 1730s and 1740s, which had a particularly strong response in Boston and its region. But most Congregational ministers recoiled from the strong emotionalism that characterized the revival and preferred a "reasonable" religion. In fact their theology was evolving away from strict Calvinism with its tenets of predestination and the essential depravity of humankind inherited from the fall of Adam and Eve. In its place they believed in the basic goodness of human nature and the ability of people to avoid sin through the exercise of their free will (Arminianism).

At the same time, some of these "liberal Christians," as they preferred to call themselves, also began abandoning the traditional Christian and Calvinist doctrine of the Trinity, which taught that Father, Son and Holy Spirit were distinct persons of the godhead, but all sharing the same divine essence. They believed that the Trinitarian doctrine, formally pronounced only in the 4th Century, was unsupported in Scripture. The debate centered on the figure of Christ, but there was no agreement on this issue among the anti-Trinitarians. Some saw Father, Son and Holy Spirit as being merely three distinct modes of action of God, as in acting now as Creator, now as Redeemer and other times as Sustainer (Modalism or Sabellianism). Some, perhaps most, saw Christ as a special creation by God, who ranked somewhere between God and the angels (Arianism). Others saw Christ as Jesus, a man who was perhaps especially attuned to the mind and will of God, but who was nevertheless entirely human and incapable of performing miracles (Socianianism or Humanitarianism).

In time all these varieties of anti-Trinitarian theology came to be labeled Unitarianism, but at the end of the 18th Century that term, as it was used in England, usually referred only to the view that Jesus was a man and nothing more (Socinianism), which most of the "liberal Christians" would have denied. Indeed many of the early Unitarians never accepted the appropriateness of the term in describing their theology.

The progress of anti-Trinitarianism in the latter half of the 1700s and the early years of the 1800s is difficult to chart. It happened as more and more "Unitarian" ministers appeared and were able to convince their congregations to agree with them. But these clergymen did not proclaim their theology from the pulpit, so the more conservative Congregationalist ministers rarely had a public target to attack. And the organization of the Congregational church in Massachusetts, which made each congregation independent and in charge of its own affairs, meant that Trinitarian Congregationalists, who made up the majority of its ministers and congregations, could do nothing to prevent individual pastors and churches from adopting a Unitarian theology.

Congregationalists in Massachusetts were strongly divided geographically on the Trinitarian question. Unitarians were largely confined to the easternmost parts of the state and were especially centered on Boston. Perhaps Boston, with its bustling port, with merchants and seamen who traveled the world, simply had a more cosmopolitan and tolerant outlook in general, but also Unitarians dominated the teaching of theology at Harvard College and most Congregational churches in Boston and its vicinity called recent Harvard graduates to be their pastors. The Trinitarians viewed with alarm the spread of Unitarian theology, which they viewed as heretical, within their church.

The division between Trinitarian and Unitarian Congregationalists burst out into the open in 1805 with the appointment of the Unitarian Henry Ware, Sr., to fill Harvard's Hollis Professorship of Divinity. Moreover, the presidents of Harvard were henceforth also Unitarians and these events together marked the institutionalization of Unitarian theology at that school. With Harvard seen by conservatives as a virtual Unitarian seminary, they founded Andover Theological Seminary in 1807 for the training of Trinitarian clergymen.

It had been the practice among Congregational pastors to "exchange pulpits" with other pastors on a monthly basis. But the spread of Unitarianism led some Trinitarian ministers to refuse to exchange pulpits with fellow Congregationalist clergy who denied the full divinity of Christ, a movement that slowly spread in the first two and a half decades of the 19th Century.

The distance between the two wings of Congregationalism continued to widen as a result of the war of books, pamphlets, tracts and sermons. The conservatives endeavored to present the liberals in the worst light possible, even questioning if they could be considered Christian. The ablest spokesman for the Unitarians and their de facto head was William Ellery Channing (uncle of the Transcendentalist poet of the same name), who was a Harvard graduate and long-time pastor of Boston's Federal Street Church (1803-1842). Moreover he was mentor in theology to New North's Francis Parkman. Throughout his pastorate he ably and vehemently defended Unitarianism in sermons and published articles.

By the early 1820s, the younger generation of Unitarian ministers were tiring of the constant attacks by the Trinitarians who clearly wanted them purged from the ranks of Congregationalism. In 1825 they met and formed the American Unitarian Association. Their first choice as president was William Ellery Channing, who declined the office. He was wary of creating yet another denomination and hierarchy with yet another creed, and Unitarian churches in general gave only tepid support to the new organization.

But Boston was well represented among the first officers of the AUA. Ezra Stiles Gannett (a Harvard graduate and Channing's pastoral colleague at the Federal Street Church) was chosen as the organization's secretary and worked tirelessly to promote and expand Unitarianism. Henry Ware, Jr., a Harvard graduate and at the time pastor of the Second Church, was named to the executive committee. In 1830 he resigned his pastoral position to become the first incumbent of Harvard's Professorship of Pulpit Eloquence and Pastoral Care, established by New North's Francis Parkman. His successor at Second Church was Ralph Waldo Emerson (1829-1832). Also elected to the Executive Committee was Samuel Barrett, a Harvard graduate recently appointed as the first pastor of the newly formed 12th Congregational Society, a position he held until 1861.

By the time of the formation of the American Unitarian Association, Unitarianism was dominant in Boston. Eight of the nine Congregational churches in the city were Unitarian. The intelligentsia, the wealthy, the leaders of the community were all Unitarian. In 1825 the Trinitarians fought back by establishing a new church of their own, the Hanover Street (later Bowdoin Street) church, and in 1826 they called the formidable and determined Trinitarian Lyman Beecher (father of Henry Ward Beecher and Harriet Beecher Stowe) to be its pastor. When he arrived he found an almost hopeless situation, writing "All offices were in the hands of Unitarians." His daughter Harriet added, "All the literary men of Massachusetts were Unitarians. All the trustees and professors of Harvard College were Unitarians. All the elite of wealth and fashion crowded Unitarian churches. The judges on the bench were Unitarian." In 1832 he gave up his futile role as Boston's chief Trinitarian to become president of the newly founded Lane Theological Seminary in Ohio.

The greatest threat to Unitarianism came not from the conservative Trinitarians, however, but from within the ranks of the Unitarian clergy, from the Transcendentalists and Universalists. The leading Transcendentalist was Ralph Waldo Emerson (1803-1882), a graduate of Harvard's divinity school and for three and a half years Unitarian pastor of Boston's 2nd Church. But in 1832

Emerson resigned because of his inability to accept many of the beliefs and practices of his church and he never returned to an active pastorate. In 1838, over the protests of their faculty, the graduating class of Harvard Divinity School asked him to preach their graduation sermon. Emerson called upon them not to be too concerned with Christian traditions, with miracles or even with the figure of Jesus. Rather they should seek God within themselves and preach what was revealed to them there. Many questioned whether Emerson could in fact be called a Christian.

Ralph Waldo Emerson

One of those in full agreement with Emerson's sermon was Theodore Parker (1810-1860), a graduate of Harvard Theological School and pastor of the West Roxbury Unitarian Church. Parker came to preach against the supernatural character of supposed biblical miracles, seeing the Bible as error prone and Jesus as inspired only as all persons are capable of being inspired by God. Thus neither the Bible nor Jesus had a claim to special religious authority. To conservatives the scandal was even worse because Parker, unlike Emerson, remained an active Unitarian minister and a member of the Boston Association of Congregational [i. e., Unitarian] Ministers. The conservatives were quick to charge that Parker could not be considered a Christian and to argue that Unitarianism was simply a disguised disbelief in Christianity. Despite having most Unitarian pulpits closed to him and the failed efforts of many of his fellow Unitarian clergy to expel him from the Boston Association of Congregational Ministers, Parker remained an active member of the Association even after he became pastor of the new 28th Congregational Society, organized for the purpose of providing Parker with a pulpit in Boston.

Thus by the mid-point of the 19TH Century Unitarianism was split into two factions just as the waves of Irish immigration began to alter the demographic makeup of Boston's neighborhoods. Moreover, Boston's elite began to abandon Unitarianism in favor of the Episcopal Church. Unitarianism began to fade in Boston and numbers of Unitarian churches and chapels, including the New North Church, began to dissolve or merge with other Unitarian churches. The heyday of Boston Unitarianism was over.

Francis Parkman's Legacy

The pastorate of Francis Parkman (1788-1852) is the last of the line of long-tenured ministers at the church, serving from 1813 to 1849. Parkman was the son of Samuel Parkman, a wealthy Boston merchant, and grandson of Rev. Ebenezer Parkman, a highly respected Congregational minister in Westborough, Mass. He received a sound classical education at the Boston Public Latin School and received the school's prestigious

The Rev. Francis Parkman

Franklin Medal, for excellence in scholarship and conduct, in 1804 and then entered Harvard College. Graduating in 1807, he began studying theology under William Ellery Channing, the leading Unitarian theologian of the day.

In 1810 Parkman went to Britain and continued his theological studies in Edinburgh and preached in several pulpits in England, many of them Unitarian. He was offered the position of associate pastor at the Unitarian church in Liverpool, which he declined in order to return to Boston, where he preached in various churches before being picked by the New North Church to succeed Rev. John Eliot, who had died in February 1813. Parkman was installed as pastor in December 1813.

At the New North Church, Parkman was remembered not for being a great churchman and outstanding theologian, but for being a captivating preacher, a caring pastor and kind and congenial person. Such was his interest in preaching that he founded the Professorship of Pulpit Eloquence and Pastoral Care in Harvard's theological school, which continues to this day as the Parkman Professorship. He was very active in the nascent Unitarian movement in Boston and shortly before his death in 1852 he was elected president of the convention of Unitarian ministers.

In 1817 Francis Parkman married Sarah Cabot, who died in 1818 shortly after giving birth to a daughter (see Chapter 9 for his tribute). In 1822 he married Catherine Hall, a descendant of the formidable Puritan minister John Cotton and of Rev. Edward Brooks (the father of Peter Chardon Brooks, "the richest man in Boston"). Several children were born to this marriage, including Francis Parkman, Jr., the renowned 19th Century historian (Chapter 5, Famous Personages).

On July 8, 1827, the church adopted the Unitarian form of service. This replaced the beginning choir anthem or voluntary with a hymn or Psalm, dropped the Watt's version of the Psalms and adopted the Cambridge Collection of psalms and hymns. For members joining, it adopted a new Unitarian Covenant, when they professed their faith.

THE COVENANT OF 1827

"The following is the form of this ancient Covenant, as now revised and adopted by us," (from church minutes):

"You do in the solemn presence (of God) give up yourself, even your whole self, to the true God in Jesus Crist, promising to walk with God, and with this church of his, in all his holy ordinances, and to yield obedience to every truth of his, which has been, or shall be made known to you, as your duty, the Lord assisting you by His spirit and grace.

"We then, Church of Christ, in this place, do receive you into our fellowship, and promise to walk towards you, and to watch over you as a member of this church, endeavoring your spiritual edification in Christ Jesus."

Pastor Parkman congratulated the Society on "their cordial adoption of the excellent selection, distinguished for its pure devotional sentiment, its entire freedom from sectarian theology, and enriched by the choicest productions of our most gifted Christian poets. May it help us to render our worship more acceptable to God, more salutary, and graceful to ourselves."

New North Declines

Despite his congenial nature, Parkman appears to have been prone to depression and melancholy, which made it difficult for him to perform his duties as pastor of New North Church.

In 1842, a pastoral colleague to Parkman was called, Rev. Amos Smith (1816-1887), who was also a graduate of Harvard Theological School. Smith now performed the bulk of the pastoral duties at the church with Parkman occasionally preaching and otherwise assisting his junior colleague. Most of the church records in this period continue to be in Parkman's hand.

However, in 1848 Smith resigned from New North Church to answer a call from the Unitarian Church in Leominster, MA. By this time, New North Church was in a severe crisis that threatened its existence—the flood of Irish immigrants fleeing the potato famine. In 1847 alone, Boston saw an influx of 37,000 arrivals from Ireland. Boston's North End was on its way to becoming predominantly Irish, generally poor and uneducated and, more importantly, Roman Catholic in religion. Boston churches were neighborhood churches and people expected to be able to walk to church, but now the Yankee Protestant population of the North End began moving out, leaving the

New North Church with a constantly dwindling population base.

Amos Smith's resignation in 1848, whether due to the Irish immigration or not, presented Francis Parkman with his own crisis. He was unable to continue on as pastor and in February, 1849, the Rev. Joshua Young was installed at New North Church, with Parkman's own resignation being effective the next month.

Joshua Young's Short Pastorate

Joshua Young

Joshua Young (1823-1904) was a graduate of Bowdoin College and a recent graduate of the Harvard Theological School. Unlike his long-tenured predecessors, Young was pastor at New North Church for only three years, resigning in 1852. Young was an ardent abolitionist and in Boston he was a member of the Vigilance Committee, which aimed at frustrating the Fugitive Slave Act, and active in the underground railroad, hiding escaped slaves and assisting them to escape to Canada. In 1849, the church began a Sunday School program for the 60 – 70 young people attending, thinking "may this school be the recovery of the church." Young people, however, liked the Baptist and Methodist churches better. Young also said he was leaving because there "was no trust between the congregation and the pastor." See page 61 for later history on Joshua Young.

Fuller Succeeds Young

Young's successor at New North Church was Arthur Buckminster Fuller (1822-1862), installed June 1, 1853. He was the Boston-born son of a U. S. Congressman, who, like his predecessors, was also a graduate of Harvard's Theological School. Like Joshua Young, Fuller was an abolitionist, but he was also a dedicated evangelist who believed in

41

ORDER OF SERVICES

AT THE

Installation of Rev. Arthur B. Fuller,

AS PASTOR OF THE

NEW NORTH RELIGIOUS SOCIETY,

Boston, Wednesday, June 1, 1853.

VOLUNTARY ON THE ORGAN AND ANTHEM BY THE CHOIR.

I.—INTRODUCTORY PRAYER, by Rev. AMOS SMITH, of LEOMINSTER.

II.—READING OF THE SCRIPTURES, by Rev. THOMAS S. KING.

III.—HYMN.

Our Father in Heaven! thou Being above;
Who reignest in power, yet reignest in love,
Our protector, our guide and our hope ever be,
To whom should we come, holy God, but to thee?

Oh gracious Jehovah! to thee would we raise
Our songs of petition, thanksgiving and praise;
Be near in thy mercy, thy might and thy power;
Be with us, oh Father, at this hallowed hour!

For thy approbation and grace we would pray;
We would ask for thy aid and thy blessing this day!

O grant that thy spirit may rest on *him* now,
Who before thee in faith and reliance doth bow.

Be near to him ever, in joy and in wo,
And thy mercies, thy strength without measure bestow,
Oh! here may thy truth, pure and holy be blest,
May the wand'rer return, and the weary find rest.

And when fleeting life, with its conflicts is o'er,
When this band now united, on earth meet no more,
O welcome it, Father, to temples above,
To regions of beauty, of joy and of love.

IV.—SERMON, by Rev. ANDREW P. PEABODY, D. D., of PORTSMOUTH, N. H.

V.—HYMN: C. M.

O God! thy children gathered here,
Thy blessing now we wait;
Thy servant, girded for his work,
Stands at the temple's gates.

O Father! keep his soul alive
To every hope of good,
And may his life of love proclaim
Man's truest brotherhood!

O Father! keep his spirit quick
To every form of wrong;
And in the ear of sin and self
May his rebuke be strong!

And as he doth Christ's footsteps press,
If e'er his faith grow dim,
Then, in the dreary wilderness,
Thine angels strengthen him!

VI.—PRAYER OF INSTALLATION, by Rev. SAMUEL K. LOTHROP, D. D.

VII.—CHARGE, by Rev. SAMUEL BARRETT, D. D.

VIII.—RIGHT HAND OF FELLOWSHIP, by Rev. J. I. T. COOLIDGE.

IX.—ADDRESS TO THE SOCIETY, by Rev. F. D. HUNTINGTON.

X.—CONCLUDING PRAYER, by Rev. ROBERT HASSALL, of MENDON.

XI.—ANTHEM.

XII.—BENEDICTION, by THE PASTOR.

taking God's word to the masses and was an advocate for the cause of temperance and for free public education. Fuller worked mightily to revive the New North Church, especially in his emphasis on baptism, as is seen in the records. However, the demographic trends in Boston's North End could not be changed. As Fuller recorded in 1855:

> "I found when my ministry began only 26 persons who lived in the city and had ever united with the New North Church. Of these, 12 lived in another part of the city, worshipped with other societies having wholly withdrawn from ours tho not formally dismissed from our church & recommended to any other. Thus there were only 14 who were members of the N. N. Church & worshipped with us, the rest were only nominal members. Besides these however were several persons members of other churches but worshippers with us & usually communing. {p. 383}"

This bleak situation was also described by Richard F. Fuller in the biography he wrote for his brother Arthur, *Chaplain Fuller, Being a Life Sketch of a New England Clergyman and Army Chaplain* (1864):

> His religious society was at low ebb when he entered upon his ministry; owing, in part, to a cause which might be counteracted, but not overcome. The native population was constantly receding from that section of the city, and giving place in part to mercantile and manufacturing occupation, but mainly to residents of a foreign birth and different religious persuasion. This cause was constantly operating with a greatly increased momentum. Building up the religious society, therefore, was like the stone of Sisyphus, raised only by the constant application of superior strength, and relapsing again the moment effort was intermitted. Members of the church and congregation were constantly caught away by the tide of population, and borne to southerly parts of the city; while those from whom recruits could be hoped to supply the broken ranks were, under the influence of the same law of change, departing also. ... He found his strength unequal to cope longer with the adverse current, expending upon it a toil which could not there obtain any lasting success, and he sent in his resignation, having resolved to accept a call

extended to him by a society in Watertown, Massachusetts. His society in Boston parted from him in regret, and some three years afterward, having settled no other pastor, sold their house of worship (pp. 115-6, 137-8).

Richard Fuller knew the situation well for he, too, was connected with the New North Church. His son Arthur Angelo was baptized there in 1853 {p. 318}.

As Richard F. Fuller wrote, in 1859 Arthur Fuller left the declining New North Church to go to the Unitarian Church in Watertown, Mass., but the outbreak of the Civil War brought an end to this ministry. He enlisted in the army as chaplain to the 16th Massachusetts Volunteer Infantry and was a spectacular success in this role. However, in 1862 his health began to fail even more and on Dec. 10, 1862, he was discharged from the army. But on the very next day, before Fuller could depart for home, during the battle for Fredericksburg a call went out for volunteers for a dangerous crossing of the Rappahannock River. Fuller, now a civilian, answered the call and was quickly killed in the fighting. Because he was technically no longer a soldier, his widow had no right to a pension, but his case was so dramatic that a special bill was passed in the U. S. Congress granting her the pension.

Fuller's contemporaries were sure that he would be remembered as a great Unitarian churchman, but he wrote little and spent his life as a good pastor to ordinary people rather than the intelligentsia. Thus his fame has been eclipsed by the renown of his grandson, the 20th Century architect, designer and futurist Buckminster Fuller, and that of his sister Margaret (See Chapter 5—Famous Personages).

From Fuller's departure in 1859 until April of 1863, when the building was sold to the Roman Catholic Archdiocese of Boston for $35,000 and the congregation's move to the Bulfinch Street Church, no pastor was settled. Church records are incomplete in these final years, but Harold Field Worthley in his *Inventory of the Records of the particular (Congregational) Churches of Massachusetts Gathered 1620-1805),* published by Harvard University Press in 1970, writes:

"In 1863, the 5th Church and Society undertook to merge with Boston's Bulfinch Street Church and Society, an action concluded with the dissolution of the Fifth Society in 1864, although the resulting merged church itself became extinct shortly thereafter."

His reference to 5th Church is the Congregational name for New North Church. Final Church records (page 385) say:

Bullfinch Street Church

"The New North Religious Society in the town of Boston having purchased the building previously owned and occupied by the Bulfinch Street Church and the latter organization having dissolved, at a meeting held April 21st, 1863, it was voted by the members of the New North Church to accept the Rev. William Alger as pastor and to receive into full fellowship without any further form all members of the Bulfinch Street Church in good and regular standing."

W.R Alger

The Rev. William Rounseville Alger (1822-1905) held a Harvard Divinity school degree (1847) and was a brilliant preacher. He held pastorates in Roxbury and then moved to Bulfinch St. Church in January of 1857, leaving in 1868 to form a more liberal church, preaching to 2,000 to 3,000 each Sunday at the Boston Music Hall. He must have maintained some continuing connection to New North Church despite his preaching elsewhere because he is named in the minutes of the final meeting of the church on Sunday, April 10, 1870.

After communion, Sunday, April 10, 1870, the New North Religious Society as it was then known, met and voted that the Brothers William R. Alger, Samuel Condon, and Francis Curtis be given power to sell the church's plate and silverware and to distribute the proceeds if and when such a sale be expedient, the minutes conclude.

Thus ends the 157 year history of New North (5th) Church, Boston.

Reproduction of the last page New North Church minutes,
April 10, 1870.

CHAPTER 4

Understanding
New North's Evolution

Understanding Puritanism, Congregationalism and Unitarianism is not easy and Peggy Bendroth, executive director, of The Congregational Library, Boston, has offered a brief explanation to help us understand how New North Church changed in its history.

She has served as executive director for the Congregational Library since August 2004. She received her B.A. from Cornell University and a Ph.D. in history from Johns Hopkins University. She has been interviewed by Public Broadcasting for programs on early Colonial America and she is the author of several books, including *Fundamentalism and Gender, 1875 to the Present* (Yale 1993) and *Fundamentalists and the City: Conflict and Division in Boston's Churches, 1885 to 1950* (Oxford 2005). She has also edited several other volumes, including *Women and Twentieth-Century Protestantism* (Illinois 2002). Her most recent book, *A School of the Church: Andover Newton Across Two Centuries* (Eerdmans 2008), was written to mark the school's bicentennial year. Another recent book, *The Spiritual Practice of Remembering* is available at <u>Amazon</u>.

Understanding New North's Evolution

By Margaret (Peggy) Bendroth

Puritanism was not just a system of beliefs—it was also a way of "doing church," one that today came to be known as Congregationalism.

The Puritans were Protestants, part of a movement originating in the 16th Century, upholding the authority of the Bible as the only way of faith and practice, and faith in Christ as the way to salvation. Protestants broke off from the Roman Catholic church because they opposed not just its doctrines but its practices, especially all forms of ceremony and liturgy and hierarchy; English Puritans dissented from the Anglican Church, the state church closely resembling Catholicism in belief and practice. They were convinced that only the most plain and simple forms of worship and church government would open the way to God.

English Protestantism took a variety of forms, everything from Scots Presbyterianism to Baptists and Quakers. Congregationalists, then known as Independents, were part of this mix, distinguished by their vision of the true church as a local company of believers, free of outside control. The minister served as shepherd and guide over these gatherings, referred to as "conventicles," preaching the word of God and sharing authority with the laypeople in decision-making.

The most difficult question for Independents was purity, whether they could stay within the Church of England or needed to separate to save their souls. Was the Church of England still a legitimate Christian church? Until the 1630s, most Puritan Independents believed the former, and watched the small and troublesome Pilgrim band of Separatists leave for the Netherlands and then Plymouth in 1620 with more relief than regret. But soon after that departure, the English government, under the leadership of Archbishop Laud, began a campaign of persecution, jailing and fining Puritans and forcing many into hiding.

The "great migration" of Puritans in the 1630s, bringing tens of thousands to New England's shore, may have looked like Pilgrim-style separation from the Church of England, but the understanding was very different. John Winthrop's famous sermon, delivered as the first group was preparing to leave on the *Arbella,* used the biblical image of a "city on a hill" to describe the new venture. New England would demonstrate to the world (or the Church of England at least) what the true church really looked like. It would be reformation from afar.

The first settlers arrived without a rulebook or set of standard church practices. The Congregational Way, as it was called, developed over time, as both ministers and laypeople began to work out the implications of the ideals they had held as English dissenters. The core notion was that of covenant. This idea had a long biblical precedent, describing the mutual obligations between God and the people of Israel. As latter-day Israelites (so they often thought of themselves), New England's Puritan churches adopted this model, applying it to everything from civil government to marriage.

The covenant ideal applied especially to church life. A Congregational church formed when a group of individuals (laypeople and one who would presumably become pastor) agreed to "walk together with each other and before God." This covenant agreement, put into writing and entered into the church records, marked the congregation's beginning and its ground rules for life together. Essentially it meant that the membership did not consist of assenting to a list of doctrines—it was agreeing to a

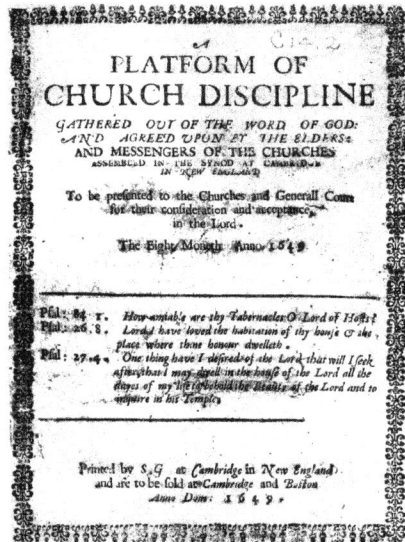

The Cambridge Platform of 1649 set standards for church governance, parts of which are followed today.

life-long commitment. In Puritan churches the fundamental test for church membership was the ability to testify to an experience of grace, a life-changing encounter with God.

This did not mean all was harmony. The New England model of independent gathered churches was unprecedented and difficult ideal to put into practice. In many ways Congregational-ism was a tightrope: ministers had authority, but not beyond what laypeople would approve—an early expression of what the United States Constitutions would later call the "consent of the governed." Local churches were independent and had full right to run their own affairs, but were also answerable to their peers. "Congregationalism" was in fact the name given to the system of local church *interdependence* in New England, an explicit rejection of their old identity as Independents.

The most difficult tensions in the Congregational Way had to do with family life. The Puritan ideal stressed the importance of the individual's relationship with God, unimpeded by church hierarchy or liturgical rules; but Congregationalism also stressed the importance of the entire church acting as one, based on the conviction that God spoke most clearly to people gathered under covenant. The balance between individual spirituality and church unity was always tricky; by the time the second generation of Puritans became old enough to stand for church membership, it was all but impossible to maintain. The Halfway Covenant, instituted in 1662, allowed non-church members to present their children for baptism, but not to participate in communion. (In other words they were half-way members.) Deeply controversial, it was to outspoken critics like Increase Mather and John Davenport an admission of failure; at the very least it was a concession to expediency. Whether out of indifference or fear, second-generation New Englanders were not joining churches in sufficient numbers: the future of the "city on a hill" was at stake. By allowing them to baptize their children, the clergy of Massachusetts Bay hoped to keep them within the sphere of church life, with the goal of having them one day "own the covenant" themselves.

This was not the only challenge the Congregational churches encountered. By the 1680s they found themselves in a new and troubling political situation, under a royal governor and the English law of religious toleration. Slowly but inexorably, Baptist, Quaker, and even Roman Catholic churches began to establish themselves across New England. But Congregationalism's troubles were only just beginning. A few years later, in the 1730s and 1740s, New England—and in fact the entire transatlantic world—was rocked by a religious revival, popularly known as the first "great awakening." Though the revival brought new converts into Congregational churches it posed new and ultimately debilitating challenges to the old Puritan way. The most fascinating, and to some disturbing, feature of the awakening was a new notion of conversion as an instantaneous emotional event. Puritan conversions could take a lifetime, and were always vetted by the entire church community. The new model was not only deeply individualistic, it was often accompanied by bizarre behaviors and experiences.

Congregationalists divided over the legitimacy of these conversions: to some they were the undisputed work of God, to others a dangerous delusion. Ultimately the center did not hold, as the pro-revival faction split off from what they believed were spiritually dead Congregational churches into Separate churches, or for those still unsatisfied, into Baptist ones. The anti-revival group would also separate from Congregationalism, into Unitarian churches. In the late-18th Century, the Unitarians' opposition to revivalism reflected new winds of intellectual, scientific, and political change in Europe, the Enlightenment and its emphasis on human reason. Enlightenment thinkers were not atheists but deists, they insisted that true religion was reasonable religion, that is, evident to any thinking person with a clear view of the world. Stories of miracles or supernatural events were not only unnecessary, they were in fact dangerous, putting credulous people into the hands of corrupt religious leaders. Reasonable religion also took issue with Calvinism and its view of God as absolutely sovereign, with power to damn or save according to his will; it also took issue with the doctrine of the Trinity and the idea of three in one, an unreasonable paradox (hence the name Unitarian).

Unitarians, then, were Congregationalists who wished for a more reasonable and intellectually respectable faith. By the early 1800s, they had become a formidable presence in Boston and its surrounding towns and angry battles over church property were fueling division. The formation of the American Unitarian Society in 1825 marked their beginning as a separate denomination, though at the time it was simply an organization for like-minded Congregationalists. In the years following, however, Trinitarian Congregationalists (as they often called themselves) and Unitarians would drift farther and farther apart into separate bodies.

The years ahead posed more challenges for Congregationalists, especially with the dis-establishment of religion and the opening of the religious "free market." Once the single largest church in British North America, by the mid-19 Century they had fallen far behind faster-growing groups like Methodists and Baptists. Though their numbers waned, their influence remained strong. From its earliest days in New England, Congregationalism stood for important principles of civic order and the rights of ordinary people, values with a deep and lasting influence on American culture.

Early Puritan Church Life Strict & Focused

By Charles Chauncey Wells
(From Memorial History of Boston, Book II, Religious History)

In Puritan America, one's life focus was on God and one's salvation. The church and worship were essential to achieve that. It was a disciplined life, so being a Puritan in early Boston took total devotion and acceptance of many rules and regulations. The Puritan church had stripped out the trappings of the English Church. There were no crosses, stained glass, statues, or ornamentation, so the Puritan worshippers really were mostly devoted to understanding the Bible and its interpretation as regards to one's salvation. There was no choir, organ or musical instruments.

Here are some distinctions from how worship is conducted today:

Family devotions were strictly observed in the Puritan home.

• Simple Services. The format: "One praying, one singing, one preaching" were the essentials to be followed.

• Sermons the highlight and were long. Most sermons were at least an hour, perhaps two, one even lasted four. The preacher had an hour glass which he used to measure time. Few used notes and were well educated in theology and the Bible so they could speak extemporaneously.

• Lord's Prayer eliminated. While the English Church used the Lord's Prayer often, the Puritans eliminated it. Holy Communion or the commemoration of the Last Supper was retained, but celebrated only one Sunday per month

• Christmas eliminated. The Lord's Day was good enough. Puritanism eliminated Christmas and special church holidays and saints days. They viewed these observances as a distraction. If you celebrated Christmas, you would be taken to court and fined.

• Church attendance mandatory. If you did not attend, you were fined.

• In earlier times, women and men sat apart and children sat in the balcony. Boys were especially watched and disciplined by the elders.

• Ministers were selected by the congregation. The church was the basic unit, eliminating bishops and archbishops. The minister often served for his whole life. If his preaching was poor or unpopular, he was dismissed.

 • All Day Services. Usually Sunday services began about 9 a.m. and lasted until noon. People went home for lunch, usually prepared the day before, rested, and came back at 2 for more prayers, singing, and sermon. Baptisms were often done in the afternoon.

Order of Service:
Pastor's prayer for about 15 minutes, perhaps more.

Bible Reading. The pastor or ruling elder would read a chapter of the Bible and might comment on it.

Psalms would be read responsively. Later these would be sung, the elder singing the line first and the congregation repeating it. After 1640, most churches used the *Bay Psalm Book*, the first book printed in British America in Cambridge.

Sermon. Finally, the Pastor's sermon for the rest of the morning. Same format would be repeated in the afternoon.

Later, in the early 1700s, churches began to modify this austerity and to add music and shorten services, but did maintain strict observance of the Sabbath Day.

CHAPTER 5

INTERESTING AND FAMOUS PERSONAGES OF NEW NORTH CHURCH

Historian Francis Parkman

Attempting a Google search on Francis Parkman, pastor of the New North Church, is greatly complicated because of the much greater fame and national prominence of his son, also named Francis Parkman (1823-1893), whose baptism is recorded on November 2, 1823 (p. 294). "Frank" Parkman was one of the best known and most influential 19th Century American historians, which was acknowledged by Theodore Roosevelt's dedication of his own four-volume history *The Winning of the West* to him. In 1967 the U. S. Postal Service issued a postage stamp to honor him in its Prominent Americans series.

Parkman's mother was Caroline, his father's second wife, who was a descendant of John Cotton, the prominent Puritan minister in the Massachusetts Bay Colony. Young Parkman disappointed his father by forsaking a career in law and pursuing his historical interests, especially the history of the American frontier. In the 1840s, when the frontier was far from being tamed, he went so far as to live for a while among the Oglala Sioux, where he gained a first-hand experience of American Indian culture.

Soon thereafter Parkman's historical works began to appear: *The California and Oregon Trail* (1849), *The Conspiracy of Pontiac* (1851), and in 1865 the first volume of his seven-volume *France and England in North America*, the last volume of which was published in 1892. He was also a keen horticulturalist who personally developed several new varieties of flowers. For a brief time he was a professor of horticulture at Harvard's agricultural college.

Robert Gould Shaw, pastor's brother-in-law

Rev. Francis Parkman's brother-in-law **Robert Gould Shaw** (1776-1853), married to Elizabeth (Eliza) Willard Parkman, was one of the wealthiest merchants in Boston at the time of his death but he had to endure early poverty after the failure of his father's and grandfather's land speculation in Maine. With the assistance of his uncles and the support of his circle of wealthy merchant families allied by marriage (his wife Eliza was the daughter of Samuel Parkman, whose first wife was Shaw's aunt Sarah). In time Shaw's wealth increased considerably and he amassed a large fleet of ships that carried on trade with Europe, the West Indies and the Far East. Shaw was one of the founders of the Boston Exchange and was a director and president of the Boston Bank. Shaw was also a Mason and used his wealth to rescue Boston's Grand Lodge (then at the corner of Tremont Street and Temple Place) during the anti-Masonic movement in the early 1830s. For a time the lodge's ownership of its property was in dispute so Shaw purchased the building from the lodge and then sold it back for the same price once the furor had settled.

Despite Shaw's close association with the New North Church (its records are filled with the baptisms and marriages of his children), he remained independent of creeds and denominations. His son Francis G. Shaw wrote of him: "He always asserted that he had the faculty of seeing visions, and that they were pleasant and delightful, or the contrary, according as he was in a spiritual or worldly state of mind at the time. In his later years, he became an enthusiastic believer in modern Spiritualism, and gave full credence to the wonderful narrations of some of the prominent mediums; but he needed no help from them to strengthen his belief in immortality, which was never shaken."

Robert G. and Eliza Shaw's eldest son **Francis George Shaw**

(1809-1882; his marriage to Sarah Blake Sturgis in 1835 is recorded on p. 168) gave up an active life in business to pursue idealist dreams and promote reform. He and his wife Sarah were early supporters of Brook Farm, the Utopian Transcendentalist experimental commune in West Roxbury, Massachusetts, where Ralph Waldo Emerson and Margaret Fuller lived. The couple was also among the most prominent radical abolitionists in the pre-Civil War period, and during the Civil War they strongly urged the formation of all-black Union military forces. Thus when the 54th Massachusetts Volunteer Infantry regiment was created, it seemed appropriate that its command was offered to their son **Robert Gould Shaw**. The unit and its commander were distinguished for their courage in the bloody, failed attack on Fort Wagner, South Carolina, in 1863. The regiment suffered heavy casualties, including the death of young Shaw. The bravery of the 54th Massachusetts and its young colonel was memorialized in Augustus Saint-Gaudens' bronze relief sculpture put up in Boston at 24 Beacon Street in 1897, and it came to national prominence again in the 1989 film *Glory*, starring Matthew Broderick as Robert G. Shaw.

Robert Gould Shaw led the Black 54th Volunteer Regiment and this monument, across from the MA State House in Boston Common, commemorates the first time that an all-African American unit fought in the Civil War. Men enlisted from all areas of the North and even from the Caribbean. He was killed in the 2nd Battle of Fort Wagner near Charleston, SC.

Another child of Francis G. and Sarah Shaw was also honored with a public monument in a major city. The **Josephine Shaw Lowell** Memorial Fountain in Manhattan's Bryant Park, was the city's first public monument with a woman as its honoree. Josephine was married to Charles Russell Lowell (nephew of the Romantic poet James Russell Lowell) until his death in the Civil War less than a year later. She never remarried but in the family tradition devoted herself to reform, especially the eradication of poverty. She founded a number of charities and was the first woman appointed as commissioner of the New York State Board of Charities.

Quincy Adams Shaw (1825-1908), whose baptism was recorded on July 10, 1825 (p. 296), was another son of Robert Gould Shaw and Elizabeth Willard Parkman Shaw and one of the few of their offspring who embraced business and finance as a career. He was a stunning success.

After graduating from Harvard in 1845 he went West with his cousin Francis Parkman, Jr., and Parkman dedicated his history of the Oregon Trail to Quincy Shaw. And it was in the West that Shaw made his fortune. In 1860 he married Pauline Agassiz, daughter of the famed Swiss biologist and geologist Louis Agassiz, responsible for establishing that the earth had endured repeated ice ages and who joined the Harvard faculty in 1847.

Louis Agassiz recognized the great potential of the copper deposits in the Upper Peninsula of Michigan, which led to the formation of the Calumet & Hecla Mining Co. Quincy Shaw invested almost all of his money in the company and became its first president in 1871. Calumet & Hecla became the greatest producer of copper in the U. S. and Quincy Shaw held more of its stock than anyone else in Massachusetts. At his death in 1908, he was the largest

Company shield, Shaft No 2, Calumet, Michigan

taxpayer in the state and the wealthiest man in New England.

True to the family tradition of using its wealth for the purposes of bettering society, Quincy and Pauline Shaw established in Boston the first kindergarten in the United States and financed day nurseries in the city as well. The Shaws were also avid art collectors and made substantial donations to the Boston Museum of Fine Art and the Royal Japanese Museum.

The baptism of Robert G. and Elizabeth Parkman Shaw's son **Joseph Coolidge Shaw** (1821-1851) was recorded at New North Church on May 20, 1821 (p. 291). After graduating from Harvard in 1840 he left for a three-year tour of Europe. While in Rome he became attracted to Roman Catholicism, to which he converted and in 1847 he was ordained to the Catholic priesthood. In 1850 he entered the novitiate of the Society of Jesus (Jesuits).

However, he soon contracted tuberculosis, which proved lethal for him. He took his vows as a Jesuit on March 4, 1851, and died six days later. He left his large personal library to what was to become Boston College and his books formed the core of the college library. Shaw House at Boston College is named in his honor.

Thomas Parkman Cushing (1787-1854; two of his marriages are recorded on pp. 161, 165) was another relation to the Parkman family. His mother Sarah was the daughter of Rev. Ebenezer Parkman and thus the aunt of Rev. Francis Parkman. He was another Boston merchant, like Robert Gould Shaw, who had a limited education but became fabulously wealthy. His dying bequest was an endowment that led to the establishment of the Cushing Academy in Ashburnham, MA, in 1865.

A business partner of Thomas Parkman Cushing was the wealthy merchant **Edward Tuckerman** (1775-1843), the third consecutive holder of that name in Boston. His father Edward II (1740-1818) began the family fortune as a large-scale baker and real-estate investor. Edward III's first wife was Hannah Parkman (her death in 1814 is recorded on p. 462), who was the daughter of Samuel Parkman and his first wife Sarah Shaw. Tuckerman's second wife was Sophia May. The baptism of their son **Edward Tuckerman IV** (1818-1886) is recorded on p. 287. This Edward Tuckerman became a renowned botanist, especially in the field of lichens and Alpine plants, and historian at Amherst College. He married Sarah Elizabeth Sigourney Cushing, the daughter of

Thomas Parkman Cushing. Another son was **Samuel Parkman Tuckerman** (1819-1890; for his baptism, see p. 288), who achieved fame as a church organist and author of books on church music. He was organist-choir master at Boston's St. Paul's Episcopal Church and at Trinity Church in New York City. A third son was **Frederick Goddard Tuckerman** (1821-1873, whose baptism is recorded on p. 291). He gained a significant reputation in the mid-nineteenth century as a Romantic poet. His works are still studied and appear in literary anthologies today.

School Master John Tileston

The death of John Tileston, former writing master of Boston's North Writing School, at

IN 1713 THE FIRST SCHOOL HOUSE WAS BUILT ON THIS LOT BY CAPT. THOMAS HUTCHINSON KNOWN AS THE NORTH LATIN AND NORTH GRAMMAR SCHOOL; RECOMPENSE WADSWORTH WAS THE MASTER.
IN 1718 A WRITING SCHOOL WAS BUILT ADJOINING THE GRAMMAR SCHOOL.
A PUBLIC SCHOOL HAS BEEN MAINTAINED ON THIS SITE SINCE THAT DATE. HENRY TILESTON MASTER. JOHN TILESTON TAUGHT FOR MANY YEARS.

the age of 92 is noted Oct. 17, 1826, on page 479 of New North's records. For almost 65 years, until his retirement in 1819 in his mid-80's, Tileston taught writing, then regarded as one of the essential elements of a proper education, to three generations of schoolboys from Boston's North End.

As an infant Tileston fell into a fire and severely burned his hand, which was left permanently impaired. For most purposes he was unable to use his hand deftly but it was perfect for holding a pen and a career was born. It has been suggested that Tileston was the model for the character Johnny Tremain, who was forced to leave his apprenticeship as a silversmith because of severe burns to his hand, in Esther Forbes's 1943 novel *Johnny Tremain.*

Tileston, who was remembered with affection by his schoolmate John Adams, was revered by his students, who, in time, rose to prominence and power in Boston. Upon his retirement the city officials voted to continue his school-master's salary (which was continued to his widow Lydia after his death). Moreover, he received the highly unusual honor of having a street renamed for him while he was still alive, as Love Street became Tileston Street in 1821. Lydia Tileston's death at age 95 appears on May 24, 1831, in New North's records (p. 484).

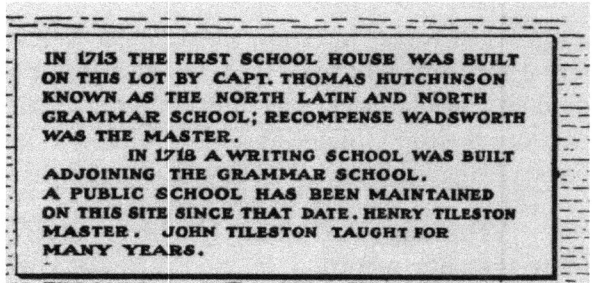

Brilliant History Unfolds for Pastor Joshua Young

After he left the New North Church, Joshua Young became pastor of the Unitarian Church in Burlington, Vt., a northern terminus of the underground railroad, and Young was a prominent figure in moving escaped slaves to freedom.

John Brown

As a radical abolitionist, he sympathized with the efforts of John Brown to fight slavery and the spread of slavery in the United States, by force if necessary. The culmination of Brown's career was his bloody attack on the weapons armory at Harper's Ferry, Va., in October 1859. Brown was captured by Federal and Virginia militia forces, tried and executed by hanging on Dec. 2, 1859. While many saw Brown as a murderous fanatic, to Joshua Young he was a hero and a martyr. Brown's body was returned to his home in North Elba, N.Y., for burial.

Young went to the funeral, intending merely to be one of those in attendance, but as there was no other clergyman present, Brown's widow asked Young if he would preside at the service, which he did. As the body was being placed into the ground, Young repeated the words of St. Paul, "I have fought a good fight, I have finished my course, I have kept the faith. Henceforth there is laid up for me a crown of righteousness ..."

Young immediately found himself a national celebrity, both hailed and vilified. Upon his return to Burlington, he discovered that several prominent families had quit his church and many would not even speak to him. The controversy and social ostracism made his position at his church impossible so he resigned. Despite his fears that his pastoral career had come to an end, Young continued to serve as a minister until just before his death. See page 41.

Margaret Fuller, Sister of Pastor Fuller

Margaret Fuller may well have been the most famous American woman of her day. She was involved in the Transcendentalist Movement,

was an early advocate for women's rights and education, advocated an end to slavery, and wrote in defense of the rights of American Indians.

In her journalistic career, she was the first woman to be editor of the *New York Tribune*. In Europe, she was involved in the revolutions in Italy in the mid-1840s, during which she met the marquis Giovanni Angelo Ossoli, by whom she had a child (Angelo Eugene Philip Ossoli) although it is not clear if the couple ever married. The three of them were returning to America, but died in a shipwreck in a storm off Fire Island, N. Y., in July 1850. Arthur B. Fuller remembered his sister's family when he named his son Arthur Ossoli, baptized in 1856 {p. 320}. Another of Arthur's sisters was Ellen Kilshaw Fuller, who married the Transcendentalist poet William Ellery Channing. Their son Eugene Giovanni, apparently also named to remember Margaret's family, was baptized October 1, 1854 {p. 319}.

Prince Hall, A Name Still Known Today

Prince Hall (1735-1807) was the most prominent African American of his day in Boston. Today he is remembered for the Prince Hall Lodges of Freemasons that he started and which he served as Grand Master from 1791-1807 in Boston. Race has separated black and white Freemasons and Prince Hall Lodges operated without recognition from mainstream state Grand Lodges. This now has changed and today there are 26 state Grand Lodges which recognize and interact with Prince Hall Lodges, mostly in the north. A plaque on Castle Island in Boston Harbor tells this history:

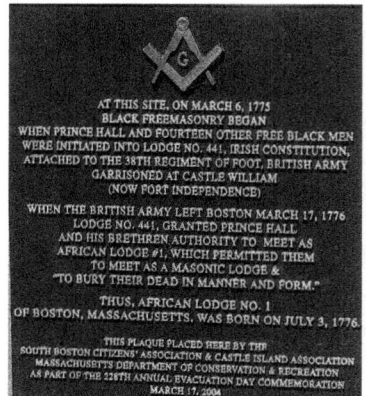

"At this site on March 6, 1775, Black Freemasonry began when Prince Hall and 14 other free black men were initiated into Lodge No. 441, Irish Constitution, attached to the 36 Regt. Of Foot, British Army, garrisoned at Castle William. . .

"When the British Army left Boston on March 17, 1776, Lodge 441 granted Prince Hall and his brethren authority to meet as African Lodge No.1, which permitted them to meet as a Masonic Lodge and 'to bury their dead in manner and form.'"There are more than 2,000 Prince Hall Lodges in the U.S., Canada, the Caribbean, and Liberia. Prince Hall is also known for his work to establish a school in Boston for black children, arguing that blacks paid taxes just as white citizens did and deserved to have a public school. However the selectmen did not listen to him. He started a school on his own, moving to African Society House on Belknap Street where his son Primus continued it. He was also a major early voice for abolition of slavery both in Boston and in America. He died Dec. 7, 1787, as a New North member and lies buried in Copp's Hill Burying Ground.

Deacon John Wells Gave Volume III

Deacon John Wells (1763-1832) donated our Book III volume for keeping New North Church records on Dec. 23, 1813. He and his half-brother Benjamin Tuttle Wells were coppersmiths and made the cannon reamers for "Old Ironsides," along with a variety of pots and pans and other household items including bed warming pans in the collections of the Smithsonian in Washington and Winterthur Museum in Delaware. He was a captain in the Ancient & Honorable Artillery Company (1793) and charter member (1795) with Paul Revere of the MA Charitable Mechanics Assn. to promote U.S.-made goods, train apprentices, and offer welfare benefits to survivors and families. The brothers lived in adjoining condominiums in the Wells-Adams house, 117-118 Salem St., torn down in 1894, one of the last wooden structures on the North End. He represented Boston

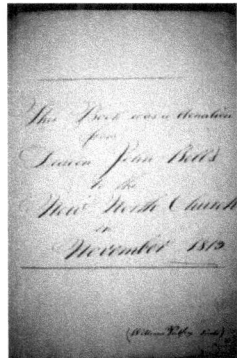

in the General Court (state legislature). John Wells served 20 years as deacon of New North from March 13, 1812 until he died, Oct. 14, 1832, age 69, "an honest man in the truest sense." He was buried in the Wells-Tuttle Tomb 96 in Copp's Hill. Benjamin Tuttle Wells figures prominently in the Appleton-Wells Bible at the back of this book.

OTHER DEACONS & ELDERS AT NEW NORTH CHURCH

In the Puritan and Congregational Churches, there were elders and deacons elected by the congregation. Elders had a higher rank, worked with the pastor overseeing church affairs and participated in the service by reading the lessons or psalms. There was usually only one at a time. At New North Church, the office lasted from 1720 into the 1750s, when it was discontinued as being too hierarchal. Deacons worked with the congregation in administrative functions and there was usually more than one deacon at the same time. They would, for example, receive the collection money, distribute alms to the poor, and oversee the maintenance of the building.

John Baker (1681-1742?)

He was the first elder of New North and served from 1720 until he died. He worked as a brass craftsman and was a member of the Ancient & Honorable Artillery Company (1703) and civically active as trustee of Boston's funds and moderator of the town meeting. He is buried in Tomb 8, Copp's Hill

Ephraim Hunt (1681- after 1732) joined the church in 1716 and became a deacon in 1725/6. Originally a blacksmith, he was appointed justice of the peace in 1702 and special justice of the Court of Common Pleas in 1712. He joined the Ancient & Honorable Artillery Company in 1717 and was sergeant in 1719 and then rose to the rank of colonel in the militia. He had 7 children and is buried in Copp's Hill.

Caleb Lyman (1678-1742)

He was a founder, deacon from 1714-1720 and elder from 1720-1742, when he died without any heirs. He was a shopkeeper, active in Boston town affairs and very generous both to the church--500 pounds or $111,000 at this death, and to the town, giving 30 pounds toward the building of a new workhouse to house and employ the poor. He was lieutenant and captain in the Artillery Company (1732). In 1704 in the Indian Wars, he led a bloodthirsty raid upon an Indian camp nine days up the Connecticut River from Northampton, MA, killing and scalping 7. He was a Boston assessor and selectman and is buried at Copp's Hill.

Deacon John Simpkins

Died Dec. 4, 1831, age 91. "For more than 55 years, deacon of the Church, being chosen in 1776 and for many years the senior deacon of the Congregational churches in Boston. He was the last of 73 persons who have died within the 18 years of my ministry whose age exceeded 70," Pastor Francis Parkman wrote. He was an upholsterer, sold furniture and became very wealthy. He was active in early Revolutionary activity, served as captain in the Artillery Company (1769) and as commissary distributed 20,000 pounds to the families of soldiers serving in the Continental Army. He is buried in Tomb 159 at Copp's Hill. Even though he lived near Brattle Street Church, he remained at New North.

John Dixwell (1681-1725) is noted both for his own life accomplishments and for the history of his ancestors. He was grandson of John Dixwell, one of three "regicides" who fled to Hartford in 1664 following the execution of Charles I by Parliament in 1649. Regicides were members of English Parliament who had signed Charles I's death warrant, which was followed by the Puritan Revolution and Oliver Cromwell's leadership for about 10 years. The father lived under the alias James Davids in Hartford to avoid detection and possible extradition to England for execution by Charles II, the king's son who regained the throne in 1660. Dixwell confessed his true name only on his deathbed in 1689. His son John, a goldsmith, immediately retook the name John Dixwell, and came to Boston, where he was one of the original founders of New North and served as deacon in 1720, ruling elder 1725 and died in 1725.

Samuel Barrett (1670-1736).

When he died in1736, he had been ruling elder for 10 years. He was a member of the Artillery Company (1717) serving as sergeant, 1718, and then lieutenant, 1722. A mason, he joined two others in 1728 to construct the town granary on Mill Creek, which divided the North End from the center of Boston. He built his own masonry tomb, No. 21, in Central Burying Ground on the Common.

William Parkman Jr. (1685-1775)

His father, also Wm. Parkman, was one of the founders and the 12th signer of the Articles. This Wm. Parkman, the son, was chosen as the last ruling elder in 1743. He was a joiner, a specialized carpenter that cuts and fits joints in building construction, and was very active civically. Jobs included scavenger, constable, assessor, measurer of boards and timber, and viewer of shingles. In 1734, he received permission to build and operate Boston's Charlestown ferry dock for 30 years. He was a member of the Artillery (1711) and served as sergeant. A great nephew, The Rev. Francis Parkman, served as pastor from 1813 – 1849.

John B. Hammatt (1778-1864) was elected deacon in 1835 and again in 1849 under The Rev. Francis Parkman. He became wealthy as an upholsterer and wall paper-stainer and was involved in a number of activities: Artillery (1801) as 3rd sergeant and was a very prominent Freemason. It was said there were "few positions either in the Lodge, Chapter or Commandery that he had not held." He was grand master of the Grand Commandery of MA and RI. "His exemplary and useful career, through a long life, earned him the high esteem in which he was universally held."

Henry Fowle Had Remarkable Life

Today, Henry Fowle (1766-1837) would scarcely be remembered except that he wrote an autobiography that details his birth in 1766 in Medford, his coming to Boston at the age of 16, to his death in 1837. He attended New North Church for over 40 years. Except for time during the War of 1812, when Boston was in depression, he made a good living as a pump and block maker. It is a trade unknown today, but important for pumps to pump the water out of the bottoms of sailing ships and block and tackles to raise the sails and lift cargo. He was an active Freemason and orator and master from 1810-1820 of St. Andrew's Lodge, which is associated with the Boston Tea Party of 1773. He helped form the MA Knight's Templar, served as its grand commander for 20 years and then went on high offices in the General Grand Encampment of the United States for that order. He traveled widely and knew many prominent Masons in New England, but died poor and his son William, a well-known education reformer, provided for his widow and children. Despite this, he was buried with full Masonic honors in Newton: *"Primus inter pares,"* First among equals.

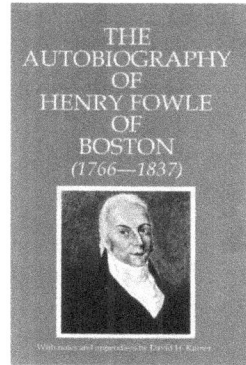

Simon Skillins & Descendants

Simeon Skillins, also Skillin/Skilling (1716-1778) led a family of famous Boston carvers and his sons John and Simeon carved the woodwork in 1801 for the present New North Church. About 80 per cent of it survives today. These carvers included both Skillins and Fowle descendants and this family's work continued to about 1869, moving from signs for tradesmen and taverns to decorative ship carvings of figureheads, trail boards, and stern boards. Their later work includes chairs and furniture. This family is associated with New North Church from 1739 until about 1795. Simeon Skillins and his wife Ruth are buried at Copp's Hill.

Doing His Public Duty Saddened His Life

John Bray, who's death at age 68 in 1829 is noted on page 482, was one of the most popular men on the North End. He was a cooper or barrel maker and packer of fish, beginning poor and becoming very rich, owning Bray's wharf and serving as customs officer. He was active in Boston affairs as selectman, active Freemason, and member of both the Ancient & Honorable Artillery and founder of North End's Columbian Artillery. He had 12 children and "his house was a hospitable resort of old and young, whose enjoyment he delighted to witness, and he was charitable and kind to his poor neighbors."

"Every day, precisely at 11, he would put down his tools, put on his coat and start for Walsh's lemon-stand on Dock Square. The only foreign fruit to be had at that time in Boston was sold in the street from small stands at three or four places," an Artillery biographer wrote.

"When lemons were very expensive, he would take out a handful of change and tell Walsh to help himself, as he did not wish to know the cost. He would then go home with his lemon, prepare his punch and take his dinner, and by 1:30 p.m. was always back at work again at his wharf."

One day in 1821, as he was driving his carriage with his wife on the Medford Pike, he was robbed by a famous robber named Martin of $14 and his gold watch. Mrs. Sally Bray asked Martin if he wanted her gold watch, too, to which Martin replied that he robbed gentlemen only.

Martin was caught, tried, and sentenced to hang, which greatly distressed John Bray. He wanted Martin pardoned or his sentence commuted because Martin was convicted on the basis of Bray's testimony. So, on the day of execution, John Bray was determined to visit Martin, but was prevented from approaching the scaffold by his friends and family. The execution greatly weighed on his conscience and he could think of nothing else. Where before he had been a large and heavy man, he shrank and became emaciated. He had entertained frequently and lavishly and that stopped also. "Conviviality was no longer agreeable to him, and the pleasures of company were so irksome that his festive board was less frequently spread until it was wholly laid aside." His former happy life ended leaving him mentally unbalanced and depressed, his possessions and position meaningless. When he died, he owned Bray's Wharf and a large brick house with gardens on Salem Street.

CHAPTER 6

PARKMAN MURDER HAS ITS ROOTS IN NEW NORTH

One of Boston's most famous murder cases has its roots in New North Church. In 1849, Professor John Webster murdered Dr. George Parkman. How Webster disposed of the body and how he was convicted is still memorable today. Though New North isn't mentioned now in connection with the case, it nonetheless figures into the history of the story.

Both men and their families were members of New North and the church's pastor Francis Parkman was brother of the murdered man.

Church records show that on April 1, 1821, Sarah Hickling Webster, daughter of the murderer Dr. John Webster and his wife Harriet was baptized by the Rev. Francis Parkman.

Two Sundays later on April 15, 1821, Harriet Eliza Parkman, daughter of Dr. George and Eliza Parkman was

Professor John Webster

Dr. George Parkman

baptized at New North Church, also by Pastor Francis Parkman.

Then under Deaths, page 149, we find:

"1849—Nov. 22. George Parkman, M.D. (Murdered at Medical College), 59 yrs."

"1850—Aug.30. Prof. John White Webster of Harvard University. Executed for murder of Dr. Parkman, both once members of NNRS (New North Religious Society), 57, 10 months."

Earlier, George and Eliza Parkman had a son George Francis on Jan 26, 1817, but he died 29 months later.

The Websters had an even more extensive history with New North. Both became members on May 30, 1819. They had two children who died: John Redford Webster, born May 29, 1818 and died Nov. 1, 1820, and Harriet Wainwright Webster, born Nov. 22, 1822, who died in infancy. Another daughter, Mary Ann Webster, was baptized on March 20, 1825. Two additional Webster daughters were born: Catherine Prescott Webster, 1827, and Harriet Wainwright (it was common to name a child after the one who had died), 1830, but by then the family was attending First Church in Cambridge.

The murder case itself is one of the most famous in Boston history, reaching worldwide attention and press coverage. Even Charles Dickens when he visited Boston wanted to see the room at Harvard Medical College where the gristly murder took place.

The murder was unprecedented. It involved two prominent Boston high society men and such events just didn't happen here. It was charged with lurid details and it was so important that it was prosecuted in the Massachusetts Supreme Court. It had sensationalism and the press devoted columns to it. There was international interest in its unfolding. And it seriously disrupted the lives of the two families involved.

Professor John White Webster (1793-1850) was a native Bostonian. He graduated from Harvard in 1811, Harvard Medical College in 1815, and then went to London to Guy's Hospital for what we today would call his residency, then called "surgeon's pupil, physician's pupil, and surgeon's dresser." In 1818, he was a doctor in Fayal, Sao Miguel Island in the Azores, where he met and married Harriet Fredrica Hickling, daughter of the American vice consul there. He returned to Boston to set up his own practice, but soon moved on to become a lecturer in chemistry, mineralogy and geology at Harvard Medical College.

Old Harvard Medical College

Oliver Wendell Holmes Sr., physician, author and father of the noted Supreme Court justice, described Webster as "pleasant in the lecture room, but rather nervous and excitable." Some related that Webster liked to liven up his demonstrations with fireworks and the college president warned him that some of his demonstrations were dangerous and could cause a possible accident. Professor Webster also authored several works in his field that were viewed favorably.

Poet Henry Wadsworth Longfellow, a family friend, describes the professor's bizarre sense of humor and an unfortunate harbinger of things to come when he was entertained at dinner in the Webster home:

"Lowering the lights, fitting a noose around his own neck, and lolling his head forward, tongue protruding, over a bowl of blazing chemicals, he gave a ghastly imitation of a man being hanged."

With four daughters, a wife used to upper class life, and a mansion in Cambridge, it seemed that his salary couldn't stretch to cover the bills. He was making about $800 a year for his normal lectures and then was boosted to $1,200 when he became Erving Professor of Chemistry at the college.

His tastes and expenses simply outstripped his income. He had quickly run through the money inherited from his father by building a mansion in Cambridge some called "Webster's Folly." Then he borrowed heavily from friends. That didn't help and he was forced to give up his mansion and rent a more modest home. George Parkman, who Webster knew as a benefactor of Harvard Medical College and as a member of New North Church, was a money lender in addition to being a real estate mogul and doctor. Webster borrowed $400.00 and another $2,000.00 later and had not made any payments on the debt for two years.

To add insult to injury, Webster had leveraged his valuable rock and mineral collection as collateral for the Parkman loan when at the same time he mortgaged it to Robert Gould Shaw, Parkman's brother-in-law. Webster also had been writing bad checks on the Cambridge Bank where he had no account.

Dr. George Parkman (1790-1849) was a generous man, but a hard man with the dollar if you owed him money. Avoiding the cost of a horse, he could be seen walking around Boston personally collecting rents on his properties.

Parkman came from one of Boston's richest families, investing mostly in Boston real estate. Studying in Scotland and Paris, he was a medical doctor for many years, especially interested in mental illness and help found the *New England Journal of Medicine*. Later he turned to money-lending and land development on Boston's West End. His other interest was in philanthropy and he endowed Harvard with the Parkman Professorship of Anatomy and Physiology and donated land for the Harvard Medical College which opened in 1846 and where he was murdered three years later. Being strung along on the debt and at the same time being flimflammed on its collateral set the stage for a confrontation with Webster. He was last seen on a Boston street at 1:45 p.m. on Fri., Nov. 23, 1849.

The confrontation took place later that afternoon when Dr. Parkman went to Professor Webster's basement laboratory to get his money. It appears both men became angry and Webster apparently stabbed Parkman in the ribs with a hunting knife. Webster later said he hit Parkman over the head, but marks on the body pointed to stabbing.

Panic stricken by what he had done, Webster proceeded to dismember the body. Some parts he hid, some he dropped down his privy, and others like the head he burned in the furnace. Then he acted like nothing had happened.

It appeared that Dr. Parkman had totally disappeared.

The family put out 28,000 circulars advertising a $3,000 reward for information on the whereabouts of Dr. Parkman. Leads came into the police, but what cracked the case five days later was when the medical school's building's janitor Ephraim Littlefield told police about suspicious events in Dr. Webster's lab. This led police to find the various body parts in various places. Professor Webster was arrested a week after Dr. Parkman's disappearance.

SPECIAL NOTICE!

$3000 REWARD. DR GEORGE PARKMAN, a well known citizen of Boston, left his residence, No 8 Walnut street, on Friday last; he is 60 years of age, about 5 feet 9 inches high, grey hair, thin face, with a scar under his chin, light complexion, and usually walks very fast. He was dressed in a dark frock coat, dark pantaloons, purple silk vest, with dark figured black stock and black hat.

As he may have wandered from home in consequence of some sudden aberration of mind being perfectly well when he left his house; or, as he had with him a large sum of money, he may have been foully dealt with;—the above reward will be paid for information which will lead to his discovery if alive; or for the detection and conviction of the perpetrators of any injury that may have been done him.

A suitable reward will be paid for the discovery of his body.

Information may be given to the City Marshal.

ROBERT G. SHAW.

Boston, Nov 26, 1849.   istc   nov 27

Boston Evening Transcript, November 27, 1849.

During the 12-day trial, beginning March 19, 1850, it is said that up to 60,000 people saw portions of it in the courtroom. Tickets for $5 were sold for 15-minute increments to be seated in the courtroom.

New North Church pastor, the Rev. Francis Parkman, who had resigned his pastorate due to depression by the time of the murder, testified at the trial. He said that Professor Webster came to his home about 4 p.m. the Sunday after his brother went missing. Professor Webster's visit primarily centered on his maintaining that he had paid the debt and that Dr. Parkman had marked it paid, but that he could not find the paper. The prosecution made much of the fact that Webster offered no words of concern to the Rev. Mr. Parkman about his brother's disappearance or concern for the Parkman family.

Professor Webster's attorneys did an adequate job presenting a parade of character witnesses and of attacking the janitor's testimony as just wanting to collect the $3,000.00 reward, which he did eventually. Even Webster's three daughters: Harriet, Catherine and Mary Ann testified in behalf of their father.

However, one of the problems for the defense was Professor Webster himself. He had to have the last word, about 15 minutes of last word.

He told the jury that he had offered evidence to his attorneys that they had not presented in court. That information alone would exonerate him, he said. His friend's testimony in court showed he was beyond reproach, he said. Then he proclaimed he was not connected to this murder in any way in a loud and dramatic voice and sat down.

Judge Lemuel Shaw

Judge Lemuel Shaw, presiding judge of the Massachusetts Supreme Court then proceeded to instruct the jury for more than two and a half hours.

Two important points of law were established.

1. Before this case, *Corpus Delicti*. meant that, for there to be a conviction, there must be a whole body. Corpus delicti literally means "the body of the crime," referring to the body of evidence that a crime has occurred, or, in a murder case, the corpse of the deceased is the corpus delicti. Circumstantial evidence could not establish Corpus Delicti.

"In the eyes of the law, the state had not proven that the remains found in the lab were Parkman's. Even if the remains were Parkman's," the defense continued, "the state had not shown how he was killed," one trial analysis quoted the defense as saying.

In this case, the court ruled that the sum of what all that the police detectives discovered and that the prosecution presented amounted to *Corpus Delicti*.

Judge Shaw told the jury:

"It has sometimes been said by judges that a jury never ought to convict in a capital case unless the dead body is found. That, as a general proposition, is true. It sometimes happens, however, that it cannot be found, where the proof of death is clear. Sometimes, in a case of murder at sea, the body is thrown overboard on a stormy night. Because the body is not found, can anybody deny that the author of that crime is a murderer?" a New England Publishing Associates book, *Great American Trials*, quoted the judge.

2. This trial is one of the first in America in which forensic evidence of medical experts was used to convict a defendant. Dr. Parkman's partly burned false teeth, which were found in the furnace, were identified by his dentist Dr. Nathan C. Keep. Because of the length of Dr. Parkman's jaw, they were especially intricate. He testified that these were the very ones he had made for him years earlier. In addition, Parkman's private parts were identified by his wife. And the family identified from the torso the peculiar heavy hair that Dr. Parkman had on his stomach and back.

On March 30, 1850, in less than three hours of deliberation, the jury convicted Webster of murder with malice, an automatic death sentence. On April 1, Judge Shaw sentenced Webster to death by hanging.

Professor Webster was his own worst enemy. If he had not dismembered the body and had confessed immediately, he probably would have been charged with manslaughter or murder without malice and gotten off with a prison sentence. As it was, he did later confess to the crime in making his appeal for clemency to the governor of Massachusetts, but the heinous nature of the murder and intense public outcry precluded the governor from acting favorably on his pleas.

John White Webster was executed at 9 a.m. Aug. 30, 1850, at Boston's Leverett Street Jail. He was denied burial at Mt Auburn Cemetery in Cambridge. No one knows for certain where Professor Webster's body is buried because it was done in secret later that night. Witnesses do say it is definitely in Copp's Hill Burying Ground, possibly in the old Webster Family Tomb 4 or possibly in an unmarked spare grave.

The secrecy was supposed to avoid grave robbers, prevent crowds, and dampen down publicity. Instead, it gave rise to a false story that Professor Webster wore a harness during the execution and escaped to the Azores to spend the rest of his life. Newspaper reporters wandered far from truth in their stories and this an example of that.

Both men's families suffered for years afterwards.

The George Parkman home at 8 Walnut St, Boston, is still is there today. His wife Eliza died in 1877 and is buried with her husband in Mt. Auburn Cemetery, Cambridge. The children, George Francis and Harriet, became recluses and never married. The estate passed to them and, when George Francis died in 1908, about $ 5.5 million was left to the city of Boston. It is one of the largest bequests it has ever received.

Harriet Webster steadfastly maintained her husband's innocence until he confessed in his clemency plea to the governor. She continued to visit him along with the daughters up until the execution. Police tried to shield them from the press and the curious.

Their old friends, the Appletons collected $5,000 for their welfare and the murdered man's wife, Eliza Parkman, was a generous contributor. Most of the Webster household effects were sold at auction for $450. A family friend, Samuel Cunningham, donated a home at the corner of Ash and Mt. Auburn Streets in Cambridge for Harriet to live in. She died October, 10,1853, less than three years after the trial, and is buried in Mt. Auburn Cemetery.

Henry Wadsworth Longfellow said in his journal:

"Mrs. Webster is dead—dead of a broken heart—worn out, she swooned away into death without any other disease than this! The only wonder is she did not die before. What a life! With the stigma of her husband's crime upon her."

She was admired both in life and in death. Her pastor William Newell preached a

Henry Wadworth Longfellow

76

long sermon the Sunday after her funeral and told how admirably she had lived her life under such difficult circumstances.

Earlier in October, 1845, the oldest daughter Sarah Hickling Webster had married John Dabney, son of the consul in Fayal in the Azores. Then in September, 1849, their son Charles was baptized by Pastor Francis Parkman at the Webster home in Cambridge.

Harriet (1830-1924), married John's brother Samuel Wyllys Dabney, who was courting her at the time her father was executed, and they went to live in the Azores.

Catharine Prescott Webster (1827-1909) married Thomas Jackson Lothrop, a tutor to the Dabney boys in Fayal, Azores. Mary Ann (Molly) (1825-1909) never married and lived in the Azores to the age of 100. Catharine and Mary Ann left Boston to join their sisters in the Azores right after the funeral.

Even if their mother had no happiness, it seems the girls did live fulfilled lives after all the heartache they had gone through with their father.

Lemuel Shaw, presiding judge in the case, retired from the bench at age 80 in 1860 and his ruling on circumstantial evidence continues to be cited today as the means test for this type of defense plea in a murder case. In an earlier case in 1843 involving attorney George Bemis as defense attorney, Judge Shaw's ruling set the precedent on insanity pleas in criminals defenses. Later, George Bemis was hired by the Parkman family to assist the prosecutor. He did a full account of the trial, the most detailed record of the police investigation and trial transcript ever written on it.

Judge Shaw's daughter Elizabeth married Herman Melville in 1850 and Melville was famous for the stories *Moby Dick* and *Billy Budd*.

NOTE: Simon Schama, famous for his book *The Story of the Jews,* and the PBS documentary of the same name, devotes the better part of his historical novel *Dead Certainties (Unwarranted Speculations),* published in 1991 by Vintage Books, to the Webster murder of Dr. Parkman. In it he gives a well-researched and interesting narrative for modern readers.

CHAPTER 7

AFRICAN AMERICANS AT NEW NORTH

It is indeed surprising to us today to think of slavery in Boston, but it did indeed exist and Massachusetts was the center of the slave trade in New England. Possibly as early as 1624, but certainly by 1638, when Indian captives from the Pequot War were exchanged in the West Indies for Africans, slavery had gained a foothold. It is estimated that Boston ship owners were selling slaves to Connecticut by 1680 and Rhode Island in 1696. At its height, the slave population from 1755 to 1764 was never more than 2% or 4,500 of Boston's population. Large slaveholdings were simply not economically viable in New England because the farms were smaller and basically family owned. If a farm had any, it would have only one or two slaves. In Boston and Massachusetts villages, slaves worked in the crafts and trades with their owners in either ship or home construction or in producing products. Because of court cases, slavery had effectively ended by 1810. Slaveholders often freed their slaves and then paid them wages to continue. Others converted them to indentured servants and they had a set time to earn their freedom.

Free blacks made up a much larger part of the population, about 10% in 1752. Many were laborers or worked in shops and some even owned their own businesses. Women worked as domestics or as hotel maids.

At New North Church, African Americans did not receive equal treatment and discrimination did exist. Blacks had to sit in the balcony. Prince Hall, the most prominent black member of New North, had to suffer these indignities, but he stayed. America's first published poet, Phyllis Wheatley (1753-1784), attended 1st Church and likely suffered these same indignities and yet also still stayed a member there and is likely buried in its Granary Burying Ground tomb for the poor.

Why did Prince Hall continue to be a New North Church member when he and Flora could have joined an African American congregation? Possibly this is the one place he could freely associate with whites and was respected. Certainly he had an impact as one of the few blacks in a white congregation, a very positive influence against segregation. He also was an abolitionist and these views were popular among many parishioners. The Halls continued to be members until their deaths: "April 7, 1798: Mrs. Flora Hall wife of Prince Hall, a member of the Church" and on Dec. 7,1807: "Prince Hall, church member, age 72 years."

In this book, we are not continuing that segregation. However, because of the difficulty of researching African Americans and also because of their relatively low population in early-day Boston, African Americans are listed separately in this chapter by category. People of color in Volume III are indexed and cross referenced, but those in Books I and II are not indexed, so the researcher needs to look through the short lists below for a complete knowledge of African Americans at New North Church. Then on to the Book III listings.

Book I & II—1714-1812
Book I

Page 14: Admissions
  1721, Dec. 20 (f) Zipporah, a Negro Woman.
  1723, Nov. 10: (f) Experience, a Malatto woman

Page 24: Admissions
     1766: Nov. 2 (f) Dinah-a Negro Woman belonging to
                    Capt. Nichels

Page 26: Admissions
     1775: Aug. 27 (f) Susanna Williams. . .free Negro
     1777: Feb. 2: (f) Chloe Negro servant to Capt. John Bradford

Page 27: Admissions
     1782: Aug. 11: (m) Pompey Edes—Free Negro

Page 30: Admissions
     1804: Sept 9: (f) Lucy Pollard, black

Page 80: Covenant
     1773: May 2: Peter Mitchell, a free Negro
     1781: Dec 2: Samuel, a Negro Man belonging to Col. Jackson

Page 81: Covenant
     1789: Aug. 2: Billah Cary, a Negro
         Covenant Entries end with 1812

BAPTISMS
Acceptance of Black Baptisms:
Book I, Page 260, Church Business:
1764, June 10 Lord's Day:
     The Pastor (Andrew Eliot) laid the following case before the Brethren:
     A Negro Woman, who from years ago professed Christ, was baptized in this Church: Desired the privileges of the Covenant for her offspring.
     It appears she was a person of sober conviction; that she had contracted with the Person who is now her husband by the consent of both their masters and mistresses, but had not been married by the forms prescribed by the law of the Province for white people. The master of the Negro man not consenting to such marriage.
     VOTED: That this child or any other under like circumstances may be baptized.

Baptisms Pages 91 – 200
(Jan. 14, 1714 – Dec. 30, 1781)

Page 96: Baptisms
    1719: March 8: (f) Zipporah, a Negro Woman. Adult
Page 102: Baptisms
    1723: Nov. 3: (f) Experience, a Molatto Woman
Page 115: Baptisms
    1732: March 26: (m) Abraham, a Negro man servant to Mr.
        S. Gardner
Page 117: Baptisms
    1732: June 3: (m) Sampson, a Negro Man servant to Mr.
        John Baker
Page 119: Baptisms
    1734: Dec. 29: (m) Benjamin, a Free Negro. Adult
Page 120: Baptisms
    1735: Oct. 5: (f) Tilipah, a Negro woman Adult Servant to
        Abiul Walbry?, Esq.
Page 123: Baptisms
    1737: Aug. 7: (m) Robin, a Negro Man servant to Deacon
        Webb
Page 124: Baptisms
    1738: Aug. 6: (m) Caesar, a Negro Man servant to Mr Barret.
Page 129: Baptisms
    1741: Aug. 30: (f) Pricilla, Negro woman servant to Capt.
        Caroll?
        Aug. 30: (m) Will, Son to Priscilla, Negro &c (Capt.
        Caroll)
Page 132: Baptisms
    1743: May 15: (m) Jack, a Negro Man servant to Mr.
        Edward Cheever.
        May 15: (m) Salem, a Negro Man Servant to Mr.
        John Harrod
Page 133: Baptisms
    1744: April 15: (f) Qualheba, a Negro Woman Servant to
the Honorable Samuel Watts, Esq.
        April 29: (f) Mary, Negro Daughter to Qualhaba Negro

Page 134: Baptisms
>1744: Nov. 18: (f) Flora, a Negro Woman servant to Mr. J. Richey
>
>1744: Nov. 18: (f) Sarah, a Negro child, daughter to Flora above
>
>1745: Feb. 24: (m) Caesar of Jenny, Negro woman servant to Capt. Viscount

Page 135: Baptisms
>1745: April 7: (m) Mark Anthony of Boston & Flora, both Negros

Page 136: Baptisms
>1746: March 2: (f) Rose of Sampson, Negro servant to Mr. John Baker & Dolly, Negro servant to Mr. Afton Stoddard

Page 137: Baptisms
>1746: Sept. 14: (f) of Boston, Negro servant to Mr. John Brock, and Flora, Negro.

Page 139: Baptisms
>1747: Jan.31: (f) Jenny of Caesar & Jenny, both Negros

Page 140: Baptisms
>1748: Sept. 4: (m) Boston of Boston & Flora Negro servants

Page 141: Baptisms
>1749: Nov. 12: (m) Suranam, Negro servant to Robert Parish

Page 145: Baptisms
>1751: Oct. 27: (m) Cato of Boston & Flora, both Negros

Page 148: Baptisms
>1753: July: (f) Rose of Surrinam & Rose, both Negros

Page 149: Baptisms
>1753: Nov. 4: (m) Mark Anthony of Boston & Flora, Negro servants

Page 150: Baptisms
>1754: June 9: (f) Elisabeth of Jack & Lydia, both Negroes

Page 154: Baptisms
>1756: Aug. 8: (f) Flora of Surrinam & Rose, both Negros
>
>1756: Dec 12: (f) Dinah, a Negro Servant belonging to Captain Barber

Page 167: Baptisms
>1764: June 17: (m) Adam of Dinah, both Negroes

Page 185: Baptisms
>1773: May 16: (f) Susanna of Peter & Ruth Mitchell, free
>Negros

Page 191: Baptisms
>1777: Aug. 10: (m) Peter of Peter L Mitchell and . . . Sura
>Domo, Negro

Page 195: Baptisms
>1779: Nov. 28: (f) Susanna Franklin of Susanna Franklin,
>free Negro

African American baptisms end here, although white Baptisms in Book I continue through Page 331 ending in 1797. Possibly there were no black baptisms because blacks may have joined other churches after that time. For example, Boston's African Baptist Church was organized in 1805.

MARRIAGES

"The slavery of Negroes was among other abesses which gave origin to the practice of denying them the privilege of contracting marriages according to the laws of the land.

"The simple consent of the master and mistresses of slaves was all the ceremony which was deemed necessary for them to become man and wife. This was the cause of much irregularity among them.

"In this instance, the master of the Negro husband would consent to no other mode of marrying," Ephraim Eliot wrote.

So the issue of marriage came before the full church meeting about 1765. The church body voted that it would henceforth baptize any Negro infant who was presented by their parents regardless of formal marriage contracts or vows.

It could not deal with the problem of Negro marriage contracts and had to wait until slavery was abolished in Massachusetts in 1783 when the Massachusetts Supreme Court ruled slavery unconstitutional based on the 1780 Constitution. All slaves in Boston and the rest of the state were immediately freed.

Source: Eliot Papers by Ephraim Eliot, Boston Eliot Family Papers, Massachusetts Historical Society, page 17.

Book I—Marriages 1744-1783
Page 43: Marriages

  1744: May 24: Boston, Negro servant to Jno (John) Pomeroy?
         Gloria, Negro Servant to Jno Proctor?

Page 50: Marriages

  1753: June 28: Boston, N. Servant to Mr. Nathaniel
         Holmes
      Susanna, N. Servant to Capt. Samuel Hawkins

Page 51: Marriages

  1754: June 18: Will, Negro servant to Samuel Hinton
         Ann, Free Negro

Page 58: Marriages

  1756: Sept. 22: Harriet Free Negroes
         Silva
  1756: Dec. 23: Archlais, Negro Servant to James Barray
         Esther, Negro Servant to Alexander Sears

Page 56: Marriages

  1760: Jan. 7: Jack, Negro Servant to Sarah Lewis
         Lydia Gleson, free Negro
  1760: Nov. 20: Boston, Negro Servant to Nathaniel Holmes
         Phyllis, Negro Servant to Abigail Labb

Page 59: Marriages

  1763: Jan. 4: Peter, Negro Servant to Mr. McTineak?
         Jenny, Negro Servant Mr. Richie

Page 62: Marriages

  1765: Nov. 28: Sambo, Negro Servant to Francis Ritchie
         Jane, a free Negro
  1766: Feb. 6: Prince & Poll? Negro Servants to Mr. Afton
         Stoddard

Page 64: Marriages

  1768: March 17: Yong? Negro Servant to Joseph Jackson
         Prudence, Negro Servant to Abagail Williams
  1768: May 12: Boston, Negro Servant to Edward Foster
         Bellah, Negro Servant to Joseph Roby

Page 65: Marriages

  1769: Sept. 28: Salem, Negro servant to Nathaniel Greenwood
         Rose, a free Negro

Page 66: Marriages

    1772: July 15: Walt, servant to Samuel Hawes
                   Nancy, servant to Ebenezer Jacobs

Page 71: Marriages

    1780: Feb. 13: Henry & Grace, Negroes

Page 72: Marriages

    1780: (No month, day) Yarrow, Wilett, Negros

Ends with 1783 Marriages and continues on Page 333 with Marriages from Rev. Webb's Private Book. The only marriages of African Americans are below. It would seem there would have been more black marriages than that in those 13 years.

Page 345: Marriages

    1796: Oct. 9: Thomas and Dolly Ball, Blacks

Page 337: Marriages from Rev. Webb's Private Book (1744-1783)

    1789: Nov. 14: Prince Holmes & . . . . (Listed because Prince is a black name) There is no bride mentioned.

Page 345: Marriages

    1796: Oct. 9: Thomas and Dolly Ball   Blacks
                  End of Marriages for Book I

Book II Marriages 1798 -1812
Page 93: Marriages

    1799: Sept 5: (Unreadable) Blacks

Page 97: Marriages

    1803: Aug. 2: William Clifford and Ruby Smith   Blacks

Page 103: Marriages

    1808: March 14: Thomas Welles and Joanna Brown Blacks
    1808: April 27: Sylvester Richmond and Sally Tyler Blacks
    1808: Aug. 14: Thomas Amibal and Esther Faybls? Blacks
Page 104: Marriages
    1809: July 7: John Olin (Blin) and Sarah Desse Blacks

Page 105: Marriages

    1810: Aug. 19: John Jackson and Jane Johnson Blacks

Marriages for Book II end at Dec. 31, 1812.

DEATHS
Book I--Pages 351 – 360 Deaths
Page 352:
    1792: Feb. 10: Mr. Prince Hipaire?? 70 yrs. a black
Page 356
    1795: August 29: In this month died also a black woman 78
        – James Hawkes (probably owner).
Page 360
    1797: Jan 22: A child of Isabella, black, 8 mos.
    1797: Feb. 9: a negro woman, about 50. "a stranger."
    1797: Aug….: Harrison Mortimer, black, 60 yrs.

NOTE: In 1759, Buried in the Town of Boston: Whites 565, Blacks 54 total 576

1760: Whites 508	Blacks 68	Total 576
1761: Whites 390	Blacks 66	Total 456
1762: Whites 448	Blacks 83	Total 531
1763: Whites 344	Blacks 63	Total 407
1764 Whites 471	Blacks 77	Total 548
1765 Whites 494	Blacks 51	Total 545
1766 Whites 389	Blacks 44	Total 489

No listing 1767 through 1769

1770 Whites 404	Blacks 79	Total 483
1771 Whites 423	Blacks 59	Total 482
1772 Whites 458	Blacks 59	Total 517
1773 Whites 533	Blacks 62	Total 595

Book II--Pages 132 Deaths
1797 Yellow Fever Epidemic in Boston: August – October
    No African Americans Listed
Pages 133:
    1798: April 7: Mrs. Flora Hall wife of Prince Hall,
        a member of the Church
Pages 144:
    1803: July 21: Harriet Hall, Black, 36 years, A church
        member

Pages 145:

1804: Jan. …: Violet Greenough. Black widow, age 77 years

1804: March 9 Miss Coffin

………Also a black woman, 44 years.

Pages 148:

1807: Dec. (no date; It is Dec. 7): Prince Hall, church member. 72 years.

Ends Nov. 20, 1813.

Volume III—Indexed by Name, then event.

Those identified as "black," "colored" or "of color" in Volume III.
These are cross referenced for marriages

Armstrong, John H., married Mrs. Ann Stevens, Oct. 15, 1818, p. 155

Benson, Laben, married Rhoda Gibson, May 3, 1819, p. 155
Bowen, Lucy , married Thomas Cooper, Dec. 19, 1827, p. 163
Bowen, Lucy T., married Cato Prince, Feb. 18, 1825, p. 161
Brown, Abigail, married John Mitchell, June 29, 1815, p. 151
Brown, Cecilia, married Thomas, Cooper, Mar. 11, 1832, p. 166
Brown, John, married Harriet Potter, Nov. 12, 1820, p. 157
Butler, Henry, married Judith Flancy, Sept. 10, 1818, p. 155

Cæsar, Jane, married Jefferson Didea, Oct. 17, 1832, p. 166
Clark, Thomas, married Mary Evens, June 21, 1821, p. 158
Colburn, Nancy, married Perry Cole, Aug. 17, 1820, p. 157
Cole, Mary-Ann, married Henry Thacker, Nov. 30, 1820, p. 157
Cole, Perry, married Nancy Colburn, Aug. 17, 1820, p. 157
Cooper, Thomas, married Cecilia Brown, Mar. 11, 1832, p. 166
Cooper, Thomas, married Lucy Bowen, Dec. 19, 1827, p. 163
Cross, Lois, married Peter Spiwood, Mar. 25, 1821, p. 157

Deetes, Titus, married Eliza Evans, May 30, 1824, p. 161
Didea, Jefferson, married Jane Cæsar, Oct. 17, 1832, p. 166
Dunkinsfield, William, married Nancy Guss, April 26, 1816, p. 152
Durant, Mary, married James Williams, April 12, 1819, p. 155

Evans, Eliza, married Titus Deetes, May 30, 1824, p. 161
Evans, Mary, married Thomas Clark, June 21, 1821, p. 158

Faguins, Adeline, married Daniel Low, Nov. 30, 1823, p. 160
Flancy, Judith, married Henry Butler, Sept. 10, 1818, p. 155

Gibson, Rhoda, married Laben Benson, May 03, 1819, p. 155
Gould, Jane A., married John Williams, July 20, 1821, p. 158
Gray, Peter, married Betsey Windship, Oct. 23, 1823, p. 160
Guss, Nancy, married William Dunkinsfield, April 26, 1816, p. 152

Hall, Susanna, member, p. 363
Hall, Mrs. Sylvia, deaths, Dec. 7, 1836, p. 494
Howard, Hannah, married Adam S. Ray, Oct. 12, 1826, p. 162
Howard, Richard, married Hannah Waters, July 1, 1821, p. 158

Levear, Hannah B., married John D. Silver, Sept. 21, 1826, p. 162
Lewis, Hannah, married John Williams, June 20, 1819, p. 156
Lewis, Joseph, married Adeline Williams, Aug. 12, 1847, p. 174
Long, Almira, married Samuel Sampson, Mar. 14, 1819, p. 155
Low, Daniel, married Adeline Faguins, Nov. 30, 1823, p. 160
Lyndes, George, married Catharine Robbins, April 11, 1824, p. 161

Macoy, Abraham, married Elizabeth Williams, Oct. 14, 1829, p. 164
Mitchell, John, married Abigail Brown, June 29, 1815, p. 151

Pollard, Lucy, member, p. 364; death, Dec. 12, 1831, p. 484
Potter, Harriet, married John Brown, Nov. 12, 1820, p. 157
Prince, Cato, married Lucy T. Bowen, Feb. 18, 1825, p. 161

Ray, Adam S., married Hannah Howard, Oct. 12, 1826, p. 162
Robbins, Catharine, married George Lyndes, April 11, 1824, p. 161
Russ, Mrs. Abigail, deaths, Jan. 11, 1823, p. 472

Sampson, Samuel, married Almira Long, Mar. 14, 1819, p. 155
Silver, John D., married Hannah B. Levear, Sept. 21, 1826, p. 162

Spiwood, Peter, married Lois Cross, Mar. 25, 1821, p. 157
Stearns, Mary, married Alfred Williams, Oct. 07, 1827, p. 162
Stevens, Mrs. Ann, married John H. Armstrong, Oct. 15, 1818, p. 155

Thacker, Henry, married Mary-Ann Cole, Nov. 30, 1820, p. 157
Thacker, Henry, married Deborah Westley, April 15, 1828, p. 163
Thacker, Henry James Walker, child of Henry & Mary A Thacker,
        baptized May 14, 1822, p. 293
Thacker, Mary Ann Webster, child of Henry & Mary A. Thacker,
        baptized Aug. 10, 1823, p. 293
Thacker, Rachel Matilda, child of Henry & Mary Thacker, baptized
        July 17, 1825, p. 296

Waters, Hannah, married Richard Howard, July 01, 1821, p. 158
Westley, Deborah, married Henry Thacker, April 15, 1828, p. 163
Williams, Adeline, married Joseph Lewis, Aug. 12, 1847, p. 174
Williams, Elizabeth, married Abraham Macoy, Oct. 14, 1829, p. 164
Williams, James, married Mary Durant, April 12, 1819, p. 155
Williams, John, married Hannah Lewis, June 20, 1819, p. 156
Williams, John, married Jane A. Gould, July 20, 1821, p. 158
Williams, Alfred, married Mary Stearns, Oct. 07, 1827, p. 162
Windship, Betsey, married Peter Gray, Oct. 23, 1823, p. 160

Unnamed foreigner, deaths, April 27, 1823
Unnamed servant of Mrs. [Joanna] Lakeman, deaths, Feb. 23,
1856, p. 508.

CHAPTER 8

THE NORTH END TODAY

For 300 years, the site of New North Church has been a church. From 1714 – 1802, it housed the New North's first church, which began as Puritan, changed to Congregational and ended up Unitarian. The present Charles Bulfinch-designed church was dedicated May 2, 1804 and it housed the New North Religious Society until about 1863.

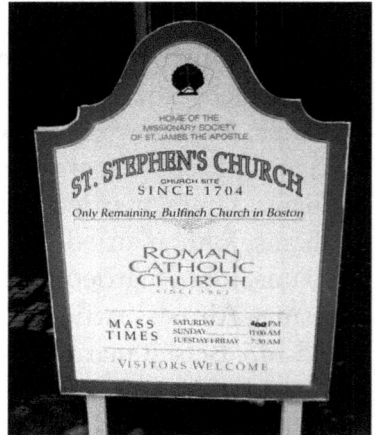

Beginning in the 1840s, Irish immigrants flocked to the North End by the thousands for its low-cost housing as it gradually went downhill and native Bostonians moved to other parts of the city. The North End became almost entirely Irish and they were Roman Catholic and did not embrace Unitarianism.

Shortly after the Unitarian congregation disbanded in 1863, the building was sold for $35,000 to the Most Rev. John B. Fitzpatrick, Roman Catholic bishop of Boston. He bought it for use of St. John the Baptist parish, whose church on Moon Street had become too small. Rev. George Foxcroft Haskins, a Harvard graduate and Roman

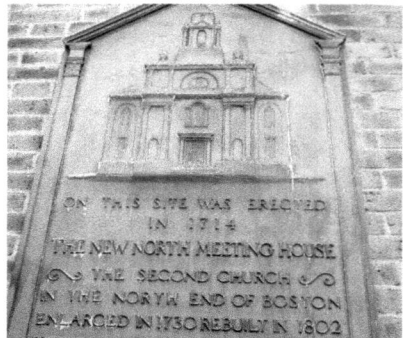

Catholic convert, became priest in charge of the parish, renamed St. Stephen's Church. It was remodeled for Catholic worship.

Interior front view with altar

In a detailed history, Sister Fidelma Conway, C.S.J., St. Stephen's historian, has related:

"St Stephen's underwent many changes. In 1869, it was moved back 12 feet when Hanover Street was widened. A few months later it was raised 6.5 feet to make room for a basement church. In 1874-75, an addition of 30 feet was added to the rear to increase seating capacity from 1,000 to 1,600."

Fire gutted the church in 1879 and from the insurance settlement the building was repaired and electricity installed. In the 1920s to commemorate Boston's 300th Anniversary, the "dirty gray paint was removed and it was restored to its original

Back of church with organ in balcony.

beautiful red brick and white paint. The dome was also gilded. Mrs. Charles Knowles Bolton of Boston raised $3,121.00 for the work and one of the contributors was John F. Fitzgerald (Honey Fitz), Boston mayor, who was baptized there in 1863. He was grandfather of President John Fitzgerald Kennedy. Rose Fitzgerald Kennedy, the President's mother, was also baptized there and later buried from St. Stephens in 1995.

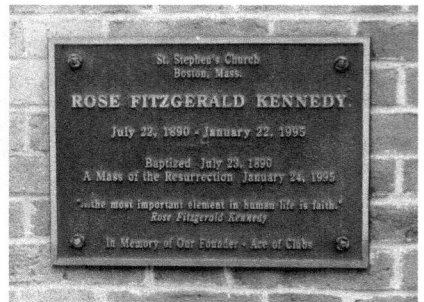

"...the most important element in human life is faith."
–Rose Kennedy

Rose Kennedy funeral, 1995

Senator Ted Kennedy emerging from church with family.

"By 1964, St. Stephen's suffered the fate of most other inner city churches. The congregation was depleted and there was no money for upkeep and repairs. After consulting experts and studying alternatives, Richard Cardinal Cushing decided not only to save the church, but also to restore it to the Bulfinch design at a cost of over $1 million," Sr. Conway relates.

"The first task to lower the church to its original level was done by Isaac Blair & Co., Inc., of Cambridge, the same company that raised it in 1870.

"When the belfry was stripped, the original dome, covered with sheet copper and held together with wrought iron nails, was found underneath a false cap. Shortly after the copper and nails were authenticated by Columbia University and the original bill from Paul Revere was found.

"Other than the pews, about 80 per cent of the woodwork is original. The Doric and Corinthian Columns are one-piece pillars of pine. The capitals of the Corinthian columns were carved by Simeon Skillin, one of the foremost woodcarvers of the 18th and early 19th Centuries. He is also noted for the figureheads on ships that sailed from Boston.

"A Hooper bell is in the belfry. It was placed there by the City of Boston in 1853 when the original, believed to be from the Paul Revere Foundry, cracked while being used by the city for a fire alarm," she wrote.

The church still holds services and since 1968 it is the international headquarters for the Missionary Society of St. James the Apostle, an organization of diocesan missionary priests who serve in Peru and Ecuador.

Today St. Stephen's Church is listed on the National Register of Historic Sites and is the only Bulfinch church remaining in Boston. Services are weekdays at 7:30 a.m.; a Vigil Mass on Saturday at 4 p.m. and Sundays at 11 a.m. with organ and cantor.

The North End itself has undergone many changes. In the

first half of the 1800s, along Fulton, Commercial and Lewis streets businesses and warehouses developed. Housing went downhill and one area became known as "Black Sea," an area of prostitution. By the 1840s, the North End was Boston's worst slum. Housing was low cost and Irish immigrants came here because they could afford it, but moved on as they got better jobs and had more income. Next came Eastern European Jews and the Italians who populate the area even now.

Health related problems like TB and typhoid always caused early deaths in the North End largely because of families lived so tightly packed together and drank water from wells located near privies. At that time, houses were from 400 to 800 square feet, with a density of 10.57 people per house city wide. We find that Ward 2, the east half of the North End, had density of 17.8 people per house, the highest in Boston. In 1849, a cholera epidemic killed 700. In 1918, the Spanish Flu killed so many parents that the Boston City Government created the Home for Italian Children to care for the orphans

Beginning in the 1880s, the four and five story brick apartment buildings with commercial space on the first floor we see today replaced the falling down wooden houses. The city built North End Park & Beach, Copp's Hill Terrace, and the North End Playground. Michelangelo School and the Paul Revere Mall followed and greatly improved the North End. In 1912, Prince Spaghetti was founded in a storefront at 92 Prince St. by three Sicilian immigrants from the same village. It outgrew its North End factory and moved to Lowell in 1941, but a recent TV ad featured Anthony of the North End rushing home because Wednesday is "Prince Spaghetti Day."

In 1919, molasses was being used to make World War I munitions and it was stored in a huge tank above Commercial Street. The tank burst creating a 15-foot wave of molasses rushing down Commercial to the waterfront killing 21, injuring 150, and causing $100 million in damage.

Completion of Boston Central Artery/Tunnel Project in 2007 put the elevated I-93 highway underground and opened access to the North End from the rest of Boston. It has Boston's finest Italian restaurants and bakeries, the Freedom Trail runs through it on the way to Bunker Hill Monument. Paul Revere House, Old

North Church and Copp's Hill Burying Ground draw thousands of tourists. Younger and more affluent Bostonians are moving here. The North End today has a brighter future than ever before.

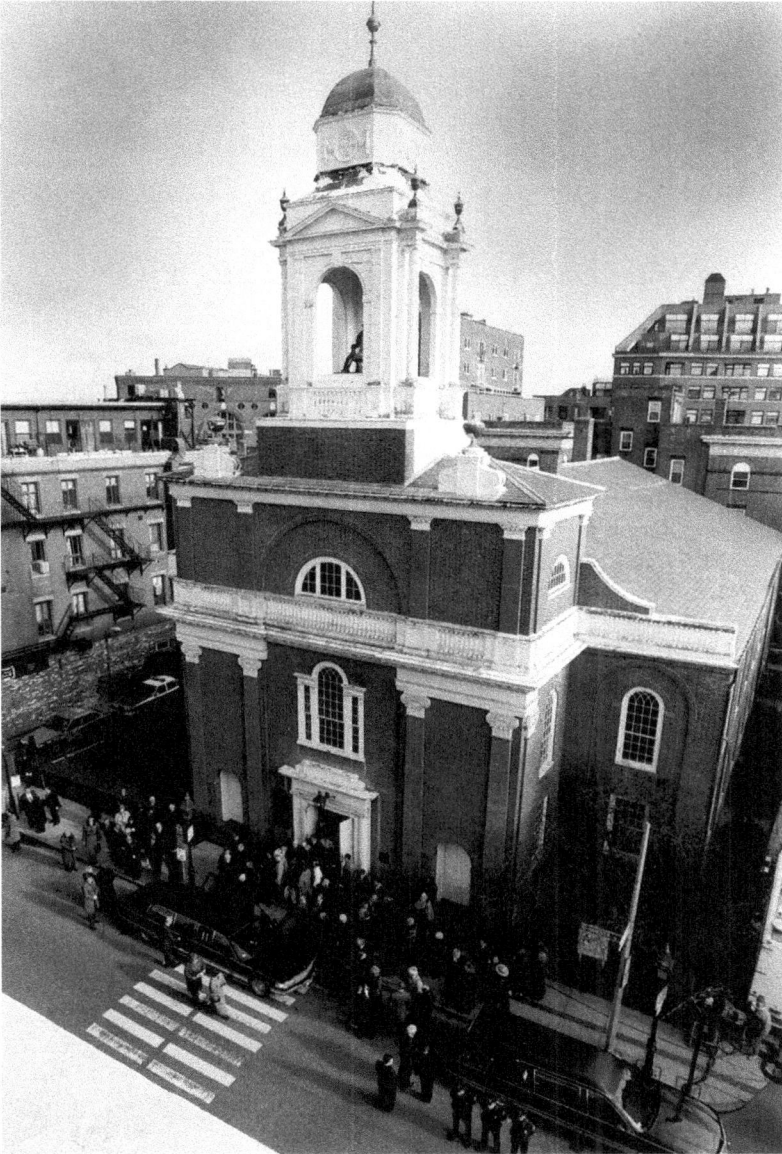

Mourners entering church for Rose Kennedy funeral, 1995.

Photos: 1995 Rose Kennedy funeral photos by Mike Adaskaveg. staff photographer, Boston Herald. Current photos by Erin Ryan Lordan.

CHAPTER 9

VOLUME III RECORDS SECTION

By Steven Fanning

Parish records of the New North Church of Volume III begin with the commencement of the pastorate of the Rev. Francis Parkman (1788-1852) and are printed as they were written. Page numbers show how they are written by the various parish scribes and we have added an index to those pages at the back so you can easily find who you might be looking for.

Earlier Vol. I & II contain records from the church's beginning. Vol. I is from 1714 – 1797 and Vol. II is from 1798 – 1812. These are extracted and indexed in *The New North Church 1714,* compiled by Thomas Bellows Wyman and transcribed and edited in 1995 by Robert J. Dunkle and Ann S. Lainhart and published by Clearfield Publishing Company and printed by Genealogical Publishing Co., Inc., Baltimore, 1995. Original Vols. I & III are located in the Rare Books Division of the Boston Public Library and are available on microfilm there. New England Historic Genealogical Society in Boston has original Vol. II and microfilm Vols. I & III.

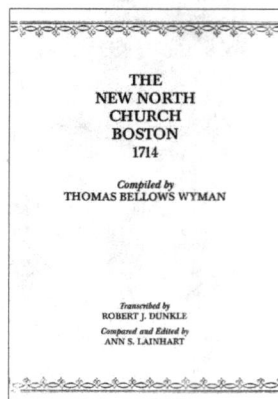

THE
NEW NORTH
CHURCH
BOSTON
1714

Compiled by
THOMAS BELLOWS WYMAN

Transcribed by
ROBERT J. DUNKLE
Compared and Edited by
ANN S. LAINHART

As a record keeper, Parkman was meticulous. His writing is careful and clear and his entries are usually complete. He showed considerable interest in the role that extreme heat and cold played in causing increased deaths in Boston and he consulted city records as he traced the number of deaths each year due to consumption (tuberculosis), intemperance (alcoholism) and suicide.

In keeping with his scholarly achievements at the Boston Latin School, Parkman sprinkled Latin phrases throughout his records. Most of them concern the location of baptisms, *sua domo* (at their own house), *domi* (at home). But occasionally, especially concerning tragedies in his own family, Parkman made longer Latin entries. After he noted the baptism of his daughter Mary-Agnes in 1827, he later added "mortua, igne erepta, Dec. 1829" ("died, taken away by fire). When he recorded his daughter's death in the death records, he wrote even more, "Heu! Igne nobis erepta filia mihi carissima" (Alas! Taken away from us by fire, dearest daughter to me). When his father Samuel died in 1824, Parkman wrote "Pater mihi dilectissimus atque venerandus" (Most beloved and venerable father to me), and when his mother Sarah died in 1835, he wrote in a similarly loving fashion, *mater mihi carissima* ("dearest mother to me").

The most extensive use of Latin by Parkman was when he recorded the death of his wife Sarah following childbirth in 1818:

> *Cara, vale, ingeniô præstans, pietate, pudore,*
> *Et plusquam conjugis nomine cara, vale.*
> *Cara, mi Sara, vale. At veniet felicius ævum*
> *Quando iterum tecum, sim modo dignus, ero.*
> *Cara, redi, læta tum dicam voce amicus*
> *Eja, age in amplexus, cara mi Sara, redi.*

Farewell, dear one, outstanding in talent, piety and modesty,
  And beloved more than by the name of wife, farewell.
My beloved Sarah, farewell. And may a happier age come
  When once more I will be with you, if I might be worthy.
Beloved one, return, and then I will say with a friendly voice
  Oh, rush into my embrace, my beloved Sarah, come back.

As tender and touching as this memorial is, it is not original. It was adapted from a well-known piece of neo-Latin, written by Robert Lowth, renowned grammarian, poet, biblical scholar, and soon-to-be bishop of London, upon the death of his daughter

Mary in 1768 and inscribed as an epitaph on her tomb. Parkman had changed the wording to make it appropriate for a wife named Sarah instead of a daughter named Mary. See page 161 for his death tribute.

Pastor Arthur B. Fuller, in contrast with Francis Parkman, is a disappointment as a keeper of church records. His cursive writing is a terrible scrawl and his information is often incomplete. For example, in March 1855 he recorded the death of "a child of Mr. and Mrs. [blank]," {p. 507} and it is common for him to omit the first names of his parishioners.

In a manner strangely similar to the death of Francis Parkman's wife Sarah following childbirth, so did Arthur's wife Elizabeth die following the birth of their son Arthur Ossoli in March 1856. And, like Parkman, Fuller wrote a touching memorial to his wife {p. 508}.

Logic would dictate that the records would be: Births, Marriages, Deaths, and perhaps Membership in the Church. However, the actual order is: Marriages (151-181); Baptisms (282-321); Members (361-386 and 426-427) and Deaths (462-512). The beginning pages are Proceedings of the Church and the last pages are Letters to the Church and Invitations to and Attendance at Church Councils, not annotated here. There are gaps between sections for additional information to be added. These pages are blank.

MARRIAGES AT NEW NORTH CHURCH

{MARRIAGES, p. 151}
1813.
Dec. 19. Dexter Dana & Mary P. Eustis – of Boston

1814.
March 20. William Mills Jun. & Abigail Soal Curtis – of Boston
May 5. George Ainslie & Martha Whitcomb – of Boston
May 12. Andrew Barcolm & Harriet Kittredge – of Boston
July 17. Robert Lord & Susanna Morse – of Boston
July 24. Joseph Hart & Betsey Eustis
D[itt]o. Joshua Cheever & Harriet Cutter
August 14. David Belcher & Nancy Tippen
December 1. Moses Clough & Rhoda Jones
- - - - -   Henry Fowle & Ruth Skimmer
                                                    Total 10

1815.

Feb. 5. ‡ John W. Beals & Julia Rumney

Feb. 6. + Isaac Gregson (Roxbury) & Nancy Nevers

May 29. James Kettell & Sarah Payne

June 5. Capt. William Smith & Caroline Smith

June 7. Thomas Wells & Eliza Tuttle

June 22. Samuel Leach & Phebe Leach

June 25. Peter Seaver & Sally Clark

June 29. John Mitchell & Abigail Brown, of color

July 1. Henry Rasmasson & Dorcas Howard   Boston

Aug. 3. Mr. Elisha Parks of Boston & Miss Mary-Ann Austin of Long Island, N. York

Oct. 12. Aaron L. Darrow & Ruthy Vinton   Boston

Oct. 16. ‡ Robert Davis (of Concord) & Eliza Tapley Hall of Boston

Oct. 29. ‡ Benjamin Ticknor (of B.) & Hannah Gardner of Abington

{MARRIAGES, p. 152}   1815

Nov. 12. Edward Tuttle & Catharine Vannever Geyer [both] of Boston

Nov. 26. Henry Bartlett & Mrs. Elizabeth Gilbert

Dec. 10. Enoch H. Snelling & Sally D. Jones

Dec. 24. ‡ Samuel Low & Abiah Page Lillie

Total 17 Attest F. Parkman

1816.

Jan. 13. Mr. Joseph Johnson, of New York, & + Miss Sarah Palmer, of Boston

- - - . Josiah Peirce & Mary Lincoln

Jan. 20. Edward King & Mary Bell

Feb. 13. Nathaniel S. Magoon & Abigail Danforth

Feb. 15. George Lewis & Elizabeth Jones

Feb. 29. ‡ Eleazer Wheelock, of Sturbridge, & Abigail Wheeler, of Boston

March 5. William Thompson Jun. & Mary Burrows Fullerton

March 24. William Blaney & Sally A. Leach   Recorded in the Town book

April 26. William Dunkinsfield & Nancy Guss [both] of color

May 19. ‡Enos Cobb & Eliza Weld

{MARRIAGES, p. 153}

July 8. William Parsons Shelton & Mary-Ann Curtis [both] of Boston

August 4. + John Boardman & + Lydia White

Sept. 29. John Jones & Margaret Curtis

Oct. 6. Joseph G. Spear & Hannah Blodget

Oct. 6. Simon W. Robinson & Hannah T. Danforth

Oct. 17. Capt. Andrew Blanchard, of Medford, & Lydia Stanwood, of Boston

Oct. 31. William Grubb & Eliza Bridge

Nov. 3. + Levi Younger & Catharine P. Jones

Nov. 28. Thomas L. Hutchinson & Catharine Cade

Dec. 26. + Charles Jennison & Ruth Beals   20 Total F.P.

1817

Jan. 12. Charles Mountfort & Ann Smith

Jan. 12. Moses Emerson, of Madbury, N. H., & Eliza H. Pike, of Boston

Jan. 19. Adam C. Goldback & Lydia Bodge Married Sunday at Noon

{MARRIAGES, p. 154}

Mar. 30. John Tileston Fracker, of Boston, & Nancy Wood

June 29. Levi Whitcomb & Elizabeth U. Francis

July 17. William Baker & Susan Wilson

Aug. 24. Joseph S. Waterman & Mrs. Jane P. Richardson

Sept. 25. + Samuel Gerry & Sarah W. Newell

Oct. 12. George Geyer & Mary Cutler

Oct. 21. + Caleb Hartshorn & Frances Hunt

Nov. 27. Joseph Clark & Mary Barnes

Dec. 25. Samuel Aspinwall & Atlanta Hill (of Charlestown)

12 Couple F. Parkman

1818

Jan. 20. Thomas Kendall & Lydia H. Singleton

Jan. 20. Caleb G. Loring & Miss Harriet Tuttle

Feb. 23. Parker H. Pearce & Hannah Withington

June   Ellis Gray Blake & Sarah Blake Wiswall

{MARRIAGES, p. 155}

July 19. Charles Melander & Mary Barber

Sept. 10. Henry Butler & Judith Flancy [both] of color

Sept. 17. John B. Tremere & Sarah F. Burrows

Sept. 20. William P. Main & Mrs. Susan S. Cox

Sept. 23. William Bentley Fowle & Maria Antoinette Moulton

Oct. 15. John H. Armstrong & Mrs. Ann Stevens [both] of color

Nov. 22. Thomas Hendy & Mary-Ann Cushman

Nov. 22. George Kirkpatrick Edgar & Sally Nowell Jenks

12 Total F. Parkman

1819

March 14. Samuel Sampson & Almira Long [both] of color

April 12. Lewis J. Bailey & Sally Fenno

April 12. James Williams & Mary Durant [both] of color

May 3. Laben Benson & Rhoda Gibson [both] of color

May 30. Samuel Tuttle & Mary Silsbee

{MARRIAGES, p. 156}

June 13. Elisha Webb & Sophia Charlotte Leach

June 20. John Williams & Hannah Lewis [both] of color

Sept. 2. John Knowlton, of Portsmouth, & Sally Adams Knowlton

Sept. 16. George Revere & Abigail Tufts

Total 9 Attest Francis Parkman

1820

Jan. 9. Josiah M. Barnett, of Charlestown, & Lydia H. Wiswell, of Boston

Jan. 26. Reuben Heywood & Dolly B. Wood

Mar. 5. John Ellms & Sarah Andrews

Mar. 26. Richard Austin & Mary P. Harris

April 20. Amasa T. Wild, of Acton, & Sarah B. Babb

June 14. Phineas Sprague, of Duxbury, & Hannah Brown, of Boston

July 9. John Fenno Jun, & Charlotte Frecker

July 25. Daniel Messenger Jun, & Mary-Ann Smith

Aug. 3. Seth Webber, of Boston, & Mary Bourne, of Middleborough

{MARRIAGES, p. 157}

Aug. 17. Perry Cole & Nancy Colburn   [both] of color

Sept. 13. William D. Cobb & Hannah B. Hutchinson

Sept. 21. Joshua B. Fowle & Elizabeth D. Austin

Oct. 7. William Knight, of New-Bedford, & Mary P. Colesworthy, of Boston

Nov. 12. John Brown & Harriet Potter   [both] Boston, of color

Nov. 23. Charles Holbrook & Nancy Oakman

Nov. 30. Henry Thacker & Mary-Ann Cole [both] of color

Dec. 21. George Archbald & Mary-Ann Pratt

Total 17 couple.   Attest F. Parkman

1821

Jan. 8. John Spear Jun & Mary Simpson   [both] of Boston

Feb 12. Hawkes Lincoln Jun & Sarah Webb

March 1. Lewis Lyman, of Hartford, Vermont, & Mary B. Bruce, of Boston

March 25. Peter Spiwood & Lois Cross   [both] of color

March 30, 1821. S reported for Record in the Town Books. F. Parkman

{MARRIAGES, p. 158}

April 6. Mr. William Emerson & Miss Eliza Rogers Simpson [both] of Boston

April 6. John Vannevar & Susan Cutter   [both] of Boston

June 21. Thomas Clark & Mary Evens   [both] of color

July 1. Richard Howard & Hannah Waters   [both] of color

July 20. John Williams & Jane A. Gould   [both] of color

Aug. 20th. Nathaniel H. Stevenson & Sibbel Grubb

Aug. 30. Thomas Crocker & Ann Boylston Trott

Sept. 6. William Perkins & Phebe Allen

Oct. 13. Adolph Frederickson & Sarah Russell

   William Kemp & Nancy Atwood Rider [both] of Wellfleet

Oct. 30. Ralph Webster & Ann Eliza Cushing

Nov. 21. William Pike & Elizabeth Baker

Total 16 Couple   Francis Parkman

{MARRIAGES, p. 159}
1822

Jan. 27. William Howard & Mary Allen French

April 16. Charles P. Dexter & Sarah R. Blake
June 17. Abraham Millet & Abigail Smith
July 7. Thomas D. Francis & Eliza Curtis
July 31. John Brown & Cornelia Romana Susana Little
Aug. 26. William W. Cole[s]worthy & Ann Maria Bucknam [Buckman*]
Sept. 1. Isaac Ward, of Plymouth, N. H., & Prudence H. Eaton
Sept. 15. Henry Roaf & Emeline Copeland
Sept. 18. Joseph N. Howe Jun & Elizabeth Kneeland Harris
Nov. 28. Charles Gilbert Singleton & Esther Abbot
Dec. 8. Nathaniel Blake & Bridget Shelton

11 Couple

1823
Jan. 5. Thomas G. Bangs & Elizabeth Ann Tucker
Feb. 27. John W. Tuttle & Eliza H. Cade

{MARRIAGES, p. 160}
Mar. 11. Amos Farnsworth, M. D., & Mrs. Mary Webber
Mar. 18. Benjamin Clark Jun & Theresa E. Ingalls
April 27. Orramel H. Throop & Mary B. Harris
June 5. Amos Cotting & Harriet Tuttle
July 6. John Singleton Luckis & Louisa Tippen
Aug. 4. John Grubb & Adeline White
Oct. 1. James Bingham & Eliza Pickett
Oct. 23. Peter Gray & Betsey Windship   [both] of color
Nov. 2. David Orcutt & Dorcas W. Hall
Nov. 17. Charles Foster, of Charlestown, & Lydia Webb
Nov. 24. Josiah Snow, of Provincetown, & Ruth Dyer
Nov. 30. Daniel Low & Adeline Faguins   [both] of color
Nov. 30. Andrew Townsend Hall & Lydia Young Wells

15 Reported for record to City Clerk F. Parkman

{MARRIAGES, p. 161}
1824
Feb. 1. Elisha Meriam & Sarah Pike
Feb. 10. John Albree, of Pittsburgh, Pa., & Nancy Shepherd, of Boston
Feb. 16. Joel Stone & Eliza Ann Sigourney
April 11. George Lyndes & Catharine Robbins, of color
April 18. Leonard W. Spaulding & Emily Eaton
May 30. James Young & Nancy Trask
- - - -. Titus Deetes & Eliza Evans, of color
July 18. George Jacobs & Rebecca L. Jones
Aug. 22. Scammell Penniman & Hannah Hammond
Oct. 5. John Dominise & Mary Jones
Oct. 14. Anthony Baptist, of Genoa, Italy, & Martha Lock
Oct. 31. Gilbert Nurse & Maria S. Hall

Nov. 5. Thomas Parkman Cushing & Sarah B. Sigourney
Nov. 28. Isaac Hall & Ann Payson
Dec. 6. Hosea Bates of Camden, Maine, & Mrs. Susan Hunstable, of Boston

                                                 15 Couple

1825
Jan. 25. Elijah J. S. Corlew & Evelina Trott
Feb. 18. Cato Prince & Lucy T. Bowen, of color
Feb. 25. Elisha Wales & Abigail R. Arnold
Sept. 11. William Grubb Jun & Sarah Tuttle
Oct. 3. Horace P. Moore & Sarah T. Howe
- - - -. Ebenezer Scott & Francis C. Russell
Oct. 23. Henry Adams & Mary D. Fitzgerald

{MARRIAGES, p. 162}
Oct. 27. Joseph Austin, Esq., & Agnes McKean
Nov. 3. Charles Arnold & Elizabeth H. Whalan
Dec. 1. Joseph Francis and Ellen Creamer

                                                 10 Couple

1826
Jan. 8. Jeremiah Hurd & Mary McMellin
May 7. Samuel Lawrence & Mary Gualt
June 21. Stephen Rhoades & Abigail B. Ward
June 28th. James H. Duncan, Haverhill, & Mary Willis, Boston
July 23. Richard K. Kellogg & Caroline A. Leach
Sept. 21. John D. Silver & Hannah B. Levear, of color
Oct. 1. Nathaniel Colesworthy & Mary Ann Brown
Oct. 10. Anthony Lebert & Jane Call
Oct. 12. Adam S. Ray & Hannah Howard, of color
Nov. 19. John Tuckerman & Catharine Tuttle
Nov. 30. John Lee, of Manchester, & Laura W. Jones
Dec. 7. George Harris & Sarah Gragg

                                                 13

1827
Jan. 17. Henry D. Wolcott & Emily Chandler
Sept. 17. Daniel C. Sampson & Emiline M. Rogers, also baptized
Sept. 20. Samuel Smith & Louiza Stockwell
Oct. 7. Alfred Williams & Mary Stearns, of color
Oct. 29. Eben Center (of Charlestown) & Emily M. Dickinson
Nov. 29. Henry Burbeck & Susan P. Hiler
Dec. 15. Dexter Dickinson & Eliza W. Dickinson
Dec. 18. John Sawin & Charlotte Lash

{MARRIAGES, p. 163}
Dec. 19. Thomas Cooper & Lucy Bowen, of color

                                                 9 Couple

1828

Jan. 3. William Read and Sarah G. Atkins

Feb. 10. Benjamin Pepper & Margaret Vannah

Feb. 21. Bradford Russell of Groton & Mary-Ann Nash

April 2. Henry Andrews & Sarah Parker Hill

1828   Reported to the Town-Clerk

April 15. Henry Thacker & Deborah Westley, of color

July 21. John F. Trull & Elizabeth Wilkinson

Oct. 17. John Greene & Mary Harvey

Oct. 19. Joseph Gardner & Elizabeth Brown

Nov. 20. Walter Miles & Abigail Ingals

- - - -. Henry W. Fenno & Rebecca H. Darracott

Dec. IV. Elbridge Lakeman, of Ipswich, & Joanna P. Adams

Dec. 28. William Henry Pomeroy & Sibella Lukis

                                    12 Couple

1829

Jan. 1st. Warren Lincoln & Nancy Parker

Jan. 27. William Fenno & Margaret N. Bailey

Jan 27. Henry Cutting & Harriet Ardelia Fenno

Mar. 2. Amos C. Mann & Hannah T. Parsons

June 14. Richard D. Blinn & Harriet Gragg

June 23. George A. Eliot and Cordelia Howe

July 1. George Harris and Phebe A. Lyscom

July IX. Henry Landerson and Nancy Ferrington

{MARRIAGES, p. 164}

July 15. Harvey Barnes and Harriet Gragg

July 29. William A. Stone, of Prospect Maine, and Clarissa Dickinson, of Boston

Oct. 1. Henry A. Little, of New-York, & Margaretta A. Little, of Boston
[both] Mr. Emerson's

Oct. 6. Robert W Holt, Liverpool, and Ann M. S. Jones

Oct. 14. Abraham Macoy & Elizabeth Williams, of color

                                    14 Couple

1830

Jan. 21. Franklin Smith and Joanna Wells

Jan. 23. Thomas H. Dolliver and Maria B. Fenno

Feb. 11. Henry Hutchinson Jun & Lavinia Stevens

Feb. 19. Joseph Goddard, Esq., Brookline, and Susan Snelling, of Boston

April 1. - - - - - - - - Reported to the City Clerk

April 8. Benjamin T. Wells & Mary-Ann Pitman

April 26. Samuel W. Hall and Margaret B. Knowlton

May 27. James Davis and Bazaine Shaw

July 8. Henry R[upell*]. Williams & Abigail H. Adams

Aug. 29. Samuel N. Dickinson & Sarah-Ann Oliver

Nov. 3. Jacob Stone, of Newbury-Port, and Eliza Atkins, of Boston

Nov. 4. Manasseh Knight & Nancy Hunstable
Nov. 18. Thomas Chamberlain & Susan Young Hill

F. Parkman

{MARRIAGES, p. 165}
Nov. 26. William Cotting & Ann Sigourney Hammatt
Nov. 29. Benjamin Comey & Nancy Howe
Dec. 9. Benjamin H. Greene & Elizabeth Clark Darracott
Dec. 30. Stephen Emmons & Alice Silsby

16 Couple

1831
March 31. Horatio Alger, of Chelsea, & Olive Augusta Fenno, of Boston
April 21. Hans Jones, of Denmark, & Elizabeth Doble
May 24. Thomas Parkman Cushing, & Martha-Ann Sigourney
May 30. John Cloase [Clouse*] & Sarah Tatman
    N. B. Here should be injected a marriage; but the names & the certificate I have lost. F.P.
Sept. 28. Henry C. Spurr & Martha Ann Stebbins
Oct. 13. Henry H. W. Sigourney & Harriet A. Williams
Nov. 6. Levi Younger & Jane Babson (Mrs.)
Nov. 25. Abraham L. Stevens Jun & Emeline N. Hutchinson
Nov. 29. Lawrence B. Johnson & Mary Howard
    N. B. In August, I married a couple, whose names are forgotten

{MARRIAGES, p. 166}
Dec. 11. Robert Restieaux & Susanna Boylston Walker
Dec. 20. Vernon Brown & Susan H. A. Nash
Dec. 22. Henry Hutchinson & Mrs. Judith Crosby
Dec. 25. Charles H. Stearns & Sarah P. Pulsifer

14 Couple   Reported to the City Clerk for record

Total of Marriages from Dec. 1813 to Dec. 31, 1831 – 244, or 14 yearly. F. P.

1832
Jan. 26. James E. Ewer & Eliza Tilden
- - - -. Alexander Brown & Susan Boynton
Feb. 16. Oren Johnson & Sarah Clark
Feb. 26. Matthias Ellis & Charlotte French
Mar. 11. Thomas Cooper & Cecilia Brown (colored)
July 8. A. H. Robinson & Mary E. S. Clark, of Lowell
July 15. Thomas Lyford & Susan Jenkins
Sept. 24. Samuel E. Holbrook and Caroline Clark
Oct. 17. Jefferson Didea and Jane Cæsar, of color
Nov. 6. George Clark & Hannah Holbrook
Nov. 29. George P. Milne & Eliza A. Lambert
Dec. 2. Edwin Bradley & Mary Jane Hammatt
- - - 3.

12 Couple F. Parkman

Dec. 3. Henry Grew & Elizabeth P. Sturgis
Dec. 6. Charles Hannah & (Mrs.) Charlotte Wilson
Dec. 16. Isaac Hall & Elizabeth Margaret Cushing
Dec. 20. Bowen Harrington & Elizabeth P. Ward   16 Couple

1833
April 4. Nathaniel Clark & Margaret Bell
April 11. Seth A. Ranlett & Mary Ann C. Stevens
       N. B. reported to City
June 3. Benjamin Dodge & Rebecca Webb Howe
June 19. George C. Barrett & Susan P. Chamberlain
July XI. George William Bond & Sophia A. May
Aug. 8. Edward Chamberlain Jun & Ann M. Powers
Sept. 4. Alexander D. McKinzie & Maria Howe
Sept. 25. Ebenezer F. Gay & Sarah C. Adams
Oct. 7. Roswell Emerson Messenger and Delia Woodward Adams
Nov. 10. Thomas Stowell & Martha Fenno
Dec. 12. Rev. Chandler Robbins & Mary Eliza Frothingham
Dec. 25. William Michael Cooper & Sophia Collingridge
          12 Couple. Total in 20 years, 270 Couple

1834
Jan. 1. Charles Partridge & Sophronia A. Flagg
Feb. 6. John Webb Hall & Sarah Ann Priest

April 25. Henry U. Dodge & Eliza N. Jones
May 29. John A. Stevens, M. D., of Cambridge, & Sarah Ann Dickinson, of Boston
June 26. John Hamilton Osgood & Adeline Stevens
Aug. 13. Josiah Woodward Kenfield & Catharine Venneever
Sept. 7. Willson Cheney & Permelia Malcomb
Oct. 5. James Gordon & (Mrs) Jane Curow
Oct. 10. Nathaniel Clark & Abigail Lane
Dec. 8. Lewis Smith & Abigail Gooding Page
       10 Couple   returned for City Records

1835
Jan. XI. Richard G. Wait & Mary T. Thomas
Jan. 29. George P. Wadsworth & Eliza Webb
- - - -. Freeman Reed & Eliza C. Malcom
Ap. 9. John Williams & Mary-Ann C. Derby
Ap. 30. Sardine Stone & Tabitha Goodspeed
May 4. James Bailey and Catharine More
June 2. Archibald Foster & Caroline E. Brown
June IX. Francis G. Shaw & Sarah Blake Sturgis

The ceremony was performed in the New-North Church, all the reltions attending. The first wedding ever solemnized here.

July 4. David Townsend Jun & Mary-Ann Gragg

July 30. Johnson Parkman, of Savannah, Georgia, and Lucy Rogers, of Boston

Sept. 1. Samuel W. Spooner, Battleboro, N. H., & Elizabeth Willard Spooner

{MARRIAGES, p. 169}

Oct. 8. John C. Hayden, M. D., & Susan A. B. Williams

Nov. 4. Ezekiel Lincoln & Mary F. Eliot

Dec. 1. George Robert Russell & Sarah Parkman Shaw

Married in the New-North Church; as were, Nov. 27, Rev. John Parkman Jun & Susan P. Sturgiss in Federal Street Church

Dec. 1. George Darracott Jun & Ann M. Clark

Total 15

1836

Jan. 31. David Adams and Jane Perkins

April 14. John Ferguson & Mary-Ann Wells

April 29. John Stablar and Christiana F. Meyers, of New-York

May 29. Henry Wise and Catharine M. Younger

June 2. Ephraim Lombard & Mary Elizabeth Hall

Aug. 22. John Stockwell & Susanna Martha Graham

Oct. 3. Eleazer D. Hartwell, of New-Orleans, & Eunice Woods, of Dunstable, Mass.

Nov. 14. William Farrow & Susanna Stanton

Nov. 27. Dresser Bacon & Mehitable Tuttle

- - - -. Cornelius A. Kelley, of Baltimore, & Mary Albert, of Boston

- - - -. Aaron R. Cloues & Lucy Ann Barnacoat

Dec. 1. William Spence & Ann Hammon   12

1837

Mar. 9. Thomas A. Williams & Mary P. Adams

These reported for City Records

{MARRIAGES, p. 170}

Ap. 30. John F. Payson & Dolly French

May 6. Samuel S. Stowers (Chelsea) & Olive F. Payson

May 21. William D. Clark & Eliza S. Mead

July 20. Nathaniel Bastow & Abby R. Hammatt

Oct. 3. Benjamin F. Snow & Elizabeth C. Gooding

Oct. 8. William Walkup & Mary Hamilton

Nov. 5. William Hart and Agnes Jones

Dec. 25. William Millett & Martha H. Skerry

1838

May 10. Nathan Hayward of Woburn & Louisa Baker

May 28. Rev. Nathaniel Hall, of Dorchester, & Sarah Elizabeth Coffin

July 3. Mr. James Longley & Sarah Eustis
July 26. Henry Dawson Dutch & Franscina M. Reed
                                    Whole number in 25 years, 320 Couple
1839
Jan. 14. Albert Crane, of Conquest, New-York , & Abigail Maynard, of Boston
Jan. 31. Theodore A. Gore & Sarah A. Kiley
Mar. X. John Gragg & Mary Jane Crawford
        Reported for City Records March 21st 1839
May 30. Samuel C. Bradshaw & Rebecca Harris
June 6. Dexter W. Wiswall & Elizabeth R. Clark
- - - -. William G. Clark & Betsey J. Babson

{MARRIAGES, p. 171}
Aug. 14. Morrill Wyman, M. D. of Cambridge, & Elizabeth Aspinwall Pulsifer
Sept. 12. Richard Robins & Susan P. Blake
Oct. 29. Lewis Keen and Caroline E. Tuttle
Nov. 6. James H. Morgan & Caroline A. Wells
Dec. 23. William Fergus & Frances A. Williams

1840

Mar. 25. Alfred Hammatt & Margaret S. White
May 13. Otis Greene and Sally Ann Hammatt
Aug. 6. Edward G. Lynes & Mary Jane Clark
Sept. 14. George B. Jones & Esther L. Cutter
    N. B. This marriage of Sept. 14 was by some error published in the papers ten
    or fifteen days before its proper date. F. P.
Oct. 11. James B. Leeds & Helen R. Peters.
- - - 18. James Hobbs & Isabell T. Barrett
- - - 31. Isaac Brooks & Jane D. Francis   7

1841
Feb. XI Reuben R. Herriott & Sophia H. Howard
- - - -. James Madison Moore & Lucy Howard
        (Reported for City Records Ap. 21, 1841)
May 6. Heman Crosley, of Manchester, N. H. & Eveline Hill, of Newton, Mass.
May XI. George W. Richardson & Sarah W. Wilkins
June XI. Thomas Cummings & Rebecca J. Williston
Aug. 19. David Morgan & Marianne Lincoln Pierce

{MARRIAGES, p. 172} 1841
Sept. 12. Thomas W. Capon, of Dorchester, & Cordelia R. Wells, of Boston

1842
Mar. 17. Lewis G. Richardson & Sarah A. Hammatt (returned for City Records)
Sept. 14. Arthur Berry of Gardiner, Me., & Mary Parr Taylor, of Crediton,
England

Oct. X. Robert Jones & Margaret Owens, of Wales
Oct. 20. Isaac Taylor & Elizabeth H. Adams

1843
Jan. 2. Nathaniel G. Eliot & Mary R. Bassett
Ap. 16. George Green & Mary Hiler (as certified by Mr. Smith)
June 21. William Parsons Atkinson & Sarah Cabot Parkman
Dec. 28. Lewis Winde & Eliza Gurney

1844
March 19. John B. Thomas & Hannah D. Rogers; both of Gloucester, Mass.
June 13. M. Johnson Mandell & Mary Jane Brown
July 8. Joseph Nason & Sarah C. Darracott, in Brattle Street Church
Oct. 21. Joseph Murdock & Caroline D. Smith
Oct. 31. James Colger & Mary Ellen Fennelly
Nov. 14. Joseph Addison Leseur & Frances Wilkinson

{MARRIAGES, p. 173}   1845
April 16. William C. Appleton of Roxbury, and Mary A. L. Smith of Boston
April 30. William Bellamy and Ann Maria Dodd
July 9. Jesse D. Bates and Mary Elizabeth Fowle
July 9. Edward Winship Morse and Olivia Kennedy Fowle
July 10. Joseph R. Gordon and Nancy Williams
Oct. VII. John R. Dabney, of Fayal [Azores], and Sarah H. Webster of Cambridge
Oct. 28. Rev. Amos Smith (Junior Pastor of the Church) and Mary Elizabeth Williams
Oct. 29. William H. Barnes and Elizabeth C. Hartt
Oct. 30. James M. Dolliver & Mary D. Gurney
Nov. 6. Andrew Corrigan and Elizabeth O'Dare
Nov. XI. Charles Rose & Rachel M. Thacker
Dec. 22. Rev. William B. Greene, South Brookfield, and Anna B. Shaw, of Boston
Dec. 25. Albert Gurney and Sarah F. Dillaway   Total 13

1846
January 15. Edward W. Barnicoat & Augusta F. Stearns
January 31. William Lasell of Boston & Sarah M. Peabody of Salem
April 11. Christian Fieldstad & Emily C. French
May 21. John G. Hall & Sarah Cushing
June 3. Daniel A. Oliver & Elizabeth W. Shaw

{MARRIAGES, p. 174}
1846
August 6. John P. Putnam & Lucy A. Harris
August 22. John W. Hodges & Charlotte A. Foss
Oct. 22. Charles Jordan (of Cambridge, Mass.) & Mary C. Bradshaw of Boston
Nov. 8. Francis P. Wells & Mary Ann F. Smith, in King's chapel
Nov. 12. James Young & Elizabeth Carnes
Dec. 20. Enoch M. Chase & Mary Jane Dunlap   XI

1847

Jan 7. Horace Cushing (of N. York) & Rebecca A. S. Lewis, of Boston

Jan. 13. Eben D. Jordan & Julia M. Clark

June 15. George Savil, of Quincy, & Catharine M. Gurney of Boston

August 12th. Joseph Lewis & Adeline Williams (of color)

1848

Jan. 4. Nahum Ward, of Marietta, Ohio, and Harriet Denny, of Boston

April 6. Benjamin T. Bradshaw and Abby W. Eastman

August 21. John C. Neal and Lucy Hunter

      Continued on next page by Joshua Young

{MARRIAGES, p. 175}
1849

April 26th. Francis Sheldon and Sarah Tremere

May 22. Andrew McMullen and Catharine Gassett

1850

May 9. James Bowker and Charlotte Nottage

June 6. Myron Shaw of Philadelphia and Mary E. Harrod of Boston – at Church

July 10. Royal S. Warren, M. D., of Waltham, and Susan Elizabeth Bates of Boston

Sept. 26. x Warren Houghton and Lydia Ann McKenney, both of Waltham

Dec. 9th. x John Tompson to Ellen Jordan

1851

May 14. x Charles E. Turner to Mary Ann Dazele

May 25. George Hardy to Jane Batie

Sept. 8. William A. Kruger to Nancy S. Harrod

Sept. 14. Amasa Beach Jr. of Worcester to Miss Mary Jane Shepherd

Sept. 25. Abram Hulin to Joanna Ryan, both of Stoneham

Oct. 20. +William Wooley to Mary Ann Pierce

Oct. 28. Samuel N. Neat to Eliza Rogers of England

{MARRIAGES, p. 176}

Oct. 28. x William A. Kendrick to Emeline Frost

Nov. 13. James Carroll to Miss Mary Ann McDonough

1852

Feb. 23. Charles R. Bradford to Miss Olivia R. Fowle (Morse)

      By Rev. Mr. [C. H.] Webster of E. Boston in my absence

April 20. Albert Carter to Margaret Munroe

      Continued on next page by A. B. Fuller, Pastor

{MARRIAGES, p. 177}
1853

March 9th. Samuel Smith & Hellen Elizabeth Gerry, both of Boston

Aug. 6. Amherst A. Allen of Boston, Georgina M. Cook of Duxbury, In church.

Aug. 29th. Francis W. Wetherbee of Cincinnati, Ohio, Ann Maria Foster of Boston, In church
Dec. 1. William W. Woodbury, Lydia R. Shepherd, [both] of Boston
Dec. 22. Charles B. Leavett, Emma D. Stearns, [both] of Boston

1854
Jan. 2. Henry W. Clinton, of Lowell, Susan B. Newell, of Manchester, N. H.
April 9th. William Parkman, Mrs. Emeline R. Fisher, both of Boston
May 4th. John D. W. Joy, Frances E. Bassett, both of Boston
May 24. Donald McClaskey, Mary Campbell, both of Boston

{MARRIAGES, p. 178}
July 3d. William A. Clark, Mary A. Harris, both of Boston
July 24. Ezra F. Tirrell, Helena Clapp, both of Weymouth
Sept. 14. William T. Clark, Sarah A. Robinson, both of Boston
Sept. 29. Henry J. Clark, of Cambridge, Mary G. Holbrook, of Boston
Oct. 1st. Ralph H. Darby, Irene P. Harris, both of Boston
          Charles S. Lambert, Sophia A. Lambert, both of Boston

1855
Jan. 1st 1855. Mr. John S. Hayes, Mrs. Augusta P. Nichols, both of Dover, N. H.

{MARRIAGES, p. 179}
Jan. 7. Mr. George H. Dodd, Miss Eliza Ann Leeds, both of Boston
Jan. 23d. George R. Spinney, Sarah E. Stearns, both of Boston
Feb. 6th. Charles H. Pratt, Rachel M. Williams, both of Boston
March 14. John Lawless, of Philadelphia, Ann Collins, of Boston
March 27. James M. Weston, of Duxbury, Abby W. Torrey, of Scituate
April 16. John F. Payson, Jr, Lizzie M. Hall, both of Boston
June 12. Freeborn F. Raymond, of Boston, Sarah E. Richardson, of Lexington
June 20. Charles R. Adams, Catharine S. Holbrook, both of Boston
July 26. McLaurin F. Cooke, Mary E. Moore, both of Boston

{MARRIAGES, p. 180}
Sept. 2. Lemuel F. Rich, Margaret Murray, both of Boston
Sept 13. William Stanton, Matilda P. Murray, both of Boston
Oct. 2d. Samuel P. Oliver, Eliza R. Harrod, both of Boston
Oct. 24. Gilbert F. Smith, of Charlestown, Sarah A. Floyd, of Boston
Oct. 31. Rufus H. Everett, Susan J. Taft, both of Boston
Nov. 13. Alfred C. Converse, of Boston, Julia A. Woods, of Hillsboro, N. H.
In 1853 I married in this city 5 couples
In 1854   "   "   10 "
 " 1855 "   "   16 "
 " 1856 "   "   4 "
 " 1857 "   "   7 "

{MARRIAGES, p. 181}
1856
Jan 16th. Grant Learned, Jr., Catharine M. Lampec, both of Boston

Sept. 24th. James N. Wentworth, of Canton, Mass., Rachel A. Smith, of Boston

[blank] Adams, [blank] Maclstrom [?], both of Boston

Dec. 3d. James D. Mitchell, [illegible: Rowena Brown*], both of Boston

1857
Jan. 14. John F. Walker, Julia E. Goodale, both of Boston

Feb. 19. Joseph L. Holton, Susan M. Bassett, both of Boston

May 25. Otis Mann, of Boston, Maria A. Falls, of Chelsea

Sept. 29. William G. Nichols, of Boston, Lillia L. Pendleton, of Searsport, Maine

{MARRIAGES, p. 182}
Nov. 11. Alfred Fisher, of Alna, Maine, Abigail H. Brown, of West Roxbury, Mass.

Dec. 1. Stephen W. Smith, of Brooklyn, N. Y., Sarah A. Taggard, of Lexington, Mass.

Dec. 9. Harvey H. Hart, Sophia Moore, both of Boston

1858
Feb. 25. Henry F. Spencer, Sarah D. Holbrook, both of Boston

April 4. Francis Stedman, Mrs. Percilla [sic] S. Haven, both of Boston

April 12. Mr. Hiram Ferry, of Northampton, Mrs. Fannie G. Thompson, of Boston

May 8. Mr. Hans Peters, of Boston, Miss Mary Feeny, of East Bridgewater

June 21. Matthew Elroy, Bridget Feeney, both of Boston

July 21. John M. Gookin, of Boston, Lorinda C. Lash, of Waldoboro, Maine

{MARRIAGES, p. 183}
July 23. George Wistar, Mrs. Margaret Lear, both of Philadelphia, Penn.

Sept. 6. George W. Banker, of Boston, Mary B. Baldwin, of Malden

Nov. 2. Charles W. Longley, of Sidney, Maine, Abbie F. Brown, of Middleboro, Mass.

Dec. 7th. Henry Connor, Elizabeth Lowe, [both of] Boston

Dec. 7th. Albert S. Pratt, Julia Dodd, both of Boston

Dec. 15. George M. Washburn, Chicago, Ill., Lucy F. Bartlett, Boston

1859
Jan 13th. James N. Clark, Mehitable Ford, [both of] Boston

Feb. 17th. John H. Chase, Eunice M. Schoff, both of Boston

March 17. Winslow L. Knowles, Henrietta Cheever, both of Boston

{MARRIAGES, p. 184}
May 13. Horatio N. Allen, Mary T. Adams, both of Manchester, N. H.

By Rev. R. C. Waterston

Dec. 22nd. Henry Leeds, Jr. & Melissa Amanda Nash, both of Boston

May 11, **1862**. George P. Richardson, Jr., & Eliza Greene Mizner, both of Boston

End of Marriages

CHAPTER 10

BAPTISMS

{BAPTISMS, p. 282}

1813

Dec. 12. M	John Eliot, son of Samuel & Mary S. Edes
__ __ M	Jonathan, son of Samuel & Eunice Howe
__ __ F	Elizabeth Dakin, daughter of Daniel & Sarah Munroe
Dec. 26. M	Joel Lyman, of Joel & Elizabeth Richardson

1814

Jan. 23. M	Francis Parkman, of Benjamin T. & Lydia Wells
Feb. 13. M	John Eliot, of Owen & Elizabeth Jones
Feb. 27. F	Sally Ann, of Charles & Isabella Hammatt
March 13. M	Henry Hutchinson – adult, when admitted to the Church
__ __ M	John Shepherd, of Abel & Mary Tompkins

__ __ F	Sarah Riggs, of Jacob & Elizabeth C. Farnsworth	
10 F	Sarah Ann, of Edward & Eunice Cutter (at home)	
April 24. F	Esther, of Parker & Anna Emerson	
May 1. F	Cordelia, of Ammi & Hannah Cutter	
May 8. F	Harriet Hill, of Samuel B. & Elizabeth Edes	
__ __, M	Nathaniel Hill, of Nathaniel & Elizabeth Clarke	
May 29. M	John West, of Isaiah & Mercy Atkins	
June 5. M	George Nathaniel }	
M	Francis Edwin } of Nathaniel & Eunice Faxon	
F	Eunice Maria }	
July 17. M	James Osmund Baptized at home	
June 12. F	Martha, of Samuel & Martha Ball	
July 3. F	Abigail Wheeler, adult – when admitted to the Church	
July 10. M	Joseph Thomas, of William & Fanny Hammatt	
__ __. F	Sarah Clark } Twins, of George & Sarah Daracott	
__ __. F	Mary Lowell }	

{BAPTISMS, p. 283}

July 17. F	Nancy, of Thomas & Elizabeth Williams	
__ __. M	Ebenezer, of Ephraim & Abigail Tufts	
__ __. M	John Eliot, of Thomas & Hannah Lillie	
July 31. F	Susanna K. Harris, adult, when admitted to the Church	
__ __. M	Robert Lyons, of Adam & Ruth Gobleck	
__ __. M	William Henry, of Richard & Margaret Hunting	
Sept. 4. M	Vernon }	
__ __. M	Albert Henry } of Stephen & Eliza Brown	
__ __. F	Caroline Elizabeth }	
__ __. M	Isaac Cornelius, of Isaac & Lydia B. Howe	
__ __. M	William, of James & Mary Brown, at home, sick	
October 14 M	James, of James & [blank] Nash	
__ __ 23. M	Edward Rumney, of John B. & Abigail Hammatt	
Nov. 20. M	Harriet Groves, of Thomas G. & Eleanor Bangs	
Dec. 25. F	Lucy Goodwin, of Isaac & Sally Atkins	

40.

1815

Jan. 29. M	John Knoar } }	
__ __. F	Nancy Paine } Barber }adults	
__ __. F	Nancy Paine their infant child	
March 12. F	Mary-Ann-Stevens, of Andrew Eliot & Elizabeth Symms	
March 20. F	Mary, of John & Lucy Hudson	
May 14. F	Helen Maria, of James & Eleanor Weld	
June 18. M	Thomas Otis, of Turell & Mary Tuttle	
June 25. M	Thomas Page, of Daniel & Nancy Lillie	
July . F	Sarah, of Benjamin & Mary Tilden (baptized by Rev. Noah Worcester)	

{BAPTISMS, p. 284}

Date	Sex	Name
July 30.	M	Frederic Augustus, of Stephen & Eliza Brown
__ __.	M.	Ebenezer Hancock, of Elisha & Meriam Field
__ __.	M	George Singleton, of Caleb B. & Mary Munroe
Aug. 20.	M	John Andrew, of Jesse & Hephzibah Bird
Sept. 10.	F	Harriet, of Ebenezer & Abigail B. Wild
__ __.	M	Christopher, of Christopher & Sally Gore
Sept. 24.	M	Francis Henry, of George & Mary Perry
		Mrs. Elizabeth Willard, sister of Mr. Samuel Parkman
Oct. 22.	M	William Daracott, of Nathaniel & Elizabeth Clark
Oct. 29.	F	Mrs. Henrietta Lamson /adult/
__ __.	F	Sarah, of Benjamin & Henrietta Lamson
Nov. 11.	M	Joseph Clark } twins of Joseph & Betsey Hart
__ __.	F.	Elizbeth Clark } Christened at home
Nov. 26.	F	Abigail, of William & Abigail S. Mills
__ __.	M	Robert Gould, of Robert G. & Eliza Shaw
Dec. 17.	F	Susan Snelling – widow
__ __.	M	Josiah } of Susan Snelling
__ __.	M	Samuel Greenwood }
__ __.	F	Sarah Clark, of George & Sarah Darracott
Dec. 24.	F	Agnes, of Owen & Elizabeth Jones
__ __.	F	Louisa, of Daniel & Sarah Munroe Total 29

1816

Date	Sex	Name
Jan. 15.	F	Sarah Ellen, of Abigail Tower, at home
___ 27.	F	Frances Ann, of Edward & Grace S. Oliver
	F	{Catharine Eustis }
Feb. 11	M	{Francis Edward } of Benjamin & Sophia Welles
	F	{Sophia Rumney }
Mar. 10.	F	Sarah Spear, of Isaiah & Mercy Atkins

{BAPTISMS, p. 285}

Date	Sex	Name
March 10	M	Samuel, of Samuel & Mary B. Parkman Jun.
__ __.	F	Lydia Oakes, of Nathaniel & Rachael Low
April 4.	M	William West, of Abimilech & Sarah F. Riggs
__ __.	F	Eliza West, of Jacob & Elizabeth C. Farnsworth
April 21.	M	Ammi Windship, of Ammi & Hannah Cutter
__ __.	M	Samuel Nichels, of Edward & Eunice Cutter
__ __.	F	Mehitable, of Nathaniel & Esther Lombard
May 5.	M	Henry Hill, of Charles & Isabella Hammatt
May 14.	F	Elizabeth Rogers }
__ __.	M	William Rogers } of Henry & Mary Simpson
__ __.	F	Mary } [The father dead; the mother presented them at her own house]
May 19.	M	+ Thomas Emery, died, of Jacob & Sarah Barstow
May 26.	M	Benjamin Clark, of Peter & Sally Seaver

116

July 14.	F	Eliza Wild, of Robert & Susan C. Lash
Aug. 4.	M	Samuel, of Samuel & Martha Ball
Aug. 18.	M	Charles Augustus, of Benjamin T. & Lydia Wells
__ __.	M	Isaac Gustavus, of Isaac & Lydia B. Howe
Sept. 8.	F	Susan Barber & } of Lot & Dolly Whitcomb
__ __.	M	Lot }
Sept. 22.	F	Mary Chamberlain, of Thomas G. & Eleanor Bangs
Oct. 6.	F	Eunice Harriet, of Samuel & Eunice Howe
__ __.	M	George Gustavus, of William & Mary Howe
__ __.	F	Abigail Carnes, of Thomas & Hannah Lillie
Oct. 20.	F	Mary-Ann Lincoln, of Josiah & Mary Peirce
Nov. 10.	M	+ Elias & }Parkman }Baptized at home
__ __	F	+ Sarah Rogers }adults }belonging to 2d Church
Dec. 1.	M	[Enoch Howes Snelling adult & his son
__ __.	M	[Enoch Howes Snelling, Jun.
		+ Not of the Society. Total 34

{BAPTISMS, p. 286}
1817

Jan. 12.	F	Margaret, of Isaac & Sally Atkins
__ __.	M	[blank], of Isaac & Mary Scott (died May 6, 1819)
Jan. 26.	M	George Francis, of George & Eliza A. Parkman
Feb. 2.	M	Josiah Quincy, of Joseph & S. Lewis
__. 16.	F	Mary Pearson, of Phillip & Joanna Adams
Feb. 23.	M	Edward Wells, of Edward & Catharine V. Tuttle
April 20.	M	Theodore Mansfield, of Joel & Elizabeth Richardson
__ __.	F	Frances Mehitable, of George & Sarah Daracott
__ __.	F	Mary Elizabeth, of Nathaniel & Elizabeth Clark
June 1.	M	Joseph Ellis Andrews } adults
	F	Sarah Andrews }
	M	Almira }
	F	Sarah-Ann } Andrews, children of J. E. & S. Andrews
	M	Joseph Ellis }
June 8.	F	Sarah-Ann, of Nathaniel S. & Abigail Magoon
__ __.	M	Thomas-Emery, of Jacob & Sarah Barstow
June 19.	M	+ Theodore (Brattle St. Church), of William & Elizabeth Spooner (at their home)
June 29.	M	Edward, of Edward & Susan Page
__ __.	F	Rebecca-Ann, of George & Elizabeth Lewis
July 27.	F	Lucy Barnicott – adult, received into the Church
__ __.	F	Mary Elizabeth, of Jacob & Mary-Ann Hall
Aug. 3.	F	[Cordelia Rosanna }Twins of Benjamin T. & Lydia Wells
__ __.	M	[Charles Gustavus }
__ __.	M	William Francis, of William P. & Mary Ann Shelton
__ __.	M	+ George (at Brattle St. Church), of Nathaniel R. & Susan Sturgess

117

Aug. 24. M   Mary, of Caleb B. & Mary Munroe

{BAPTISMS, p. 287}

Sept. 7.		[William & Caroline Smith, adults, &
__ __.	F	[Caroline Dorcas Smith, their child
__ __.	M	Benjamin, of Benjamin & Henrietta Lamson
Oct. 12.	F	Hannah Blake, of Robert G. & Eliza W. Shaw
__ __,	F	Helena Augusta, of Isaiah & Mercy Atkins
Oct. 19.		Mary Jane, of Stephen & Eliza Brown
Oct. 26.	M	Elisha, of Elisha and Miriam Field. The father died Aug. [illeg.]
Nov. 9.	M	Bernard Whittemore, adult, &
__ __.	M	Bernard Bemis, of B. & Jane Whittemore
__ __.	F	Sarah, of Daniel & Sarah Munroe
__ __.	M	Charles Thomas, of Christopher & Sally Gore
Nov. 23.	M	Henry, of Samuel & Mary B. Parkman

38 Baptisms

1818

	M	William, of William & Abigail S. Mills
Jan. 18.	F	Mary, of Parker & Esther Emerson
Feb. 8.	F	Lydia Wilson, adult, admitted into the Ch.
__ __.	M	Edward, of Edward & Sophia Tuckerman
__ __.	M	Nathaniel Goodwin, of Isaac & Sally Atkins
__ __.	F	Cornelia Torrey, of Edward & Ruth Cutter
April 19.M		Henry, of James & Mary Brown
May 4.	F	Catharine, of Levi & Catharine P. Younger
May 24.	M	Alfred, of Charles & Isabella Hammatt
July 5.	M	Nathaniel Prentiss, of Nathaniel & Charllotte Freeman
Aug. 2.	M	William Earle, of George & Sarah Daracott
Aug. 23.	F	Abigail Parker, of William & Fanny Hammatt
Sept. 13.M		Nathaniel Austin, of Elisha & M. Parks
__ __.	M	Edward Francis, of Edward & Susan Page

{BAPTISMS, p. 288}

Sep. 27	F	Elizabeth Burrows, of William & M. Thompson
Oct. 11.	F	Harriet Wild of Robert & Susan C. Lash
__ __.	F	Marcy Little, of Benjamin & Mary Tilden
__ __.	M	Charles Tidd, of Ebenezer & A. B. Wild
__ __.	F	Frances Elizabeth, of Barnard & H. Bignall
Nov. 14.	M	Edward Blake, of Daniel & Harriet Parkman, sua domô [at their house] on account of sickness
Dec. 20.	F	Mary Elizabeth, of Joseph & Mary Clark
__ __.	F	Eliza Lincoln, of Josiah & Mary Peirce

22 Total

118

1819

Jan. 17.	Sarah Elizabeth	}
__ __. Twins	{James Blake	} of Thomas & Sarah Leeds
__ __.	{Daniel Davenport	}
Jan. 24.	Charles Gould Loring, adult, &	
__ __.	Charles Frederick, of Charles G. & Harriet Loring	
Feb. 21.	Sarah Snelling	}Twins of
__ __.	Merab Hutchins	}John & Sarah Drew
__ __.	Sarah Daracott, of Nathaniel & Elizabeth Clark	
Mar. 7.	Mary Blake Bruce, adult	
April 25.	Jacob, of Jacob & Mary-Ann Hall	
__ __.	John Jones, of William P. & Mary Ann Shelton	
__ __.	Samuel Parkman, of Edward & Sophia Tuckerman	
May 2.	Sarah Elizabeth, of Samuel & Eunice Howe	
_ __.	William Ede, of Alexander & Betsy Vanneever	
__ __.	Sarah Anne, of Enoch H. & Sarah Snelling	
May 9.	Sarah Cabot, of Francis & Sarah Parkman	
__ __ 29.	John Redford, of J[ohn]. W[hite]. & Harriet Webster	

{BAPTISMS, p. 289}

June 6.	Powell Mason, of Samuel & Mary B. Parkman	
June 13.	George, of Nathaniel & Esther Lombard	
July 4.	{William & Susan Baker, adults, &	
__ __.	{William Baker, their child	
July 19.	Ann	}
__ __.	Eliza	} of Nathaniel & Eliza Francis
__ __	Nathaniel	}
Oct. 17.	Emily Frances, of Benjamin T. & Lydia Wells	
__ __.	Thomas Eliot, of Thomas & Eliza Wells	
__ __.	Gardner Howland, of Robert G. & Eliza Shaw	
Nov. 8.	Joseph Ellis, of Joseph E. & Sarah Andrews	

Total 28

1820

Jan. 2.	George Francis, of Edward & Ruth Cutter
Jan. 9.	Edward, of Daniel & Sarah Munroe
__ __,	Eliza Seaver, of Christopher & Sally Gore
__ __.	Charlotte Rebecca, of Nathaniel & Charlotte Freeman
Jan. 23.	Sarah-Ann, of George & Susan Stanton
Feb. 7.	Caroline, of James & Mary Brown
Feb. 13.	Mary-Ann Louisa, of William & Caroline Smith
Mar. 5.	Hannah Elizabeth, of Philip & [blank] Adams, baptized by Br. Frothingham [?], at Chelsea, domi [at home]
March 15.	Nancy, of Thomas & Elizabeth Williams
March 26.	[Harriet, wife of Mr. John B. Hoffman
__ __.	[Harriet Malvina, of J. B. & Harriet Hoffman

April 2.	Ann-Fitz, of Isaac & Sally Atkins
May 14.	Mary-Elizabeth, of Henry & Mary Elizabeth Fowle
__ __,	Maria-Antoinette, of William B. & Maria-A. Fowle

{BAPTISMS, p. 290}

May 14.	William Burrows, of John B. & Sarah F. Tremere
June XI.	Augustus Francis, of Charles & Isabella Hammett
__ __.	George, of William & Abigail S. Mills
June 18.	Ann, of Samuel & Mary S. Edes
July 23.	Thomas Wells, of Edward & Catharine Tuttle
__ 31.	Horatio Bray, } of John & Sally S. Winslow
__ __.	George Chapman }
Aug. 27.	Alfred, of Benjamin & Mary Tilden
Oct. 4.	Samuel Sewell }
__ __.	Philip Reynolds }
__ __.	John West } Children of Mrs. Ann Ridgeway (widow)
__ __.	Ann Sewell } baptized at her own house
__ __.	Henry Wolcott }
__ __.	Edward Wolcott }
__ __.	Anthony Brooks }
Oct. 8.	Levi, son of Levi & Catharine P. Younger (by Rev. Mr. Gray [?]) + Baptized in August Abby [in a different hand] Louiza, of William & Mary B. Thompson
Nov. 19.	George Bradish, of Elisha & Mary Ann Parks
Dec. 3.	Franklin, of George & Sarah Daracott
__ __.	Charles Gould, of Charles G. & Harriet Loring
	34 Total 10 not of the Society

1821

Jan. 21.	Josiah, of Josiah & Mary Peirce
Feb. 4.	Frances Mehitable, of Nathaniel & Elizabeth Clark
Feb. XI.	Evalina Elizabeth, of Alexander & Betsey Vannevar
Mar. 25.	Charles Morrison }
__ __.	Charles Staples } Children of the Boston Asylum for Indigent
__ __.	Joshua Eaton Barker } Boys

{BAPTISMS, p. 291}

March 25.	Charles Greenwood }
__ __.	George Shute Grover }
__ __.	James Laurence Boyd }
__ __.	Charles Warren Bucknam } Children of the Asylum for
__ __.	Ebenezer Parsons Bullock } Indigent Boys presented
__ __.	Silas Lewis } by the Matron & by Benjamin
__ __.	William Whitmarsh } Greene, Esq., President of the
__ __.	John Quincy Adams Conery } Society
__ __,	William Beers }

120

__ __.	Thomas Cushing. }	13
April 1st.	Sarah Hickling, of John W[hite]. & Harriet Webster	
April 15.	Harriet Eliza, of George & Eliza A. Parkman	
April 22.	Sidney, of Ammi & Hannah Cutter	
April 27.	Frederick Goddard, of Edward & S. Tuckerman	
May 20.	Joseph Coolidge, of Robert G. & Eliza Shaw	
June 24.	Thomas Curtis, of William P. & Mary-Ann Shelton	
June 30.	George Hills, of Nathaniel & E. Francis	
July 22.	Eloisa Bourne, of William B. & M. A. Fowle	
Oct. 20.	Ann Maria, of Samuel & Eunice Howe	
__ __.	John Frecker, of John & Charlotte Fenno	
Nov. 4.	[Mary Ann, wife of Mr. Daniel Messenger	
__ __.	[Daniel, of D. & Mary Ann Messenger	
__ 26,	Susan, of William & Susan Baker	
Dec. 16.	Jacob, of Jacob & Mary-Ann Hall	
		30 Total

{BAPTISMS, p. 292}

Feb. 4.	Henry J. Oliver & }adults, on admission to the church
__ __,	Sarah Oliver }
Mar. 10.	Henry Bass, of Frederick A. & Sarah A. E. Gay
Mar. 24.	Ann-Maria, of Christopher & Sally Gore
Mar. 31.	William Thomas, of Joseph & Nancy Grammar
April 14.	Henry James Walker, of Henry & Mary A. Thacker, of color, meâ domô [at my house]
May 12.	Esther Lombard, of Edward & Ruth Cutter
May 19.	John Sargent, of John B. & Sarah F. Tremere
June 30.	Charles Bradbury, of William & Mary Baker
June 30.	Henry, of William & Abigail Mills
July 7.	+ James Clark, of George & Sally Daracott
__ __.	Enoch James, of Nathaniel & Elizabeth Clark
Aug. 10	Samuel Foster, of Samuel F. & M. L. McClearey
__ __.	Catharine Elizabeth }
__ __.	Henry-Blakely } of Thomas L. & Catharine Hutchinson
__ __.	Charles Bright }
Sept. 8.	Henry Nichols }of Elijah & Mary Lincoln
__ __.	Mary Elizabeth }
Sept. 29.	Amadella Hamilton, adult
__ __.	Clarissa Sherwood } of William & [Amadella?] Hamilton.
__ __.	William Robert Grier } Presented by the mother, a widow, of Cam. Eng.
Oct. 20.	Henrietta Lamson, of Josiah & Mary Peirce
Nov. 3.	Harriet Wainwright, of John W[hite]. & Harriet Webster
__ __.	Samuel Parkman, of Charles & Isabella Hammatt

__ 10.	Henry, of Henry & Mary Elizabeth Fowle
__ 17.	Thomas Gilman, of Thomas & Eliza Wells
__ __.	Caroline Elizabeth, of Edward & Catharine V. Tuttle

{BAPTISMS, p. 293}

Nov. 24.	Lydia, of Alexander & Betsey Vanneever
Dec. 15.	William, of William & Mary B. Thompson
Dec. 22.	Charles Nathaniel Minott, of Charles & M. B. Lincoln
__ __.	Matthias, of Thomas & Ann B. Crocker
Dec. 29.	Charlotte Augusta, of John & Charlotte F. Fenno

1822   Total 32

1823

Feb. 9.	Samuel Augustus, of Elisha & Mary-Ann Parks
April 25.	William Mansir } Children of the
__ __.	Thomas Bacon (baptized at the Asylum) } Asylum for Indigent
__ __.	John Cerminati } Boys, baptized at the
__ __.	Benjamin Curtis Tuckerman } Old South Church,
__ __.	Charles Freeman Wade } at their anniversary
__ __.	Daniel Randall }
__ __.	John Hammond Perry 7
May 18.	Abigail Bourne, of William B. & M. A. Fowle
May 25.	Elizabeth Willard, of Robert G. & Elizabeth W. Shaw
June 29.	John Mills, adult, on admittance to the Church
__ __.	Henry Chapman, of Nathaniel & E. Lombard
__ __.	George James Montgomery, of George and [blank] Fracker
Aug. 10.	Abby Ann, of Nathaniel & Elizabeth Clark
	Mary Ann Webster, of Henry & Mary A. Thacker, of color, domi [at home]
Sept. 21.	Anna Maria, of James & Mary Brown
Oct. 5.	Harriet, of Charles G. & Harriet Loring
Nov. 2.	George Francis, of George & Eliza A. Parkman

{BAPTISMS, p. 294}

Nov. 2.	Francis, of Francis & Caroline Parkman
Nov. 9.	John Doak, of Nathaniel and Bridget Blake
Nov. 16.	Tappan Eustis, of Nathaniel & Eliza Francis
Nov. 30	Sarah Eliza Curtis, of Thomas D. & Eliza Francis
__ __.	Nathaniel, of Nathaniel & Joanna Hopkins
__ __.	Sarah Blake Bruce, adult, & received into the Church
Dec. 7.	Amasa Stetson, of Nathaniel & Charlotte Freeman
Dec. 28.	Elizabeth Clark, } of Joseph & Betsey Hart
__ __.	Sarah Ann, }
__ __.	Martha Elizabeth, of Joseph N. & Elizabeth K. Howe

28 Total. 1823 Number of Baptisms in 10 years 315

1824

Jan. 4.	Martha Elizabeth, of Charles & Martha B. Lincoln
Feb. 8.	Ann Maria Colesworthy, adult
__ __.	Ann Maria, of William W. & A. M. Colesworthy
__ __.	Mary Elizabeth, of Amos & Mary Farnsworth
__ __.	Lydia Fish, of Alexander & Betsey Vanneever
__ __,	+ Risdon (named for Rev. R. Daracott a friend of Dr. [Philip] Doddridge & minister in England, who died in 1759), of George & Sarah Daracott
__ __.	Harriet Mehitable, of Joseph & Mary Clark
Mar. 14.	Eliza Hopkins Tuttle, adult
__ __.	John Wells, of John W. & Eliza H. Tuttle
Mar. 28.	Lynde Walter, of Samuel F. & Maria L. McCleary
May 9.	Mary Elizabeth, of John & Mary Mills
May 16.	Amos Cotting, adult
__ __.	Ebenezer Francis, of Amos & Harriet Cotting
May 23.	Mary }of Daniel & Sarah Munroe
__ __.	Daniel }

{BAPTISMS, p. 295}

May 23.	Harriet Ardelia, of John & Charlotte Fenno
__ __.	John Fenno, of Lewis & Sally Bailey
__ __.	Joseph Henry, of Joseph & Eliza Fenno
June 27.	Benjamin Burrows, of John B. & Sarah Tremere
__ __.	Sarah Elizabeth, of William & Susan Baker
July 25.	William Bowles, of [blank] Austin
__ __.	Susan }
__ __.	Charles Marsh } of Edward & Susan Page
__ __.	Edward } baptized suâ domô [at their home]
August 8.	Mary-Ann Austin, of Elisha & Mary-Ann Parks
__ __.	Isabella Maria, of Thomas L. & Catharine Hutchinson
__ __.	Sarah Winslow Copeland, of Elijah & Mary Lincoln
__ __.	suâ domô { Sarah Catharine, 12 years, of Mrs. Sybbel Feno, widow
__ __.	[at their home {John Blanchard, of John Fenno Payson, the mother dead
August 15.	Olivia, of Henry and Mary Elizabeth Fowle
Sept. 26.	Samuel Aspinwall, of Joseph & Nancy Grammar
Oct 10.	Francis Hall, of Christopher & Sally H. Gore
Oct. 17.	William Henry Hemmenway }
__ __.	William Long } Children of the Asylum
__ __.	George Washington Hollis } for Indigent Boys,
__ __.	Nathaniel Low } Baptized together at the
__ __.	Stephen A. H. Bullard } Asylum House,
__ __.	John Haven } presented by the
__ __.	Charles Walter White } Managers, and
__ __.	David Thompson } Governess

123

— —.	John James Hall	} Children of the Asylum for Indi-
— —.	Samuel Ballough	} gent Boys, Baptized together at the
— —.	William Henry Allen	} Asylum House, presented by the
		Managers, and Governess

{BAPTISMS, p. 296}

Oct. 17.	Horatio Davis	} Children of the Asylum for
— —.	George Hubbard Nichols }	Indigent Boys 13
— —.	John Adams Bates, of Edward & Ruth Cutter	

Total 46, 13 of the Boy's Asylum

1825

Jan. 30.	Frances Mary, of William & Mary B. Thompson
Mar. 20.	Mary-Ann White, of John W[hite]. & Harriet Webster
May 29.	Enoch James, of Nathaniel & Elizabeth Clark
May	James William Goodman } 4 Children of the Asy-
	Otis Crosby } lum for Indigent Boys,
	John Mansur } presented at the Asylum
	James McFarlane } by the Managers
June 26.	Lawrence Curney, of Levi & Catharine Younger
July 10.	Quincy Adams, of Robert G. & Eliza Shaw
— —.	Mary Jane, of Thomas D. & Eliza Francis
17.	Rachael Matilda, of Henry & Mary Thacker,
	of color, domi [at home]
31.	Mrs. Mary Tittle, on admission to the Church
Sept. 18.	Caroline Hall, of Francis & Caroline Parkman
_ 25.	Gilbert Stewart, of William & Mary Baker
Oct. 16.	Mrs. Harriet Loring, adult
— —.	Mary-Ann, of Caleb G. & Harriet Loring
Oct. 30.	Sarah Roby, of Josiah & Mary Pierce
— —.	Sarah, of John B. & Sarah F. Tremere
— —.	John James, of James & Eliza Bingham

19 Total

{BAPTISMS, p. 297}

1826

March 12.	Nathaniel Goodwin, of Isaac & S. Atkins
	James Risdon, of George & Sally Darracott
	James Henry, of Nathaniel & Elizabeth Clark
April 3.	Edward, of James & Mary Brown
_ 23,	Benjamin Tuttle, of Samuel & Eliza Bradshaw
— —.	David Sears, of Amos & Harriet Cotting
— —.	Alpheus Worcester } Children of the Boy's Asylum,
— —.	Samuel Gragg Newell } presented by the Governess, at
— —.	William Beers } the House
— —.	Theodore Lillie 4 }
May 7.	Maria Louisa, of S. F. & M. L. McCleary
— —.	Maria Louisa, of Joseph & Betsey Hart

124

__ __.	Walter Ingraham, of Walter & Esther Frost
May 28.	William, of John & Mary Mills
June 4.	Amos Henry, of Amos & Mary Farnsworth
July 29.	Sarah Penniman, of Thomas & C. Hutchinson
Aug. 20.	Joanna Cades, of Nathaniel & Joanna Hopkins
Oct. 1.	Charles, of Nathaniel & Eliza Francis
__ 29.	Elizabeth Whalan, of Charles & E. H. Arnold
Nov. 12.	Harriet Austin, of Elisha & Mary Ann Parks
__ __.	Harriet Caroline, of John W. & Eliza H. Tuttle
__ __.	Henry Withington, of Edward & Catharine Tuttle

Total 22

1827

Feb. 11.	Edmund Bowman, of Alexander & Betsey Vanneever

{BAPTISMS, p. 300, sic}

Mar. 25.	Charles Shaw, of Edward & Ruth Cutter
May 13.	Francis Parkman, of Nathaniel & C. Freeman
__ __.	Sarah Elizabeth, of William & Sarah Tuttle
May 28.	Charles McDonogh, of Daniel & Mary G. Parkman
June 3.	Henry, of William & Mary B. Thompson
June 24.	Francis Henry, of John B. & Sarah F. Tremere
__ __.	Henry Quincy, of Henry & Mary D. Adams
__ __,	Mary Elizabeth, of Francis & [blank] Neville
Aug. 14.	John Dixwell, of Nathaniel & Elizabeth Clark

Sept 16	Sally Hayman }	
__ __.	Ann Phillips }	Children of the late Capt.
__ __.	Emiline Mary }	T. Rogers baptized at their
__ __.	James Harvey }	own desire, suâ domô [at
__ __.	Edward Augustus }	their home]

Oct. 14.	Maria Louisa, of Caleb G. & Harriet Loring
__ 28.	William Henry, of Robert G. & Eliza W. Shaw

Nov. 18.	Joseph Vincent }	
__ __.	William Proctor Holt }	of the Asylum for Indigent Boys,
__ __.	George Martin }	baptized at the house, present by
__ __.	John Davis 4 }	Joseph Austin, Esq.

Nov. 25.	John Wade, of Thomas D. & Eliza Francis
Dec. 16.	Maria Penniman, of Nathaniel & Mary-Ann Colesworthy
__ __.	Mary-Agnes, of Francis & Caroline Parkman
	(mortua, ignê erepta [died, taken away by fire], Dec.[20], 1829)

1828

April 13.	Mary-Harriet, of Daniel & Mary Parkman	
17.	Esther Rowe, }	of Levi & Catharine Younger. The father
	David Harris }	being absent and the mother dying. These
		were baptized at home.

{BAPTISMS, p. 301}

June 8.	Maynard Walter, of S. F. & Maria L. McCleary
__ __.	Thomas Albert Leach, of T. L. & C. Hutchinson
__ __.	Sarah Matilda Jones }
__ __.	Olive Ann Catharine } of John & C. F. Fenno
__ __.	Emily Dommett }
June 29.	George Frederick, of Charles & Isabella Hammatt
__ __.	Mary-Ann Barker, of Christopher & S. Gore
__ __.	William Ward, of Stephen & Abby Rhoades
__ __.	Emeline Phipps, of Charles & Elizabeth Arnold
July 27.	Martha-Ann, of Edward & Catharine Tuttle
August 10.	Emeline Foster, of Elisha & Mary-Ann Parks
Dec. 21.	Mary, wife of Mr. Benjamin Smith } Covenant & Baptism
__ __.	Thomas Beals, of Benjamin & Mary Smith } domi suæ [at their house]

16

1829

Feb. XV.	Harriet Burroughs, adult, grand-daughter of Deacon Simpkins
April 27.	Abraham Farnsworth } Children of the Asylum for
__ __.	John Shivers Matthews } Indigent Boys suâ domô
__ __.	Thomas Mitchell 3 } [at their house]
May 25.	Amory, of Charles P. & Sarah R. Dexter
__ __.	Mrs. Susan Powers Burbeck, adult
May 25.	Susan Powers, of Henry and Susan P. Burbeck
May 31.	Edward King, of John & C. F. Fenno
June 14.	Mary-Ann, of Robert G. & E. W. Shaw
__ __.	William Francis, of William & Sarah Grubb
June 28.	+ Lowell Blake, of George & Sarah Darracott
Aug. 29.	Charles, of William & Mary B. Thompson
Sept. VI.	Thomas, of Alexander & Betsey Vanneever

{BAPTISMS, p. 302}

Sept. 20.	Mary Elizabeth, of Charles & Isabella Hammett
Nov. 8.	Agnes McKean Austin, of Henry & S. P. Andrews
__ 22.	George, of Caleb G. and Harriet Loring
__ 29.	Helen Maria, of John B. & Sarah F. Tremere

17 Total

1830

Feb. 28.	Ephraim } children of Clarissa Skerry domi suæ prop-
__ __.	Clarissa } ter res adversas [at their house on account of
__ __.	Francis Horace } difficulties
Mar. 7.	Sarah Frances, of Henry W. & R. H. Fenno
__ 14.	Francis Parkman, of Mrs. Grace Oliver, a widow, her son being twelve years.
__ __.	Thomas, a son of Mrs. Sarah Leeds, offered by her after the death of Mr. L.

May 2.	Elizabeth Waterman Palfrey (adult)
__ __.	Susan Elizabeth, of William & E. W. Palfrey
__ __.	Robert Lash }twin children of John and Charlotte Sawin
__ __.	John Pierce }
May 16.	Artemas Ward Truesdale } Children of Asylum for
__ __.	James Orman Brown } Indigent Boys
__ __.	John Willliam Tuttle }
May 23.	Augusta Maria } of [blank] & S. H. Pierce
__ __.	John Howard }
June 27.	Mary Abigail, of Joseph and Betsey Hart
July 4.	Georgianna, of Elisha & Mary-Ann Parks
__ __.	Joshua Moore }
__ __.	Margaret Augusta Fenno } of Lewis & Sally Bailey
__ __.	Nancy Noror-wood }
__ __.	Henry Fenno, of Henry and Harriet A. Cutting
July 25.	Mary-Ann, of Edward & Catharine Tuttle

{BAPTISMS, p. 303}

	Mary Brooks, of Francis & Caroline Parkman
Sept. 19.	Catharine Wild }
__ __.	William Oliver } Children of Charles & Bartha B. Lincoln
__ __.	Sarah Minott } domi suæ [at their home], Charlestown
__ __.	Henry Barry }
Oct. 18.	[blank] }
__ __.	John Tuttle } Children of John and Catharine Tuckerman

29

1831

March 13.	Sarah Blake, of Charles P. & Sarah R. Dexter, domi suæ [at their home]
April 10.	Oliver Fessenden, of Oliver & Harriet R. Lincoln
May 15.	George Augustus, of George A. & Cordelia Eliot
May 24.	John May Sylvester, æt[ate] [aged.] 9 yr.}
__ __.	Charles Adams, aged 7 yr. } Children of
__ __.	John D. Campbell, 6 yr. } the Boy's
__ __.	Benjamin C. Jones, 5 yr. } Asylum
June 19.	Ann Rebecca } of Samuel & E. Bradshaw
__ __.	Turell Tuttle }
__ __.	Edward Henry, of William & Susan Baker
June 26.	Mary Elizabeth, of Henry & Sarah P. Andrews
Aug. 21.	Charles Frederick, of John B. & S. F. Tremere
Sept. 25.	Martha Lee, of Samuel & Eunice Howe, domi suæ [at their house]
Nov. 6.	Dixwell Homer, of Nathaniel Clark (mother dead)
__ __.	Louisa Blake, of Henry W. & R. H. Fenno
Nov. 13.	Edward Thornton, of Charles & Isabella Hammatt, by Mr.

Newell
Elizabeth, of Caleb G. & Harriet Loring

{BAPTISMS, p. 304}
1832

Jan. 8.	Ann, wife of Mr. Warren Lincoln
__ __.	Caroline Parker } children of Warren & A.
__ __.	Ann Maria } Lincoln domi suæ [at their house]
Mar. 26.	Harriet Gardner, of Daniel & H. J. Denny
April 15.	Frances-Ann, of Franklin & Joanna Smith
April 22.	Susan Ellen, of Thomas & Susan Chamberlain
May 28.	+ Robert Todd } children of Fortunatus & Ellen M. J.
__ __.	+ Ellen Eliza } Cosby, ba[p]tized
__ __.	+ George Blake } at their house, near Louisville, Kentucky
__ __.	+ Alice Gray }
June 24.	Harriet Roby, of Oliver & H. R. Lincoln, domi suæ [at their house], the mother having died
July 1.	Jacob Gragg } of George & P. Harris
__ __.	George Washington }
__ __.	John Wells, of Edward & C. Tuttle
July 8.	Francis Sloan }
__ __.	Phineas Allen }
__ __.	Sterling Haynes Hopkins }
__ __.	Charles Haynes Hopkins } Children of the Asylum
__ __.	George Frederick Babson } for Indigent Boys
__ __.	George Henry Ham }
__ __.	James Bartlett Reed }
__ __.	Charles Adams Branting }
__ __.	Benjamin Spear }
__ __.	Alonzo Frederic [Ferdinand written above] Hall }
July 22.	Frances Mehitable, of George & Sarah Darracott
July 29.	Mary Hatch, of Stephen & Abby Rhoades
	+ not of my own society

{BAPTISMS, p. 305}

Aug. 5.	Charles Henry, of George A. & Cordelia Eliot
__ 26.	William Smith } of Daniel & Mary-Ann Messenger
__ __.	Susan Dorcas }
Sept. 29.	Sarah Leach, adult, domi meæ [at my house]
Oct. 21.	Eliza Willard Shaw, of Francis & C. Parkman
Nov. 25.	Isabella Harris, of Benjamin & Nancy Comey
Dec. 2.	Mary-Ann Hammatt, of William & A. S. Cotting
Dec. 30.	Adeline Augusta, of Elisha & Mary A. Parks
__ __.	George Francis, of Benjamin H. & Elizabeth C. Greene

Total 35. 4 not of the Parish

1833

— —.	William Ellis Wallace }	
— —.	Francis Henry Wallace }	
— —.	Thomas Magee }	Children of the Boy's Asylum,
— —.	Mathew Magee }	domi suæ [at their house]
— —.	John M. Hastings }	

May 9.	Charles Frederick, of Lemuel Arnold, matre mortuâ [the mother having died]
July 1.	Sarah Grace, of Henry & S. P. Andrews
14.	Geprge Walstein, of George E. Merson, of York
28.	Eliza Burrows, of John B. & S. F. Tremere
Sept. 8.	Henry Gardner, of Daniel & Harriet G. Denny
29.	Eliza Robinson, of Noah & Zoe Harrod
XI.	Total in 20 years 561.

1834

Mar. 9.	Margaret Cruft }	of William & Mary B. Thompson
	Edward William: Burrows }	of Brattle St., suâ domô [at their house]

{BAPTISMS, p. 306}

May 11.	Benjamin Franklin Mead } killed by lightening Aug. 1838.	
	Frederick Dacon House }	Children of the Boston Asylum
	Samuel Marshall }	for Indigent Boys 85 in toto since
	Daniel Carpenter }	1821. (domi suæ [at their house])
	George Adams. 5 }	

May 25.	Edward B of Robert & Susanna B. Restieaux
June 8.	Andrew Sigourney, of Benjamin H. & M. Hammatt
Aug. 17.	Samuel, of Edward & Catharine Tuttle

— —.	[blank] }	Children of Mrs. Barber, domi suæ
— —.	Henry Hutchinson }	[at their house]

Sept. 14.	John Eliot, of Francis & Caroline Parkman
21.	+ Stephen Sharp, of S. S. Brookline, Dr. Peirce's
28.	William Arnold, of Samuel A. & Mary Spear
— —.	Sarah Elizabeth, of Benjamin H. & Elizabeth C. Greene
— —.	Augustus Parker, of William & Susan Baker

Oct. .	Marianne }	of Thomas & Jerusha Andrews
	Thomas Franklin }	

Nov. 2.	Charles Edward, of Charles & Isabella Hammett
__ 16.	William Henry, of Caleb G. & Harriet Loring
— —.	Stephen, of Stephen and Abigail B. Rhoades
— —.	Thomas Edward, of Thomas & Susan Chamberlain
23.	Cornelia Eliza, of Elisha & Mary-Ann Parks
	24 (5 of Boys Asylum)

1835

Jan. 25.	Benjamin Franklin, of Franklin & J[oanna]. Smith
Ap. 18.	Lydia Cazneau, of William & E. W. Palfrey

{BAPTISMS, p. 307}

May 4.	Sarah W. Gore, of Eliza H. Tuttle, widow
— —.	Hannah Watts, of Benjamin & Nancy Comey

Henry Russell Wiley   }
James Browning   }
John Davis   }   Children of the Boy's Asylum,
Elisha Kelton   }   at the Asylum House Lt. Gov.
Avery Goudy   }   [Samuel Turell] Armstrong, Dr.
Samuel Spear   }   Tuckerman & Deacon Grant, of
Josiah Spear   }   the Managers being present
Alvan Brown   }
John Peterson   }

May 31.	Mary Ward, of Bowen & Elizabeth P. Harrington
June 14.	Daniel, of Daniel & Harriet G. Denny
— —.	Henry P. Adams, of Henry R. & A. H. Williams
Aug. 2.	George Campbell, of George C. & S. P. Barrett

Total XVII

1836

Jan. 13.	Charles Lincoln, of J. and M. Peirce (sick, domi suæ [at their house])
31.	Elizabeth Sprague, adult, on being received into the Church
May 22.	Henry H. Williams } of Henry & H. Sigourney,
	Harriet Ardelia } domi suæ [at their house]
June 13.	Benjamin Henderson, of B. H. & E. C. Green
July 17.	James Babson, of Thomas & S. Andrews (Sexton)
— —.	Elizabeth A. Pulsifer, adult, on reception to Church
Nov. 20.	Maria Brown, of Elisha & Mary Parks
— —.	Susan Rebecca, of Susan P. Barrett, domi suæ, patre mortuô [at their house, the father having died]

9

{BAPTISMS, p. 308-310}

(These copy from the Page cut out. Corrected. F. P.)

1827

April 2.	Robert T. of Robert & Susanna Restieaux
June 25.	James Everett, of Daniel & H. G. Denny
— —.	Charles Bowen, of Bowen & E. P. Harrington
July 30.	Margaret A. Hill, of Henry & Sarah P. Andrews
Sept. 3.	George Henry, of Noah & Zoe Harrod
— 17.	Eliza Atkins, } Children of Jacob & Eliza Stone + note below
— —.	Lois Parsons } domi suæ [at their house] – Newbury-Port
— —.	George F. Pearson}
Nov. 17.	Martha, of William & Ann Spence

9.

1838

April 11.	Josiah Wilson, of Thomas & Susan Chamberlain

29.	William B. of Benjamin & Hannah J. Fessenden
May 28.	Andrew Sigourney, of Thomas & Emily F. Williams
June 24.	William Waterman, of William & E. W. Palfrey
— —.	Mary L. Darracott, of Benjamin H. & E. C. Greene
	Total of Baptisms in Twenty-five years, from Dec. 8, 1813 to Dec. 8, 1838 - -
Dec. 8.	Six-hundred and twenty-five; and from the foundation of the Church in 1714 - - 7667.
1838	
Dec. 30.	Francis Parkman, of Daniel & H. G. Denny

1839

Jan.	Joseph Winslow, of Thomas & J[erusha] Andrews
Jan. 27.	Henrietta Richmond, of Henry & S. P. Andrews
Mar. X.	Warren Parker, }
— —.	Evelina Barry, } of Warren & Ann Lincoln
— —.	Susan Beals, }
Aug. 16.	Sophronia A. Partridge, adult, domi suæ [at her house]
— —.	Also, her infant child, in extremis
	+ Note. This name (Lois) changed to Louisa

{BAPTISMS, p. 311}

1840

Jan. 19.	Francis Parkman, of Elisha & M. Parks

1841

Oct. 17.	Samuel Cook, of Samuel C. & R. Bradshaw
Nov. 14.	Goodwin Atkins, of Jacob & Eliza Stone, baptized, domi suæ [at their house], the Mother being a member of my church; and three of elder children have been in like manner baptized by me Sept. 17, 1837, at Newbury-Port
Dec. 12.	Arthur Stanley, of Daniel & H. G. Denny
1842	
June 5.	[blank] of Thomas & Susan Chamberlain
Oct. 9.	Robert Bates, of William & E. W. Palfrey
Oct. 29.	Lucy Maria, of David & M. L. Pierce
Nov. 6.	Mary Eliza, of Warren & Ann Lincoln, domi suæ [at their house]
— —.	Thomas Wells, of Thomas W. & C. R. Capen

5

1843

April 30.	{ George Darracott Clark }adults, and received into the Church
	{Julia Maria Clark }
May 29.	Clarence Holbrook, of Daniel & H. G. Denny
Nov. 26.	Harriet Denny, adult, & received into the Church
Dec. 31.	Mary Jane Lynes, adult & received into Church
— —.	Elizabeth Smith, d[itt]o d[itt]o

{BAPTISMS, p. 312}
1844

Jan. 20.	Mrs. Sarah Bates, with }
	Sarah, }
	Caroline, }
	Joseph Sweetsor }
	Martin } Children of Martin and
	Susan Elizabeth, } Sarah Bates baptized domi
	John, } suæ [at their house]
	Ann Matilda, }
	Charles Sweetser, }
	Catharine, }
	Caleb Francis, }
	Jonathan, }
	Georgianna. }

Feb. 4.   Isaac Henry of Isaac & Elizabeth H. Taylor

Mar. 24.   [blank] Wheelwright of Thomas & Susan Chamberlain, domi suæ [at their house]

May 5.   Emily Frances, of Benjamin & Elizabeth Orne Fessenden

July 7.   + Francis Charles, of William P. & Sarah C. Atkinson (at West-Roxbury, Pastore absente [the pastor being absent)

Oct. 3.   x William Henry Stuart Ritchie, of William & Isabella [blank]

26.   Frances Eusebia } of Noah & Zoe Harrod

__ __,   Caroline Zoe   }

Nov. 3.   Alice, of Rev. John & Susan S. Parkman, at Dover, N. H.

                     21 Baptisms: 16 in private houses

1845

April 27   George, (aged 7 yrs, 9 ms) } of George, Jr. &

__ __.   Sarah Nason, (aged 5 ms)} Ann Matilda Darracott

Sept. 7.   Edward Morton (aged 3 years) }of Edward G. & Mary Jane Lynes

__ __.   Mary Jane (aged 10 ms)   }

{BAPTISMS, p. 313}

Nov. 16.   Alphonso, of Isaac & Elizabeth H. Taylor

1846

July 26.   Elizabeth Marietta of Benjamin & Elizabeth O. Fessenden, by Mr. Smith

Aug. 13.   An infant child (dying) child of ? [*sic*]

1847

Mar. 28.   Lucy Abby,   }

__ __.   Mary Elizabeth,   } of Nathaniel & Abby R. Barstow

__ __.   Sarah Richardson   }

Nov. XXV. Thanksgiving Day Mary Louisa, of Robert & Mary L. Shaw
__ __.   Robert Shaw, of Daniel & Elizabeth Oliver
__ __.   John Ware, of Daniel & H. G. Denny
Dec. 29   Emily, of William P. & S. C. Atkinson

Dec. 19.   Charlotte Bray   }
__ __.   Harriet Hunt   }   of Henry & Mary Elizabeth Fowle
__ __.   Abby Frances   }   at the house of Henry Fowle
__ __.   Edward Gardiner   }
__ __.   Charlotte Olivia, of Edward W. & Olivia K. Morse

1848

June IV.   Lucy Orne of Benjamin & Elizabeth Orne Fessenden,
                 At Church
September 14.   Mrs. Elizabeth Wiswall (wife of Dexter W. Wiswall
__ __.   William Dexter   } of Dexter Ward &   } At the house
__ __.   George Clark   } Elizabeth Raymond Wiswall } of Dexter W.
__ __.   Mary Elizabeth   }of Joseph Belknap & Smith } Wiswall,
__ __.   Catharine Belknap } Catharine Mears Smith   } Prince St.
__ __.   Catharine Clark, of Edward G. & Mary Jane Leynes

Continued on next page by Joshua Young

{BAPTISMS, p. 314}
1849

Sept. 14.   Charles Augustus, child of Nathaniel F. & Rebecca English
Sept.   Charles D. of John & Sarah H. Dabney, of Fayal [Azores],
             baptized at Cambridge by the former Pastor, F[rancis].
             P[arkman]. in the house of Prof. J[ohn]. W[hite]. Webster

1850

April 14.   At Church- Alice Campbell, of Thomas T. & Mary O. Haydon
"   "   Samuel Andrews &   } of Samuel A. Cushing & Caroline
"   "   Ellison Baylies   }   S. W. Cushing
"   "   Mary Elizabeth, of Joshua-Pastor of N. N. C. &
             Mary Elizabeth S. Young
             Baptized by Dr. F. Parkman – former Pastor
May 12.   x Isaac Freeman Rowe of Thomas B. & Christiana Barnes,
             At home
June 30.   Mrs. Atlanta Matilda Aspinwall   }
__ __.   Mrs. Clarissa Wilson   }   at home
__ __.   Miss Helen Elizabeth (Gerry) Aspinwall   }
July 17.   Austain Hewes Kruger, of {blank} At Grove in Reading on
             occasion of S[abbath]. S[chool]. Excursion

1851

Jan. 15.   Agnes Eliza, of [blank] Glossom

___.	Anna Jane, }	
___.	Benjamin Steward, }	of [blank] Wright
___.	Emery Seaman }	at home
___.	Daniel Gardner }	poor

{BAPTISMS, p. 315

Jan. 22.	George Henry }	of George & Frances Brown
___.	John William }	at home
___.	Mary Susan }	poor
March 30.	Arthur Henry, of Joseph H. & Eliza Cormier	
April 13.	x Charles Frederic of Nathaniel F. & Rebecca English	

1852

March 31. Grace Desor, daughter of the Pastor. Joshua Young

Continued on next page by A. B. Fuller

{BAPTISMS, p. 316}

1853 On Sunday June 26th the Pastor of the New North Church preached a discourse on the subject of Baptism, commending it to the attention of the people. On the following Wednesday 29th instant the Society made an Excursion to Bacon's Grove, Winchester, and in the P. M. forty persons, children and adults, were baptized; as follows:

Adults

Noah Harrod
William Phillips Howard
George Patridge Richardson
John Fenno Payson Jr.
Mrs. Sarah Wiswall
Lydia Reed Shepard
Sarah Lavina Shepard

Children

William Swift }children of William Phillips & Caroline C. Howard
Mary Caroline }
Mary Jane }
Albert Cabot } children of Albert & Mary Betteley
Charles }
Mary Elizabeth } children of George P. & Mary Richardson
William Henry }
John Tremere – son of William & Ellen Deblois

{BAPTISMS, p. 317}

Georgianna }
George Albert } children of George W. & Hannah Nash
Walter }
Henry Herbert }

Frances Butler　　}children of Charles P. & Frances Shattuck
Charles Henry　　}
George Blanchard　　}children of George W. & [blank] Betteley
Frank　　　　　　}
Charles Wellington – child of George & Phebe Harris
George Henry　　} children of William H. & [blank] Grueby of
Emma Frances　　}　　　　　　　　East-Boston
Francis Edwin child of Edwin & [blank] Bowker
Charles Henry – child of Thomas & Catharine Tuttle
Frederick Augustus – child of [blank] Tisdale
Catharine Louisa　}
Andrew Thomas　　}　　children of William & Mary E. Crawley
John Edward　　　}
William Henry　　}
Mary Elizabeth　　　}children of John & Mary Kell
Elizabeth James　　　}
James Clark　　}children of Eben D. & Julia M. Jordan
Walter　　　　}
Harriet Elizabeth – daughter of John F. & Dolly Payson

{BAPTISMS, p. 318}

July 17.	Louis Vasmer　　}children of Stephen & Maria L. S. Caziarc
"	Arthur Wheeler　}
"	Samuel Nathan of Samuel N. & Eliza Neat
"	Thomas Wells of Thomas & Catharine Tuttle
Sept. 1.	Arthur Angelo, son of R.[ichard] F.[rederick] & S.[arah] K.[olloch] Fuller
Oct. 16.	Charles Gustavus Wells son of Thomas W. & R. Capen

1854	Adults
Jan. 29.	Elizabeth Perry
__ __.	Edward David Hinckley
Feb.	Frances Elizabeth daughter of H. L. & Mary Dalton
Feb. 19.	Daniel Shane – child of Mr. & Mrs. D. Shane
May 28.	Sarah Elizabeth Stearns
June 4.	Raymond　　} children of Edward G. & Mary J. Lynes
	Sidney　　　}

On the 29th of June 1854 the New North Religious Society made another excursion to Bacon's Grove, Winchester, in the P. M. twenty persons of various ages were dedicated in baptism. I have been able to obtain only a portion of their names with the degree of accuracy which enable me to transcribe them here. Such names follow.

　　　　　Mrs. Mary Ann Krugman

George Albert   } children of S. B. & Mary Ann Krugman
Frank Walter   }

{BAPTISMS, p. 319}

June 28th.   Helen Amelia Severs
             Daniel Spinney
             Sarah Gerry
             Mary Amanda Harris
             Irene Putnam Harris
             Lydia Ann Nash
             Alfred Turner Nash
July 30.   Henry Derby Rogers
Oct. 1st.   Eugene Giovanni, son of W.[illiam] E.[llery] & E.[llen]
             K.[ilshaw Fuller] Channing
— —.   Edith Davenport, daughter of A[rthur]. B.[uckminster] &
             E.[lizbeth] G. Fuller
Nov. 12th.   Samuel Smith
             Morill Aspinwall, son of Samuel & Helen E. Smith
Nov. 26th.   John Plummer   }
             Anne Augusta   }   children of John P. & [blank] Ober
             Emma Francis   }

1855

March 25 1855   Maria Louisa Lusetta Caziarc
June 20.   Catharine Smith   }
             Mary Young   }
             Sarah Dyer   }   children of Jesse & [blank] Holbrook
             Flora Alabama   }
             Charles Benjamin   }
             Frances Henrietta   }

{BAPTISMS, p. 320}

June 30.   Edwin Lincoln, child of Mr. Edwin & Mrs. [blank] Shute
Dec. 29.   Thomas Leonard   }children of Thomas S. & [blank] Meizner
             Martha Elizabeth }
             In 1853 I baptized 44 persons
             " 1854 "   "   35 "
             " 1855 "   "   10 "
             " 1856 "   "   3 (one was baptized by Mr. Sears in my
church) The reason of there being so many less baptized the last year has been
the very general attendance to the subject the first two years of my ministry so
that few families are now in the society whose children have not been present in
that ordinance. Nor was any baptismal service held at the annual Sunday School
celebration. A. B. Fuller   Oct. 31, 1855

1856

March 8th 1856.   Baptized at church at the funeral of his mother my only boy Arthur Ossoli. May God bless & sanctify him. A. B. Fuller   March 13, 1856 N. B. Little Arthur was baptized by Rev. E. H. Sears of Wayland.

{BAPTISMS, p. 321}

May 25.	Mrs. Frances Spalding Shipley
Aug.	Two children, sons, of Mr. & Mrs. S. N. Neat
Sept.	Charles Franklin, son of Dr. & Mrs. Ralph Darby

1857

Jan. 1857.	Elsie Ann, daughter of Mr. & Mrs. J[ohn] Nelson
— —.	Mary Sophia, daughter of Henry L. & Mary Dalton
— —.	Louisa Zeporah, daughter of Mr. & Mrs. Lawson
April 4.	Mrs. Minerva Sellew
April 21.	Thomas Dolliver
— —.	Ida Warren infant daughter of Mr. & Mrs. Gould
May 29.	Cyrus Brown }children of Mrs. Minerva Selew
	Sarah Emma }
May 31.	Mr. Lyman Leeds }
	Mrs. Rebecca Nash } Adults baptized in
	Mrs. Hanna Nash } order to enter the
	Mrs. Susan Hewes } church
	Mrs. Martha Jennings }
	Miss Martha Elizabeth Holmes }
	Elisa Bowdoin, daughter of Mrs. M. Sellew

{BAPTISMS, p. 322}

Oct. 9.	Child of Mr. & Mrs. Lawson
Nov. 27.	Frank Herbert, child of Mr & Mrs. Saxon

1858

April 12, 1858.	Sarah Lizzie, child of Mr. & Mrs. Cook
20.	Caroline Watts
—.	Henry Augustus Floyd
—.	Josephine daughter of G. F. & Sarah A. Smith
April 24.	Thomas Leonard Mizner
—.	Eliza Greene MIzner
—.	Emma Eliza, daughter of T. S. & E. G. Mizner
June 1.	John, child of John & Elsie Nelson
Sept. 16.	Anna Cara }children of Eugene & Anna Eliza Fuller
— —.	Ellen Kilshaw }
— —.	Emily Rölker } children of William Henry & Frances E. Fuller
— —.	Julian }
Nov.	Mr. George Nash

1859

Jan. 7th 1859.	Ella Frances, daughter of Joshua T. & F. S. Davis
— —.	Caroline Blake, daughter of Edward & C. A. Sowther [?]
— —.	Charles Edwin }children of Charles A. & Elizabeth M. Walker
— —.	Marion Stimpson }
— —.	Stillman Simonds }
— —.	James Lovell }
— —.	William Henry }children of George & Mary Studley
— —.	Frances Lovell }
__ 25.	Mrs. Sarah Ann Ames

{BAPTISMS, p. 323}

Jan. 30.	Martha Elizabeth daughter of Mr. & Mrs. M. E. Keith
June 26.	Frank Langdon son of Samuel & Helen G. Smith

1862

April 27th 1862.	Elizabeth Raymond daughter of Dexter W. & Elizabeth R. Wiswell

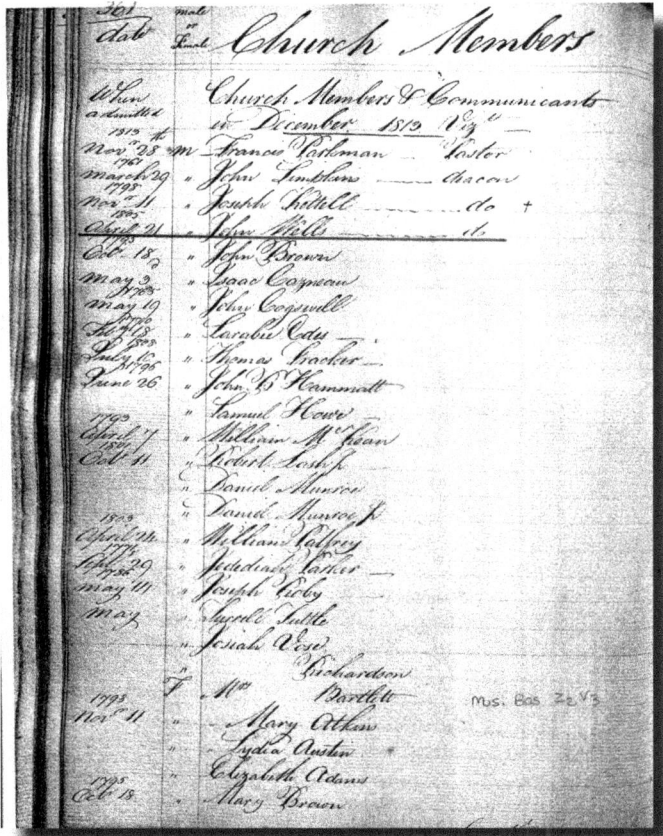

CHAPTER 11

CHURCH MEMBERS

{MEMBERS, p. 361}

When admitted	M/F	Church Members & Communicants in December 1813, Viz.	
1813 Nov 28[th]	M	Francis Parkman Pastor	
1761 March 29	"	John Simpkins	deacon
1798 Nov. 11	"	Joseph Kettell	d[itt]o +
1805 April 21	"	John Wells	d[itt]o
1795 Oct. 18	"	John Brown	
May 3	"	Isaac Cazneau	
1765 May 19	"	John Cogswell	
1770 Feb 18	"	Larabee Edes	
1808 July 10	"	Thomas Fracker	

1796 June 26	"	John B. Hammatt
	"	Samuel Howe
1793 April 7	"	William McKean
1801 Oct 11	"	Robert Lash Jr
	"	Daniel Munroe
	"	Daniel Munroe Jr
1803 April 24	"	William Palfrey
1774 Sept 29	"	Jedediah Parker
1786 May 11	"	Joseph Proby
May	"	Turrell Tuttle
	"	Josiah Vose
	"	[blank] Richardson
	F	Mrs. [blank] Bartlett
1798 Nov 11	"	Mary Atkins
	"	Lydia Austin
	"	Elizabeth Adams
1795 Oct 18	"	Mary Brown

{MEMBERS, p. 362}

1800 Oct 26	F	Susannah Bradshow, now Mrs. Parker (Jedediah)
1801 Sept 13	"	Elizabeth Bailey
1807 July 12	"	Ruth Barrett
1808 July	"	Mary Bean
1769 July 9	"	Hannah Breck
1784 Feb 22	"	Ruth Cades
1810 July 8	"	Elizabeth Clark
1795 May 3	"	Anna Cazneau
1796 Aug 21	"	Hannah Cordwell
1798 July 22	"	Mary Cathcart now Mrs. Hammatt
1800 June 1	"	Mehitable Clarke now Mrs. Hart
Dec 7	"	Elizabeth Cazneau
1801 Oct 7	"	Mrs. Mary Conant
" "	"	Miss Mary Conant
1808 Oct 6	"	Lucretia Chandler
" "	"	Abigail Chandler now Mrs. Robinson
1790 May	"	Sarah Lovering now Mrs. Cogswell (John)
1779 Jan	"	Susannah Drew
1808 Oct	"	Sally Darracott
1795 Sept 20	"	Mary H. Downs
1790 Nov 21	"	Ann Eliot
1809	"	Mary Eliot
1802	"	Susanna Eliot now Mrs. Spooner
1793 Nov 17	"	Mary Eliot now Mrs. Joy
1812 Oct 25	"	Anna Elliot
	"	Mary Edes

1809	"	Mary S. Edes
1807 Oct 10	"	Mary Eunson now Mrs. Luce

{MEMBERS, p. 363}

1808 July 10	F	Sarah Fracker
1795 May 3	"	Betsey Fullerton now Mrs. Burrows
1791 June	"	Mary Gendall now Mrs. Francis
1796 July 24	"	Mercy Gyles
1802	"	Sally Goodwin now Mrs. Atkins (Isaac)
1807 Nov 22	"	Rebecca Grammer
1780 Oct 8	"	Jane Guliker
1803 March 27	"	Sarah Greene
1795 March 8	"	Martha Gray
1796 June 26	"	Mary Hammatt
1803 Aug 14 +	"	Sarah Hammatt
1806 Jan 26	"	Nabby Hammatt
1808 March 20	"	Ann Hammatt
1806 April 20	"	Elizabeth Harris
1810 July	"	Rebecca Hill
1811	"	Elizabeth Hudson
"	"	Susanna Hall (a Black)
1811 Oct	"	Martha Haywood
1810 March 18	"	Abigail Haywood (died in May 1812) error
1808 April 17	"	Elizabeth McKean
" "	"	Agnes McKean
1812 April 12	"	Margarett Knoulton
	"	Rebecca Kettell
1808 April	"	Mary Knox
1800	"	Mary Lambert
1771 Sep 2	"	Susanna Lillie
	"	Hannah Lillie
1801 July	"	Grace Oliver

{MEMBERS, p. 364}

1800	F	Elizabeth Oliver
1803 April 24	"	Lydia Palfrey
1788 Jan 26	"	Lydia Prout
1806 April 20	"	Abigail Pico now Mrs. Prentiss
1812 Feb 16	"	Sarah Perkins *
1804 Sep 9	"	Lucy Pollard (a Black)
1807 May 8	"	Nancy Rumney – dismissed by request & recommended to the O. South Church
1808 Sep 4	"	Sarah Rumney
" "	"	Mary Rumney
	"	Elizabeth Robinson

1771 Sep 29	"	Mary Singleton
1792 Feb 12	"	Mary Simpkins
1796 March 6	"	Lydia Snelling
1798 July	"	Elizabeth Sigourney
" "	"	Martha Sigourney
1802 Jan 31	"	Margarett Skillin now Mrs. Goodwin (Nathaniel)
" "	"	Sarah Simmons
1804 June 17	"	Rebecca Stutson
1810	"	Sarah Squire
1811 Oct 26	"	Hannah Trench
1796 April 3	"	Mary Tuttle
1806 July 13	"	Mary Trevill
1780 April 12	"	Abigail Tyler
1805 Jan	"	Abul Veron
1780 Sep 10	"	Elizabeth Vernon +
1788 Nov 23	"	Abigail Wild now Mrs. Baxter +
1793 June 30	"	Hannah Webster
1800 Dec	"	Martha Wells

{MEMBERS, p. 365}

1808 July	F	Elizabeth Williams
" "	"	Catharine Williams
1765 Sep 15	"	Elizabeth Williams
1793 May 5	"	Dorothy Whitmarsh
1772 May 17	M	Benjamin Hammatt
" "	F	Ann Sigourney

{MEMBERS, p. 366}

1814		Church Members
Feb. 13.	F	Winifred Atkins
March 13	M	Henry Hutchinson
April 10	F	Maria Bigelow
_ _ _ _	F	Nancy Bigelow
_ _ _ _	M	Edward Blake Jun * & }Their connexion transferred
_ _ _ _	F	Sarah Blake } from the First Church
May 8.	M	Benjamin T. Wells
_ _ _ _	F	Lydia Wells
_ _ _ _	F	Elizabeth Greenwood
_ _ _ _	F	Mary Welsh
June 5	F	Hannah Comey
_ _ _ _	F	Sibellar Luckis
_ _ _ _	M	Nathaniel Faxon & }
_ _ _ _	F	Eunice Faxon }
_ _ _ _	F	Eliza Tuttle
_ _ _ _	M	Thomas Wells

_ _ _ _	F	Mary Howe
_ _ _ _	F	Elizabeth Langdon Eliot
July 3.	F	Hannah Cruft
_ _ _ _	F	Abigail Eustis
_ _ _ _	F	Abigail Wheeler
July 31.	F	Sarah Bray
_ _ _ _	F	Susannah Harris
Aug 28	F	Eliza Brown
_ _ _ _	F	Margaret McGaw
_ _ _ _	M	Isaac Howe Jun &
_ _ _ _	F	Lydia B. Howe

{MEMBERS, p. 367}

Sept 25.	F	Mary Jepson	*
_ _ _ _	F	Emma Bigelow	
October.			
Nov. 20.	F	Maria Kettell	
_ _ _ _	F	Charlotte Kettell	
_ _ _ _	F	Sarah C. Russell	
Dec. 18.	M	William B. Fowle	
_ _ _ _	F	Elizabeth Clark	
_ _ _ _	F	Hannah J. Hamman	35.

Number of admissions from Nov. 28, 1714, i. e. the first settlement of the church, to the present, closing the communion days of 1814 - - 1216

Francis Parkman Pastor

1815

Jan. 15	M	Henry Fowle Jun.	
Jan. 15.	F	Sarah Welsh	
_ _ _ _	F	Mary Parker Harris	
_ _ _ _	F	Esther Lombard	
Feb. 12.	F	Betsey Hart	
March 12	M	John Fenno &	
_ _ _ _	F	Olive Fenno	
_ _ _ _	M	Edward Tuckerman Jun }	by recommendation from
_ _ _ _	F	Eliza Rogers }	the Church in Federal St.
April 9	M	Thomas Lillie	
May 7	F	Eleanor Weld	
June 4	F	Abigail Tufts	
_ _ _ _	F	Mary Perry	
July 2	F	Mary Lincoln	

{MEMBERS, p. 368}

July 30	F	Isabella Johnson	
_ _ _ _	F	Eunice Cutter	*

Aug. 27	F	Sarah Munroe, by recommendation from the Church in Concord
Sept 24	F	Hannah Chamberlain
_ _ _ _	F	Elizabeth Richardson
Nov. 19	F	Abigail S. Mills
Dec. 17	F	Susan Snelling
_ _ _ _	F	Sophia Wells *

22 F.[rancis] P.[arkman]

1816

Jan. 13	F	Anna Baccoon *
_ _ _ _	F	Abigail Tower
June 30	F	Henrietta Lamson
July 28	F	Susan C. Lash
Sept. 22	F	Grace A. Hill
Oct 20	M	Isaiah S. Atkins }
_ _ _ _	F	Marcy Atkins }
Dec. 15	M	Daniel Munroe & }by recommendation of the Church
_ _ _ _	F	[blank] Munroe } in Roxbury

Total 9. F. P.

1817

June 30	F	Hannah Lambard
July 27	F	Lucy Barnicott, also baptized
Aug 24	F	Mary Scott
Oct. 19.	F	Jane Whittemore
Nov 16	M	Samuel Parkman Jun
_ _ _ _	F	Mary B. Parkman
_ _ _ _	F	Sukey Edes

Total 7. F. P.

{MEMBERS, p. 369}
1818

Feb. 8.	F	Lydia Wilson, & baptized
Sept. 20		Sarah Williams
Nov. 15. M		Joseph Clark
_ _ _ _	F	Mary Clark
_ _ _ _		Ruth Barnes
_ _ _ _		Eliza Barnes
_ _ _ _	M	Daniel Parkman Total 7.

1819

Jan. 10		Sarah Austin
Mar. 7.		Sarah R. Blake
_ _ _ _		Mary Blake Bruce, & baptized

144

May 30.	John W. Webster &	
_ _ _ _	Harriet Webster	Total 5.

1820

Feb. 7	Hannah Cutter	
June 25	George Fracker	
Dec. 10.	Sarah Wilson	3

1821

Jan 7.	Sarah Parker Hill	
Feb. 4.	John Fenno Jun &	
_ _ _ _	Charlotte Fenno	
Mar.	Susan Baker	
April	Mary Elizabeth Fowle	
Dec.	Mary White	6.

{MEMBERS, p. 370}

1822

Jan 6.	Margaret S. Palfrey	
_ _ _ _	Elizabeth Palfrey	
Feb. 4.	Abigail Lambert	*
_ _ _ _	Henry J. Oliver &	} also baptized
_ _ _ _	Sarah Oliver	}
Mar. 3.	Elizabeth Cruft	
31.	Naomi Taylor	
April 28	Mary Adams Emery	
May 27	Caroline Parkman	
Total 9.		

1823

June 29.	John Mills &	
_ _ _ _	Mary Mills	
Nov. 30	Hannah Parkman Tuckerman	
_ _ _ _	Sarah Blake Bruce	
	4. Total from 10 years from Dec. 1813, 107.	

1824

Jan. 25	Susanna Huntstable	
Oct. 30	Mary Ward	
_ _ _ _	Hannah Lock	
Nov. 28	Nathaniel Francis &	
	Eliza Francis	
	Bridget Blake	
	Total 6	

1825

Feb. 27.	Caroline Cutter
Mar. 27	Mary Lincoln, widow
_ _ _ _	Catharine Hutchinson

{MEMBERS, p. 371}

May 29	Mr. Nathaniel Clark	
June 26	Mrs. Mary M. Lincoln	
July 31	Mrs. Mary Tuttle *	6.

1826

Jan. 30	Mrs. Harriet Hudson	
Feb. 26	* Mr. Samuel Tuttle	
Oct. 31.	Miss Ardelia Williams	
Nov. 26	Mr. Cazneau Palfrey	
Dec. 31	Miss Eliza Wild	5.

1827

July 30.	Thomas L. Hutchinson	
Nov. 25	Eliza Lincoln	
_ _ _ _	Beza Lincoln	
_ _ _ _	Henry Atkins Jun.	
		4.
Dec. 30	Henry Atkins Sen. Ætat[e, aged] 83. The oldest member of the Society.	

1828

Jan. 28.	Rachael Faxon	
Feb. 24	Sarah Drew	
March 30.	Susan Blake	
_ _ _ _	Sarah P. Shaw	
	Eliza Atkins	
	Mary G. Atkins	6.

1829

Feb. XXV.	Martha Burrell

{MEMBERS, p. 372}

Feb. 28.	Mrs. Clarissa Skerry	
June 27.	William Palfrey &	
_ _ _ _	Elizabeth W. Palfrey	4.

1830

Oct. 31.	Rebecca S. Lash
_ _ _ _	Susan R. Lash
Dec. 26	Benjamin H. Greene & (by letters from Sister Church

146

_ _ _ _	Elizabeth C. Greene	
_ _ _ _	Henry W. Fenno &	
_ _ _ _	Rebecca H. Fenno	
_ _ _ _	Olive A. Fenno	7.

1831

May	Mrs. Cordelia Eliot	

1832

Jan. 29.	Oliver Lincoln	
_ _ _ _	Warren Lincoln	
_ _ _ _	Ann Lincoln	
Feb. 27.	Susan A. Pratt	
Mar. 25	Harriet J. Denny	
Sept. 30	Henry H. W. Sigourney }	
_ _ _ _	Harriet A. Sigourney }	
_ _ _ _	Thomas H. Williams } family of Mr. T. Williams	
_ _ _ _	Mary E. Williams }	
_ _ _ _	Nancy Williams }	
Oct.	Sarah Leach	11

1833

Jan.	Mary Hall	
Mar.	Margery B. Whalan	

{MEMBERS, p. 373}

Mar. 30	Edward Blake	
_ _ _ _	Abigail R. Hammatt	
April 28	Margaret Clark	5.

1834

Feb. 23.	Elizabeth Floyd	
_ _ _ _	Sarah Lamson	
_ _ _ _	Mary-Ann Peirce	
April 27.	Catharine Sibley	
June 29	Susanna B. Restieaux	5

1835

Jan. 25	Eliza Hall	
May 31.	Eliza H. Tuttle	2.

1. Total numbers of admissions into New-North Church from it's [sic] establishment in 1714, and during Rev. Mess. Webb's & Thacher's ministry, to the
Ordination of Rev. Andrew Elliot in 1742, 28 years, <u>650</u>, annual average, 23.

2. From Dr. A. Eliot's ordination to his death, Sept 1778, 35 years, <u>364</u>, annual average 10 ½ .
3. From death of Dr. A. Eliot to death of his son, Dr. John Eliot, Feb. 1813, being 33 1/3 years, <u>166</u> admitted; an[nual] average, 4 5/6.
4. Whole number admitted through the century, from 1714 to 1814 <u>1216</u>, an[nual] average, 12 1/6.
5. Total admitted from my ordination, in Dec. 1813 to Dec. 1838, or twenty-five years, one hundred & seventy-five.

F. Parkman

{MEMBERS, p. 374}
1836

Jan.	Elizabeth Sprague, also baptized.	died Jan. 1839
April	Eliza Lincoln Peirce	
_ _ _ _	Elizabeth Aspinwall Pulsifer	
_ _ _ _	Harriet Wild Lash	
June	Helen A. Atkins	
Aug.	Mary H. Eliot	6.

1837
Dec.   Sarah Cabot Parkman

1838

Sept.	Emily Foster Williams, died Dec. 21.
Dec.	George Sturgis
_ _ _ _	Sarah Snelling Drew
	N. B. 175 received since Dec. 1813, or during my ministry

1839

Sept.	Caroline Smith }
	Caroline Dorcas Smith } Mother & daughters
	Mary-Ann Louisa Smith }
_ _ _ _	Sarah Ann Cutter, died Dec. 20th

1840
Mar.   Louisa Bray

1842

April	Emily Frances Wells
Nov.	Henrietta Lamson Peirce
_ _ _ _	Sarah Roby Peirce
Nov. 27.	Amos Smith (by recommendation from a colleague Pastor (the Pastor of the Federal St. Church

1843
March   Catharine A. Pettes

_ _ _ _	Elizabeth F. Pettes

{MEMBERS, p. 375}

April 30	Elizabeth Clark & her children	
_ _ _ _	Julia M. Clark	} baptized by Mr. Smith
_ _ _ _	George D. Clark	}
May 28.	Elizabeth Hobbes	
Nov. 26	Harriet Denny, baptized	
Dec. 31.	Elizabeth Smith baptized	
_ _ _ _	Edward G. Lynes	
_ _ _ _	Mary J. Lynes baptized	

10.

1844

Jan. 29. Sarah Bates (Mrs.) & baptized suæ domi [at her home]

Feb. 24. Susanna Payn Barrett (Mrs.)

_ _ _ _   Rebecca Page Chamberlin

1845

Jan. 26. Mary Doak (admitted by Mr. Smith

July 17. Mary Abigail Hartt. (Admitted, and the ordinance administered, at her own house.)

1846

Sept. 27. Thomas G. (Gilman) Wells}

_ _ _ _   Martha Tuttle   }   admitted by Mr. Smith

_ _ _ _   Rachel Davenport   }

1849

Jan. 20.   Joshua Young, from the church in Bangor, Me., and now
                          Pastor elect of N. N.

{MEMBERS, p. 376

1849   Members of the Church

The following is a list of the church Members at the commencement of my ministry. Joshua Young.

M	Isaac Cazneau
F	Mary Ward, Mrs.
F	Hannah Lock, Mrs.
F	Catharine A. Pettes, Miss
F	Elizabeth F. Pettes, Miss
F	J. W. Green, Mrs.
F	Elizabeth Hobbes, Mrs.
M	Benjamin Fessenden
F	" " Fessenden, Mrs.
F	Lydia Wells, Mrs.
F	Martha Tuttle, Miss

F	Eliza Tuttle, Mrs.
M	Warren Lincoln
F	" Lincoln, Mrs.
M	Elijah Stearns }fr[om] Mr. Robbins Soc[iety]
F	" Stearns, Mrs. }
M	William Palfrey
F	Elizabeth W. Palfrey, Mrs.
F	Elizabeth C. Palfrey, Miss
F	Margaret S. Palfrey, "
F	Lydia Palfrey, Mrs.
F	Mary Adams, Miss
F	Joanna Lakeman, Mrs.
F	Benjamin Hudson, Mrs.

{MEMBERS, p. 377}

F	Agnes Austin (Not)
F	Eliza Wild
F	Elizabeth Wild, Miss
F	Susanna Parker, Mrs.
F	Mary Emery, Mrs.
F	Elizabeth Floyd, Miss
F	Charles Lincoln, Mrs.
M	Charles Lincoln
F	Mrs. Porter (Irish)
M	John B. Hammett
F	" " Hammett, Mrs.
F	[blank] Rumney, Mrs.
F	Martin Bates, Mrs.
F	Eliza Brown, Mrs.
F	Julia Jordan, Mrs.
F	James Clark, Mrs.
M	Robert Lash
F	Susan Rand Lash / Episcopal
F	Rebecca S. Lash
F	Benjamin Lamson, Mrs.
F	Mary E. Fowle, Mrs.
F	Priscilla Greenwood Hooper (fr[om] Mr. Robbins Society)
Total 48	

{MEMBERS, p. 378}
When Admitted
1849

March 25th	M	(Daniel W. Lillie fr[om] Dr. Beecher's
_ _ _ _	F	and wife)
Aprill	F	Isabel H. Comey

F	Hannah W. Comey
F	Olivia F. Morse Mrs.
M	Samuel Aspinwall
F	Mrs. Samuel Aspinwall
F	Helen E. Gerry
F	Harriet Tuttle
F	Mrs. Samuel Cushing

{MEMBERS, p. 379}
1853

June 26th F	Betsey Green Edes
"	M Charles Gustavus Wells

{MEMBERS, p. 380}

The following is a list of regular members of the New North Church who partake of the Lord's supper & in other ways act with us at the Commencement of my ministry. This list does not include a large number who are members of this Church & in good standing but have removed to other parts of the City or out of town or who from any cause do not commune with us. Nor does it include many who regularly commune with us but have never transferred their relations from other churches to this. Consequently many names on my predecessor's list will not be found on mine. A. B. Fuller

Arthur B. Fuller
John B. Hammatt
Robert Lash
Beza Lincoln
Benjamin Fessenden
Charles G. Wells admitted June 1853
Warren Lincoln
Mrs. Nabby Hammatt
" Lydia Wells
" Susan C. Lash
" Mary E. Fowle
" Benjamin Lamson

{MEMBERS, p. 381}

Mrs. Martin Bates
" Charles Lincoln
" Rachel Davenport
" Elizabeth O. Fessenden
" Warren Lincoln
Margaret S. Palfrey }
Elizabeth W. Palfrey } dismissed to South Cong[regational] Church
" " C. Palfrey }
Lydia Palfrey

Mary A. Emery
Emily Frances Wells
Catharine A. Pettes
Elizabeth F. Pettes
Elizabeth F. Carnes
Julia M. Jordan
Betsey Green Edes admitted June 1853
Mrs. Maria Davenport

{MEMBERS, p. 382}

Octl 30th 1853	Samuel Aspinwall
	Atalanta M. Aspinwall
	Noah Harrod
	George Harris
	Mrs. George Harris
	Mrs. Joanna Lakeman
	Mrs. Mary A. Ferguson

Transferred from other churches to New North
J. Veasey
R. J. Veasey
Elijah Stearns
Sarah B. Stearns
Christiana Barnes
Sarah Douglas
Mary Washburn
Ann Howe
Priscilla G. Hooper
Margaret Anderson
Nancy Pitman
Mary Adams
Tabitha Clark
Mrs. N.[oah] Harrod
Who [?] admitted by profession

Jan 29 1854	Mrs. Elizabeth Perry
	Mrs. Helen D. Cummings
	Edward David Hinckley
Feb 26 1854	George P. Richardson Jr.
	Mrs. Mary Richardson
May 28th "	Lucy Faxon Bartlett
	Sarah Elizabeth Stearns

{MEMBERS, p. 383}

Nov 26th 1854	Mrs. Mary Leeds
Dec. 31 "	Mrs. Mary D. Adams
	Mrs. Cordelia R. Capen

March 25th 1855	Mrs. M. L. S. Caziarc
June 30 1855	Edwin Shute
	[blank] Shute
Oct 28 "	Mr. John Nelson

I found when my ministry began only 26 persons who lived in the city and had ever united with the New North Church. Of these 12 lived in another part of the city worshipped with other societies having wholly withdrawn from ours tho not formally dismissed from our church & recommended to any other. Thus there were only 14 who were members of the N. N. Church & worshipped with us, the rest were only nominal members. Besides these however were several persons members of other churches but worshippers with us & usually communing.

    During 1853, 23 persons joined the church, 14 by letter, 9 by profession.

{MEMBERS, p. 384}

	In 1854, 10 joined the church, 1 by letter, 9 by profession.
	In 1855 4 joined the church, all by profession
May 25 1856	Mrs. Frances Spalding Shipley
Oct 5th 1856	Mr. John Townsend Maccomber
April 4 1857	Mrs. Minerva Seller [Selles?]
May 2	Mr. Thomas Dolliver
May 31 1857	Mr. Lyman Leeds
" " "	Mrs. Rebecca Nash
" " "	Mrs. Hannah Nash
" " "	Mrs. Susan Hewes
	Mrs. Martha Jennings
	Miss Sarah F. Ellis
	" Anna C. Ellis
	" Martha E. Holmes
	" Elizabeth J. Crawley
	" Harriet E. Tuttle
	" Flora A. Holbrook
Jan 31 1858	Mrs. E. L. Dickinson
	Miss Martha E. Dickinson

{MEMBERS, p. 385}
1858

April 25	Henry Floyd
" "	Miss Caroline Watts
	Mrs. Eliza Greene Mizner
	Miss Eliza Frances Floyd
Jan 27 1859	Mrs. Sarah Ann Ames
" " "	Mrs. Sarah E. Keith
March 25th 1860	Mr. Timothy Hall
" " "	Miss Elizabeth W. Hall

April 21st 1863. "The New North Religious Society in the Town of Boston" having purchased the building previously owned and occupied by the Bulfinch Street Church, and the latter organization having dissolved, at a meeting held April 21st 1863, it was voted by the members of the New North Church to accept the Rev. William R. Alger as pastor, and to receive into free fellowship, without any further form, all members of the Bulfinch Street Church in good and regular standing.

{MEMBERS, p. 386}
New Members received May 3d 1863
> Frances L. Davis
> Elizabeth P. Sawyer
> Frederick W. Leach

April 11th 1870. A duly appointed and notified meeting of the communicant members of the New North Church was held on Sunday April 10th 1870, and the ordinance of the Lord's Supper administered. Bro. E. R. Frost was chosen clerk. Bro Francis Curtis was chosen Deacon in place of George P. Richardson who had removed from the city and ceased to attend the services of the New North Religious Society. It was unanimously voted that Bros. William R. Alger, Samuel Condon, and Francis Curtis be clothed with full powers to dispose of all the plate, or silver ware property of the church, and to appropriate the proceeds in such manner as they may agree upon, should circumstances at any future time in their judgement render a sale of it expedient.

> A true record of the proceedings. Attest E. R. Frost, Clerk

COVENANTERS

{COVENANTERS, p. 426}

When received

1813

Dec. 26	F	Elizabeth Richardson
March 13	M	Jacob &

1814

	F	Elizabeth C. Farnsworth

1815

Jan 29.	M	John Knoar Barber
_ _ _ _	F	Nancy Paine Barber
Oct. 29.	M	Benjamin &
_ _ _ _	F	Henrietta Lamson (baptized)

1816

Mar. 10.		Samuel Parkman Jun & Mary B. Parkman
April 8	M	Abimilech, &
_ _ _ _	F	Sally F. Riggs
May	F	Sally Seaver
Sep.		Lot & Dolly Whitcomb
Nov.		{ Enoch H. and { Sarah D. Snelling

1817

Feb.	{M	Edward and
_ _ _ _	{F	Catherine V. Tuttle
June		Edward &
_ _ _ _		Susan Page
_ _ _ _		George &
_ _ _ _		Elizabeth Lewis
_ _ _ _		Joseph E. &
_ _ _ _		Sarah Andrews
_ _ _ _		Abigail Magoon
July 27		Jacob & Mary-Ann Hall
Aug 3.		William P. & Mary-Ann Shelton
Sept 7.		William & }baptized Caroline Smith }
Nov. 9.		Bernard Whittemore baptized

1818

		Levi & C. P. Younger
Sept. 13		Mary-Ann Parks
26		Mary B. Thompson
Oct. 11		Harriet Bignall

1819
Jan. 20   Caleb G. & Harriet Loring
                                William & Susan Baker
                                Nathaniel & Eliza Francis

1820   John B. & Harriet Hoffman
                                John B. & Sarah Tremere

1821   Mary-Ann Messenger

1822   Frederick A. & Sarah Gay
Mar. 31   Joseph & Nancy Grammar
Aug. 10   Thomas & Catharine Hutchinson
Sept 8   Elijah & Mary Lincoln
    29   Amadella Hamilton
Dec. 22   Charles & M.[artha] B. Lincoln
_ _ _ _   Ann B. Crocker
1823
Nov. 9.   Nathaniel & Bridget Blake
Nov. 30   Thomas D. & Eliza Francis
_ _ _ _   Nathaniel & Joanna Hopkins
Dec. 27   Joseph N. & Elizabeth K. Howe

{COVENANTERS, p. 427}
1824
Feb. 8.   Amos Farnsworth, M. D.
_ _ _ _   William W. & A.[nn Maria] Colesworthy
March 14.   John W. & E.[liza] H. Tuttle
May 16.   Amos & Harriet Cotting
May 24.   Lewis J. & Sally Bailey
_ _ _ _   Joseph & Eliza Fenno

1826
Oct. 29   Charles & E.[lizabeth] H. Arnold

1827
Nov.   N.[athaniel] & M.[ary Ann] Colesworthy

1830
April   J.[ohn] & C.[harlotte] Sawin
July 4.   Henry & Harriet A. Cutting

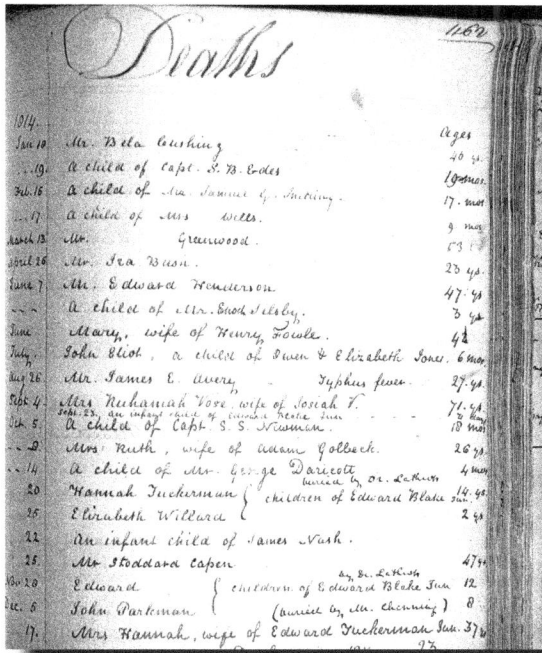

CHAPTER 12

DEATHS

{DEATHS, p. 462}
1814

Jan. 18.	Mr. Bela Cushing	40 ys
___ 19.	A child of Capt. S. B. Edes	19 mos.
Feb. 16.	A child of Mr. Samuel G. Snelling	17 mos.
___ 17.	A child of Mrs. Wells	9 mos.
March 13.	Mr. [blank] Greenwood	53
April 26.	Mr. Ira Bush	23 ys.
June 7.	Mr. Edward Henderson	47 ys.
___ ___.	A child of Mr. Enoch Silsby	3 ys.
June	Mary, wife of Henry Fowle	42
July	John Eliot, a child of Owen & Elizabeth Jones	6 mos.
Aug. 26.	Mr. James E. Avery Typhus fever	27 ys.
Sept. 4.	Mrs. Ruhamah Vose, wife of Josia V.	71 ys.
Sept. 23.	An infant child of Edward Blake Jun.	21 days
Oct. 5.	A child of Capt. S. S. Newman	18 mos.
___ 8.	Mrs. Ruth, wife of Adam Golbeck	26 ys.
___ 14.	A child of George Daricott	4 mos.
	Buried by Dr. Lathrop	
20.	Hannah Tuckerman }children of Edward Blake Jun.	14 ys.

25.	Elizabeth Willard }	2 ys.
22.	An infant child of James Nash	
25.	Mr. Stoddard Capen	47 ys.
	By Dr. Lathrop	
Nov. 28.	Edward } children of Edward Blake Jun	12
Dec. 5.	John Parkman }	8
17.	Mrs. Hannah, wife of Edward Tuckerman Jun.	
	(buried by Mr. Channing	37 ys

Deaths during 1814 – 23
1815

Jan. 2.	Miss Mary Laughton	82
__ 20.	[blank] Wife of Mr. Israel Town	21
	An infant child of Mr. John James	

{DEATHS, p. 463}

Feb. 13.	Widow Elizabeth Adams	82
__ 20.	Deacon Joseph Kettell (chosen to his office Oct. 1789, his relation being afterwards transferred from the church at Charles-Town to the N. North	74
__ __.	Mr. Samuel Vaughan	69
March	An infant child of Capt. S. Newman	
May 4.	Mr. Thomas K. Emery fever	32
June 3.	A child of Mr. J. Gray	5
July 5.	Mrs. Rebecca Hill	84
__ 10.	A child of Widow A. Smith	
28.	A child of Mr. Thomas Williams	17 mos.
Aug. 20.	+ A child of Mr. [blank] Hayden	
__ 24.	+ Mr. Isaac Richardson	29 ys.
Sept. 7.	+ Wife of Mr. Hayden	28
Sept. 24.	Samuel G. Snelling	30
__ 28.	Elijah Swift	30
Sep. 27.	+ + Mrs. Elizabeth Willard	75
Oct. 16.	A child of Mr. Averill	mos.
18.	Mrs. Elizabeth Mitchell	45 ys.
Nov.	Mr. William War Sea captain=died from home	52
Nov. 13.	Miss Sarah Hammatt	30 ys.
Nov. 20.	Mr. J. Robinson died abroad	35
Nov. 22.	Mrs. Mary, wife of Ephraim Eliot	45
Dec. 10.	A child of Mr. Isaiah Atkins Jun. (burnt to death)	5
__ 11.	Mrs. Mary Card	58
__ 12.	Mrs. Elizabeth Burbeck	57

Total 26 – 3 not of N. North

1816

Jan. 15.	An infant child of Mr. Thomas M. Payne	
Feb. 11.	+ Mrs. Elizabeth Dupee	35 y.
Feb. 20.	An infant child of Mr. Isaac Howe	
__ 27.	A child of Mr. Henry J. Oliver	
	+ not of the New-North	

{DEATHS, p. 464}

Feb. 29.	Miss Mary Lash		72
Mar. 1.	+ Mr. Isaac White Jun of the Second Church		34
Mar. 3.	An infant child of Mr. J. Silsby		5 mos.
__ 6.	Widow Mary Brazer		88 ys.
Mar. 10.	Mrs. Sophia Wells	insanity	26 ys.
	(daughter-in-law to Benjamin T. Wells, coppersmith)		
Mar. 31.	An infant child of Mr. Jacob Hall		
Ap. 2.	Mrs. Nancy, wife of John K. Barber Consumption		23 ys.
Ap. 15.	An infant child of Mr. Edward Oliver		
Ap. 20.	Mr. Nathaniel Godfrey	Consumption	26 ys.
May 1.	+ Mr. Isaac White Sen. (of the Second Church		
__ __.	Mrs. Eliza, wife of Mr. Andrew W. Symmes		25
__ __.	An infant child of Mr. J. Bannister		5 mos.
June 9.	An infant child of Mr. Bentley		
__ 15.	+ Mr. J. Gregory		40 ys.
July 20.	A child of Mr. J. Barber		4 ys.
__ 21.	Mr. Samuel Prince		56 ys.
__ 30.	+ Mrs. Elizabeth Pierpont		63
Aug. 3.	Mrs. [blank], wife of Mr. Lewis Meprate		38
__ 11.	A child of Mr. Lot Whitcomb		
__ 20.	An infant child of Mr. Benjamin T. Wells		1 mo.
Sept. 14.	Mr. Edward Baker		65 ys.
Oct. 10.	+ Mr. J. Coates		18 ys.
__ 11.	Mrs. Eunice Cutter		37
Nov. 6.	Mrs. Sibellar, wife of Joseph Lewis		27
Dec. 3.	+ A child of Turell Tuttle Jun		18 mos.
Dec. 23.	Mrs. Susanna Lillie		77 ys
Dec. 26.	+ Mrs. Elizabeth Whellen		72
	31 Total adults, 19 adults, 23 of N. North, 12 adults		

{DEATHS, p. 465}

1817

Jan. 2.	Capt. David Pulsifer	liver complaint	41
__ 10.	+ Mrs. E. Welch		60
Jan. 15.	Mr. Edward Blake Jun.		46
Feb. 3.	+ Mrs. Mehitable Simpkins, wife of Deacon S[impkins]		78
__ 4.	+ Mr. Moses Bass		82
__ 6.	+ Mr. John Quincy, grandson of Capt. Atkins		18
__ __.	An infant child of Capt. H. Atkins		

28.	Capt. Nathaniel Goodwin	72
	An infant child of Mr. Robert Lash	
March 4.	Widow Sarah Perkins	43
Ap. 10.	A child of Jacob & E. Farnsworth	
11.	a child of Mr. Nathaniel Francis	3 ys.
Ap. 12.	+ Mr. E. Dunham	44
Ap. 28.	Mrs. Elizabeth Bartlett	92
June 10.	Mrs. Elizabeth Watson	69
June 23.	+ Theodore, child of Dr. William Spooner	2 ys.
July 5.	Mrs. Ruth, wife of Mr. Samuel Tuttle	45
July 15.	Adam Golback	42
__ 16.	Mrs. Belcher	65
Aug. 12.	+ Mr. Francis Cabot Lowell	42
__ 21.	+ An infant child of Mr. Isaac Harris	17 mos.
Sept. 6.	Miss Elizabeth Clark	83 ys.
Sept. 15.	+ Mr. Blake	71 ys.
Sept. 18.	An infant child of Daniel Munroe Jun	3 ys.
__ __.	An infant child of Joseph Hart	23 mos.
__ __.	+ An infant child of [blank] Slone	2 mos.
Sept. 28.	Wife of Mr. Seward	30 ys.
Oct. 10.	+ William H. Lincoln (suicide) of Mr. Ware's	17 ys
Oct. 16.	+ Mrs. Mary Harris of Mr. Lowell's	45
Oct. 19.	+ Mrs. [blank] of Mr. Lowell's	70

{DEATHS, p. 468}

Oct. 24.	Mr. John Gore	37 ys.
Dec. 31.	Mrs. Fosdick	83
	Total 32 – 15 adults. Total 17 of N. N.	
	Those marked thus + not of the Society	

1818

Jan. 18.	An infant child of Mr. E. Page	9 mos.
23.	An infant child of Mr. J. Lewis	15 mos.
Feb. 2.	Mr. John Cogswell	80 ys.
15.	A daughter of Mr. A. Holbrook	14 ys.
Ap. 6.	+ Mr. Wiswall	61
17.	Mr. Daniel Sigourney	46
28.	+ A child of Mr. Pierce	
May 4.	A child of Mr. Joseph E. Andrews	17 mos.
8.	Mrs. Mary Jepson	83 ys.
13.	Mr. David Greene	52
June 10.	Mrs. Ann Sigourney	73
15.	Mrs. Daniel Lillie	35
July 8.	Mr. Thomas Curtis	52
14.	Mr. Thomas Oliver	60
Aug. 6.	A child of Mr. Joshua Nash	3 ys.

20.	Mrs. Joanna, wife of P. Adams	37 ys.
21.	Mrs. Eleanor Bangs suicide	31
Sep. 1.	+ Mr. James Foster	69
10.	A child of Capt. Williams	11 mos.
Oct. 12.	Mr. Nathaniel Austin	83 ys.
Nov. 6.	Miss Lombard	46
10.	A child of Mr. Henry J. Oliver	10 mos.
Dec. 23.	+ Mrs. [blank] wife of Mr. William Grubb (Mr. Ware attended)	

{DEATHS, p. 469}

Nov. 23.	Mrs. Sarah, wife of F.[rancis] P.[arkman] the Pastor of the Church, puerperal fever 28 ys [?]

> Cara, vale, ingeniô præstans, pietate, pudore,
> Et plusquam conjugis nomine cara, vale.
> Cara, mi Sara, vale. At veniet felicius ævum
> Quando iterum tecum, sim modo dignus, ero.
> Cara, redi, læta tum dicam voce amicus
> Eja, age in amplexus, cara mi Sara, redi.
> [Farewell, dear one, outstanding in talent, piety and modesty,
> And beloved more than by the name of wife, farewell.
> My beloved Sarah, farewell. And may a happier age come
> When once more I will be with you, if I might be worthy.
> Beloved one, return, and then I will say with a friendly voice
> Oh, rush into my embrace, my beloved Sarah, come back.
> *On this elegy, see Chapter 9, page 97.*

Dec. 13.	Widow Dorcas Pierce	73
Dec. 20.	A child of Mr. William Hammatt	
	Total 26. 18 adults. 23 belonged to New-North	

1819

Jan. 9.	+ Mrs. Doake old-age	81 ys.
Jan. 26.	Mr. William T. Hammatt consumption	44
Mar. 20.	Mrs. Bridgham	75
___ __.	Mr. John Eliot, son of late Rev. J. Eliot, died at N. Orleans, where he went for health 32	
May 6.	George Francis, son of Dr. George Parkman croup 29 mos.	
May 27.	Mrs. K. Webber	75 ys.
June 24.	Mr. Isaiah S. Atkins very suddenly: fits	42
July 12.	Mrs. Eliza, wife of Mr. William Grubb Jun dropsy 22	
Aug. 10.	A daughter of Mrs. Reed	11
Aug. 12.	Mrs. Harriet, wife of Mr. Daniel Parkman consumption 22	
Sept. 7.	Rebecca C. Clough rheumatic complaints, gradual decay 69	
Sept. 21.	Mrs. Elizabeth Vaughan	35
Sept. 30.	Mrs. Clap	56
Oct. 11.	A child of Capt J. Hart	4 ys.

Oct. 28.	William Leate		87
Nov. 3.	Mrs. Baker, widow		60
Dec. 1.	Mrs. McCleary, wife of S. F. McCleary, Esq.		27
		17. 3 not of society	

{DEATHS, p. 470}
1820

Feb. 26.	Mr. William Palfrey consumption		56
Mar. 19.	Thomas Eliot, infant child of Mr. Thomas Wells		
	dropsy in brain		7 mos.
Ap. 4.	Mary Singleton	decay	79
7.	George Stanton	/suicide/	32
12.	Elizabeth Williams,		
	widow of H. H. Williams, Esq.		76
May 26.	Mr. Nathaniel Low	Consumption	36
__ 30	Mrs. Lucy Windship		78
June 10.	An infant child of Daniel Munroe Jun		7 mos.
June 25.	Sarah Williams, of West-Cambridge		35
June 30.	Elizabeth Hudson		65
Aug. 6.	Andrew Sigourney Esq.		57
Aug. 26.	Mr. Samuel Barber		53
__ __.	Mr. Horace Denny		20 ys.
Sept. 9.	An infant child of Mr. Torrey		17 mos.
__ 12	+ An infant child of Mr. Cruft		12 mos.
__ __.	Mr. Thomas Merrifield		20 ys.
13.	Mr. William McKean		80
20.	+ An infant child of Mr. Dean		2 mos.
Oct. 4.	+ An infant child of Mr. Saville		13 mos.
Nov. 1.	An infant child of Dr. John Webster		18 mos.
Dec. 10	+ Mr. John Wilkinson		80
Dec. 19.	A son of Mr. Jacob Barstow		4 ys.
23.	William Warren, son of William Barnecott		9 ys.
	Total 23. 18 of Society – 9 Heads of F[amilies]		

{DEATHS, p. 471}
1821

Feb. 10.	+ Miss J. Farr		
	(from Mr. Smith's boarding-house)		58 ys.
March 5.	Mrs. Patty Hayward (widow)consumption		40
Mar. 10.	Miss Mary Leate old age		85
Mar. 16.	+ Mr. William Parker		59
Mar. 20.	Mrs. Abigail,		
	wife of Mr. George Revere consumption		26
April 19.	Sarah Blake,		
	wife of Mr. Ellis G. Blake consumption		19
May 2.	An infant child of Mr. William Mills		13 mos.

May 30.	Sarah Curtis	16 ys.
June 15.	Mrs. Hannah Lillie consumption	45
June 19.	A son of Capt Thomas Rogers measles	8
July 20.	Frederick S. Greenwood Scarlet Fever	16
July 27.	A child of Capt. Isaac Atkins	
Aug. 18.	Widow Mary Cushing old age	88
Aug. 19.	Miss Brown	35
Aug. 25.	A child of Mrs. J. Hammatt	7
Oct. 24.	Widow Sarah Clark, of Capt. J. Clark	65
Nov. 1.	An infant child of N. & C. Freeman	2 ys.
__ __.	An infant child of Mr. Josiah Pierce	
Dec. 25.	Mrs. Sally Rogers	89
Dec. 28.	A child of Mr. Noah Lincoln	5 ys.

19 Total. 16 of my Society

1822

Jan. 4.	Caroline, only child of Mrs. Eunson dropsy in the brain 14 ys.	
Jan. 20.	Mr. Benjamin French Lung Fever	19
__ __.	Mr. William B. Austin, son of Joseph Austin Esq., at sea, from Cuba 27	
Feb. 8.	Mrs. Martha Ball consumption	45
Feb. 22.	An infant child of Mr. A. Cutter Jun	3 weeks
Feb. 28.	An infant child of Mr. James Clark	2 weeks

{DEATHS, p. 472}

Ap. 16.	Mr. Benjamin T. Wells consumption	47 ys.
May 8.	Mr. Larabbee Edes decay	71
__ 14.	Mr. Thomas Hunstable dropsy	56
21.	Mr. George Gardiner B.[rain] Fever	23
Aug. 15.	Mr. John Lewis decay	75
20.	+ Mrs. Sarah L. Draper	67
22.	+ Mrs. Lydia King old age	77
Sept. 7.	Mrs. Abigail Rand	72
13.	+ An infant child of Mr. [blank] Tuttle	9 mos.
18.	+ Mr. William Hamilton	32 ys.
27.	Mr. Joseph T. Blanchard Consumption	48 ys.
	Mrs. E, wife of Capt. Robert S. Pulsifer	29 ys.
Oct. 18.	Mr. Adam French Jun	22
Nov. 10.	Benjamin, child of Caleb Eddy	2 ¼ ys.
14.	Mrs. Dorcas, wife of Capt. Benjamin Smith	57
Dec. 1.	Mr. Ebenezer Baxter	69 ys.
2.	An infant child of Mr. Nathaniel Clark	7 mos.

1822 Total <u>23</u>. 4 not of the Society

1823

Jan 9.	Mr. Adam French	57 y.

11.	+ Mrs. Abigail Russ of color	38 y.
12.	Mrs. Dolly French,	
	widow of Adam French who died Jan 9th	53 y.
24.	Miss Caroline, daughter of Samuel Howe	
	Typhus Fever	13 ys.
31.	An infant child of Mr. A. Vanneever	4 mos.
Feb. 14.	Mrs. Desire Leach, wife of Thomas Leach (Paralytic)	63 ys.
18.	Widow Ruth Barrett old age	81

{DEATHS, p. 473.

Feb. 24.	Mr. George Perry intemperance	47 ys.
Feb. 27.	Miss Sarah Austin, daughter of	
	Joseph Austin Esq consumption	33 ys.
March 6.	Mrs. Jane Gulliker decay	80
8.	+ Henry, an infant child of Rev. H. Ware	1 y.
__ 20.	Capt. William Smith consumption	33 ys.
__ 22.	An infant child of Mr. William Mills Jun	12 mos.
April 17.	Mr. William Mills Jun consumption	35 ys.
27.	+ A man of color, foreigner	40 ys.
May 25.	Miss Eliza Goff fever	23
June 4.	Thomas C. Goodwin consumption	24
June 10.	William P. Shelton	30
July 8.	Mrs. Eliza Richardson consumption	44
July 27.	Widow Abigail Pearson decay	86
Sept. 4.	Sarah A. Stanton (convulsion-fits)	4 ys.
Sept. 11.	Child of Mr. William Barnacoat	17 mos.
Sept. 17.	Mrs. Elizabeth Barnes old age with dysentery	80 ys.
Sept. 18.	Edward, son of Mr. Edward Page (croup)	5 ys.
24.	+ Mrs. Sarah Gardiner, widow of S. G. Esq	56
Octob. 1.	Mr. Jacob Gragg dysentery	27
Nov. 8.	Mrs. Elizabeth Robinson old age	82
Dec. 14.	Mrs. Elizabeth B,	29
	wife of Mr. J. F. Payson consumption	

Total 28 – 4 not of the Society

Total for 10 years, from Dec. 31, 1813 to Jan. 1, 1824 - - 247.

Of these 80 were under ten years

14 from ten to twenty

22 from 20 to 30

26 from 30 to 40

26 from 40 to 50

16 from 50 to 60

15 from 60 to 70

20 from 70 to 80

23 from 80 to 90

1 from 90 to 100

1824

Jan. 17.	Mrs. Sarah Harris	68 ys.
Feb. 7.	Mr. Charles Baxter	40 ys.
10.	+ Mrs. Elizabeth, wife of Rev. H. Ware consumption	30 ys.
28.	Henry Chapman, child of Mr. N. K. Lombard	16 mos.
Mar. 17.	Mrs. Penelope S. Nash, wife of Mr. [blank] Nash	22 ys.
April 7.	Mrs. Sarah Ann, wife of Mr. Frederick A. Gay	24 ys.
10.	Nathaniel Goodwin, a child of Capt. I. Atkins	6
17.	Simpson B. Hosea	28
— —.	William J. Swift, son of the Widow Swift, drowned at sea	17
May 17.	+ Daniel Munroe Jun, son of Mr. D. Munroe, died at sea	19
30.	An infant child of Mr. John Hoffman	15 mos.
June 11.	Samuel Parkman Esq. Pater mihi dilectissimus atque venerandus [Most beloved and venerable father to me]	72 ys.
July 10.	Mrs. Lydia Austin, wife of Joseph Austin Esq. pleurisy fever	59
12.	+ A child of Mr. Horace Bean	4 ys.
18.	Miss Lydia consumption daughter of Joseph Austin Esq	32
25.	Mrs. Maria child bed wife of Mr. Daniel Denny	36
Aug. 8.	An infant child of Mr. James Brown	14 mos.
14.	Mrs. Eliza Ann, wife of Mr. Joel Stone bilious fever (see marriages Feb. 16) "Thou destroyest the hope of man"	26 ys.
Sept. 3.	Mrs. Miriam Field brain fever, of 3 days	38
	+ Mr. Edward Tilden, at sea	24
Oct. 10.	An infant child of Nathaniel Blake Lung-Fever	15 mos.
30.	Mr. James Whalan consumption	22 ys.
Nov. 20.	An infant child of Mr. Edward Page Lung-Fever	5 mos.
Nov. 27.	Henry N., child of Mr. E.[lijah] Lincoln Lung-Fever	4 years
	An infant child of Mr. J. E. Andrews Lung-Fever	9 mos.
Dec. 4.	A twin-child of Widow Sarah Drew croup	6 ys.
10.	Miss Abigail Cushing Lung Fever	
16.	Sydney, child of Mr. Ammi Cutter Lung-Fever	4 ys.

Dec. 23.	Charlotte S., child of Mr. Elisha Webb brain fever 4 years	

__ 27.	Mrs. Jane, wife of Col. James Robinson cancer	58

Total 30. 4 not belonging to the Society.
8 Heads of families. 10 young children

1825

Jan. 2.	Mr. Elijah Lincoln consumption	29 ys.
__ 20.	+ Mrs. Sarah B.,	
	wife of Mr. T. P. Cushing Typhus Fever	22 ys.

Married November last; & dying within six months
after her sister, who had also been married only six months.

27.	+ Mr. Nathaniel Frothingham old age	79 ys.
Feb. 2.	+ An infant child of Mr. Henry Orne	16 mos.
__ 4.	Mrs. Rebecca Kettell Lung Fever	77
__ 5.	Mrs. Elizabeth Cazneau old age	92
8.	A child of Mr. Samuel Tuttle Croup	3 ys.
Mar. 1.	Major William Harris consumption	48
__ 4.	An Infant child of Mr. J. F. Payson	17 mos.
__ 5.	Risdon, a child of Mr. George Darracott [measles] 14 mos.	
__ 6.	& next day, both of measles, James Clark, next elder child of	
	Mr. D. 2 ½ years	
10.	+ Mr. William Lincoln, son of Mr. C. L.[incoln] 26 ys.	
27.	Mrs. Hannah Breck; widow	81
April 4.	Mr. David Watson decay	81
17.	Miss Sarah, daughter of Mr. T. Lillie	14 ys.
May 14.	Mrs. Lydia Wilson consumption	63
May 20.	+ A child of Mr. Noaf	2
__ 29.	A child of Mr. Knight	3
June 12.	Mrs. [blank] Stevens, widow decay	74
June 17.	Miss Mary Russell Trevett consumption	19
July 10.	Mrs. Dodd, wife of T. N. Dodd, Puerperal Fever 40	

{DEATHS, p. 478 [sic]}

July 10.	Mr. Thomas G. Bangs consumption	37 years
14.	Sarah B. Swift, child of Mr. H. S. Nantucket 5 ys.	
15.	(+note) Miss M. T. Simpkins, daughter of Deacon S.[impkins],	
	exposure to excessive heat	56
25.	Mrs. Henry, an aged domestic in Mrs. N. family 73	
31.	A child of Mr. Edward Tuttle	
Sept. 7.	Mr. Thomas Fracker	74
Oct. 27.	Mrs. Mary, wife of Capt. James Colburn consumption	25.
Nov. X.	Mrs. Charlotte, wife of Mr. John Low consumption	53
14.	+ Miss Caroline Hildreth Brighton, Dr. Fosters	17
15.	Mrs. Mary, wife of Turell Tuttle consumption	
30.	+ Mr. John Page	75
Dec. 10.	+ Miss Jane Merry consumption	25
17.	Mrs. Barnard rapid consumption	

18.	+ Mr. John Cathcart Sigourney	25

Moved to New-York & of Mr. Ware's ch,
the last of the three children of Mr. A. Sigourney;
they were married & died within 18 months. See Jan. 20

25.	Mr. Edward O. Baker consumption	24 years
		36 total. 8 not of the Society

1826

Jan. 4.	Miss Susan P. Barber paralytic	61
9.	Mrs. Mary, wife of Mr. Samuel Tuttle Consumption	

+ note: July 12-14 [1825]. The heat of the three
last days has been excessive. The Thermometer varying
at noon , in the shade, from 97° to 101°. Twenty-one
sudden deaths, of which Miss Simpkins and Miss Swift
were instances, partly from simple exposure, partly from
drinking of cold water, have been the consequence. The
whole number of deaths within these three days, from
various causes, was 45. The heat of some following days
was as great; but not so fatal.

{DEATHS, p. 479}
1826

Feb. 25.	Mrs. Mary White, widow burnt	75 years
Mar. 16.	An infant child of Mr. Ayres	3 mos.
April 15.	A child of Mr. Thompson	4 years
June 4.	+ Mr. Mark Richards consumption	42
June 10.	+ Sarah, child of Dea[con]. J[ames]. Foster Mr. Ware's	5 ys
June 24.	+ Abbot, a child of Mr. Abbot Lawrence	1 yr.
June 29.	+ A child of Mr. Shelton's	2 ys.
July 7.	John Eliot, a child of Mr. H.[enry] J. Oliver	2
July 12.	+ Mr. Henry Bartlett consumption	42
July 31.	+ Mr. Thomas Boardman Mr. Ware's	35
Aug. 3.	Mrs. Grace Hill	59
__ 6.	+ Mrs. Mary Gorham, widow of N. Gorham Esq. 67	
7.	+ Mr. Joshua Lincoln Mr. Ware's	24
12.	+ Deacon James Foster Mr. Ware's	43
24.	Mr. Jedediah Parker,	

the last of President Adam's class, which
graduated 1755   89
[N. B.: Harvard University lists Jedediah Parker in the class of
1757]

Sept. 21.	+ An infant child of [blank]	18 mos.
Oct. 17.	Master John Tileston, writing master of	

North-School in B.[oston] for the term of 70 years 92

Oct. 18.	+ Mr. Ebenezer Hutchinson	of Mr. Dean's Society
Nov. 6.	+ An infant child of Mr. Kettell Mason St.	22 mos.

Total 21. 9, only, of the Society,
of whom 5 were adults & three very old
+ Those with this mark were from other societies

1827

Jan. 27.	An infant child of Mr. J. Hart	1 mo.
Feb. 9.	+ An infant child of Mr. T. Tufts	
	Mr. Watkins', Charlestown	3 mo.
Mar. 17.	Mrs. Sarah Greene	70 ys.
April 1.	Lynde Walter, a child of Mr. S. F. McCleary	3 ys.

{DEATHS, p. 480}

Ap. 5.	Mrs. Sarah, wife of Mr. Jacob Gragg decay	56
June.	Mr. John Tuttle very suddenly	30
____.	Mrs. Ann, wife of Mr. Isaac Hall consumption	30
July.	An infant child of Mr. S. Holbrook	18 mos.
____.	Mr. Daniel Munroe old age	83
Aug. 10.	A son of Levi Younger brain-fever	7
12.	Capt. Thomas Rogers yellow-fever, abroad	57
	+ A child of Mr. George Howe Mr. Palfrey's	1
20.	An infant child of Mr. Nathaniel Clark	6 weeks
24.	An infant child of Capt. B. Smith	19 mos.
Sept. 9.	An infant child of Mr. Edward Page	14 mos.
__ 14.	Mr. Israel Rust Austin consumption	28
__ 15.	Dr. Ephraim Eliot, son of Rev. Dr. A. Eliot	
	& brother of Dr. S. E.[liot]	66
20.	An infant child of Mr. Elisha Webb	1 y.
Oct. 4.	Miss Hannah Parkman McCleary	36 ys.
Nov. 10.	Miss Hannah Cruft (the oldest member)	90 ys.
24.	+ An infant child of Mr. Daniel's	8 mos.

21,   10 adults.   2 over 80.
3 not of my own people

1828

Jan. 1.	+ Widow Sarah Floyd	52
24.	Mrs. Martha Sigourney	59
Feb. 4.	An infant child of Mr. Jacob Hall	14 mos.
Feb. 25.	William Henry, a child of R. G. Shaw	7 mos.
Mar. 15.	Henry Bright, a son of T. L. Hutchinson	6 ys.
Mar. 25.	Capt. Joshua Nash consumption	59
Ap. 4.	An infant child of Mr. William Baker	4 mos.
20.	Mr. William Howard	40

{DEATHS, p. 481}

| April 20 1828 | Mrs. Catherine P. Younger consumption | 29 |

May 9.	+ An infant child of Mr. William Emerson 6	
May 27.	Rebecca A., daughter of Mr. C. O. Fifield lung Fever	12 ys.
__ 30.	Augusta B., daughter of Mr. B. Lincoln consumption 21	
June 4.	+ Mr. John Howe (Br. Ware's)	64
__ __.	+ An infant child of Mr. Allen (Br. Ware's)	10 mo.
27.	+ Mr. William Johnson Typhus Fever 17	
July 8.	An infant child of Mr. Levi Younger 6 mos.	
Aug. 5.	Mr. John Thayer inflammatory fever 41	
30.	+ A son of Mr. Isaac Rhoades (Br. Ware's) 10	
Sept. 6.	An infant child of Mr. T. Hutchinson 9 mo.	
Oct. 4.	Mr. Edward Oliver 52	
__ 5.	+ A child of Mr. Cotton Bennett, Beverly 1 y.	
__ 10.	William H. Howe, son of Mr. William Howe 20	
__ 14.	Mrs. Mary Curtis, widow of T. C. dropsy 56	
Nov. 12.	+ Mr. Jonathan Merry (Mr. Ware's) 67	
14,	+ A child of Mr. D. Marden (Mr. Ware's) 6	
Dec. 20.	+ A child of Mr. Ezra Witton Mr. Ware's 5	
	26 Total +10 not of my Society	

1829

Jan. XII.	+ Mrs. Mary Greene (Mr. Ware's) 65	
Jan. XXI.	Mrs. [blank] Baker, widow 67	
Jan. XXV.	Mrs. E., wife of Mr. E. J. S. Corlew consumption 23	
Jan. XXVII.	+ A child of Mr. Meriam [?] burnt to death 5	
Feb. I.	Mrs. Sarah, wife of Mr. George Harris 34	
Feb. II.	Mrs. Martha Appleton, widow 81	
Feb. V.	Mr. Jeremiah Kahler (Mr. Ware's) 86	
Feb. X.	Mr. Jacob Barstow consumption (Mr. Ware's) 41	

{DEATHS, p. 482}

Feb. XI.	Mrs. Hannah Lambert old age 80	
Feb. XX.	Mrs. Elizabeth Richardson, from Scotland 89	
Mar. 4.	+ Henry May, son of Mr. J. Bridge (Mr. Ware's) 6	
April.	Mr. Benjamin Tilden very suddenly 56	
May 24.	Mary Caroline, daughter of Caleb Eddy Brain-Fever 12	
25.	+ Delia C. Hall, only child of Mr. E. F. Hall Mr. Barrett's 3	
June 14.	+ A young child of Mr. E. F. Morse Mr. Lowell's measles 4	
June 21.	+ Mr. Seth Taylor Jun. consumption 26	
25.	Frances A., daughter of D. Dickinson 14	
__ __.	+ Mrs. Frances B, wife of Judge Orne Mr. Emerson's 35	
July 27.	Mrs. Hannah, wife of Mr. Benjamin Comey 62	
Aug. X.	Mr. John Bray 68	
15.	+ An infant child of Mr. House (Mr. Emersons) 5 mos.	
XX.	An infant child of Mr. John Sawin 10 mos.	
XXX.	An infant child of Mrs. Skerry 4 mos.	
Sept. 5.	+ Mrs. Elizabeth K,	

	wife of Mr. Jos. N. Howe, East-Cambridge	27
__ VI.	Mr. Francis Gragg, son of Jacob Gragg	26
VII.	+ An infant child of Mrs. Buxton Dr. Tuckerman's	5 mos.
__ XVI.	Miss D. Sarah, daughter of Mr. William Howe 19	ys.
XXI	+ A young child of Mrs. More of Hopkington, N. H.	6
Dec. 18.	Mrs. Mary Hall, widow of [blank] Hall Esq.	80
__ __.	Miss Mary Walker, daughter of Mr. [blank] Walker	24
Dec. 20.	Mary Agnes, my youngest child.	

Heu! Igne nobis erepta filia mihi carissima   2
[Alas! Taken away from us by fire, dearest daughter to me]

23.	Lowell Blake, youngest child of Mr. G. Darracott	1
31.	Mr. Thomas Wells consumption	49
1829	Total 33. Adults 20. Children 13. 9 over 60:	

of these, 5 over 80. XI children under X.
Of this total 20 were of my own society, viz.,
15 adults (4 over 80, 7 over 60, 5 young persons)

{DEATHS, p. 483}
1830

Jan. 2.	Sarah H, daughter of Mr. Pierce	7 ys.
Feb. 9.	+ James Freeman, child of Mr. Merrill Mr. Greenwood's	2
__ 17.	Mrs. Anna M. Colesworthy, wife of W. C.	35
18.	+ Simon Peter Fish, son of Mr. T. Lane Mr. Lowell's	14
20.	Miss Caroline Cutter, of A. Cutter Esq.	24
Feb. XXII.	Mr. Edward Oliver	73
March X.	Mr. Francis Robins (in lunatic asylum)	
__ 12.	Mr. Thomas Leeds, Sexton of the Church	41
__ 16.	+ Mr. Peregrine Paddock (Br. Emersons)	19
April 6.	+ Mrs. Nancy Clarke consumption	61
April X.	Mr. George Richardson, Scotchman	80
April 16.	Mr. Charles Knight consumption	44
May 31.	+ An infant child of Mr. Jos. Hayden	1
June 1.	Mrs. Mary Pike	61
__ 25.	Mrs. Sarah Cogswell	80
__ 26.	+ Miss Elizabeth L. Eliot,	
	daughter of late Rev. John Eliot	34
__ 28.	Mr. George M, son of Mr. B. Tilden	20
July 4.	Mrs. Bridget Shelton, wife of Mr. N. Blake	32
__ 12.	Mrs. Mary Turner Hall	62
21.	+ Mr. Zeba Thayer (Mr. Streeters)	66
August 31.	Granville Mears [Sept. 6 written above the line],	
	child of Mr. J. Clark	2
Oct. 20.	An infant child of Mr. John Tuckerman	6 mos.
__ 5.	+ An infant child of Mr. [blank] Murray	14 mos.
Nov. 19.	Mrs. Ann B, wife of Thomas Crocker	28
Dec. 28.	Mrs. Abigail Bruce	89

25 - - 8 not of the Society.
Of Total of deaths from 1814, 97 were over 60. Of whom 30 were over 70, 32
over 80, and 3 upward of 92, 32 therefore between 60 & 70.

{DEATHS, p. 484}
1831

Feb. 12.	Mr. Thomas Gooding		65
Ap. 10.	Mr. [blank] French	consumption	18
__ 27.	Caroline Wentworth, daughter of Mr. Jacob Hall		7
May 3.	Mrs. Nancy Trench		71
May 7.	A child of Mr. Daniel Lillie		18 mos.
24.	++ Mrs. Lydia Tileston, widow of Master Tileston 95		
25.	Mrs. Elizabeth, wife of Mr. Nathaniel Clark 42		
27.	An infant child of Mr. John Grubb		8 mos.
June 7.	A child of Mr. [blank] Porter dropsy in the brain 4 ys.		
24.	Mrs. Hosea [blank]		65
July 23.	+ Mr. Daniel Jones (Dr. Lowell's) consumption 56		
27.	Miss Angelina Sumbardo consumption		17
30.	Mr. John Tuttle	Brain Fever	32
Oct. 22.	+ An infant child of Mrs. Kemp		1
29.	A child of Mr. Joseph Lewis		3
	+ Mr. Edward Draper, the oldest printer in Boston (Brattle St.) 82		
Nov. 30.	Mr. Turell Tuttle Sen.		72
Dec. 4.	+ Mr. Jonathan Grenough Brattle St. very sudden apoplexy 45		
__ 6.	Mrs. Sarah, wife of Capt. [blank] Hill		30
__ 12.	Mrs. Lucy Pollard, colored, member of the Church		91
14.	Deacon John Simpkins		91

For more than 55 years deacon of the Church, being chosen in 1776, & for many
years the oldest deacon in Boston. The last of 103 individuals whose years I
knew [?] who have died in the Society since the settlement of the present Pastor,
Dec. 8, 1813, of these 31 were over 70, 36 over 80, 6 over 90.

N. B. The extreme & unusual severity of cold through this month has been fatal
to many, old & young. The average of cold has been 19 degrees lower than that
of last year. [noted on attached flap]: for more than 55 years the deacon of the
Church, being chosen in Nov 1776, three years before the death of Dr. Andrew
Eliot. He was for many years the senior deacon in the Congregational Churches
in Boston; and was the last of seventy-three persons who have died within the
eighteen years of my ministry, whose age exceeded seventy. Of these six were
more than 90 years. F. [rancis] P.[arkman][on rear of flap]: Deaths. Total of
deaths from Dec. 8, 1813, to Dec. 31 1831: 354 (for 18 years) or 19 2/3 per year.]

{DEATHS, p. 485}
1831

Dec. 17.	Mrs. Mary, wife of Mr. Charles Lincoln æt[atis, aged] 65
Dec. 22.	+ Miss [blank] Freeman 58
__ 24.	An infant child of Mr. Thomas Andrews
	(Sexton of the church) 2 ys.
Dec. 25.	+ An infant child of Mr. Robert Howe 2

Total 25, 5 not of Society. 14 Adults, 6 over 70 + note

1832

Jan. 4.	Mrs. Elizabeth Lambert, the oldest in the Society XCVI
Jan. 18.	Mr. Thomas Page dropsy Æt[atis, aged] 72
19.	An infant child of Mr. Henry Cutting 2 mos.
24.	J. Q. Adams Garrett, of the Boy's Asylum 6 ys.
	(being only the third death, since its institution in 1815)
Jan. 27.	Mrs. Anna Harris, widow + 92
29.	Mrs. Sarah, widow of Thomas Page who died 17ᵗʰ Jan. 65
Feb. 15.	Miss Eliza, daughter of John Hudson 15
24.	John Elliot, a son of Mr. H.[enry] J. Oliver 5
April 8.	+ An infant child of Mr. E. P. Edwards (Brattle Street) 3
__ 27.	Mr. Thomas L. Jones consumption 27

Note 1831   The mortality in the city for the year past, and especially for the last two months, owing to influenza & severe cold has been universally great, being 1424; of whom 237 died in this cold December.

The following are the number of deaths for the last ten years within the city; 1830 – 1125. 1829, 1221. 1828, 1233. 1827, 1022. 1826, 1254. 1825, 1450. 1824, 1297. 1823, 1154. 1822, 1203. 1821, 1421

{DEATHS, p. 486}

April 27.	Mary Elizabeth, a child of Mr. C.[harles] Hammatt 3 years
__ __.	also, same week & buried together, Edward Thornton, infant
	child of C.[harles] H.[ammatt] 8 mos.
June 7.	Mr. Samuel Tuttle 62
__ 17.	Mrs. Harriet R, wife of Mr. Oliver Lincoln 25
25.	+ A child of Mr. Andrew Cazneau 7
July 27.	+ Mr. Thomas Backus, Quincy, killed at the Railway 44
29.	+ Mr. Francis Bryant, drowned in Jam[aica] Pond 18
Aug. 5.	+ A child of Mr. [blank] Goodrich (Mr. Emerson's) 2
17.	Mrs. Ann M., wife of Mr. Robert W. Holt consumption 21
__ __.	+ A child of Mr. [blank] (Mr. Emerson's) 2
Sept. 7.	Susan Elizabeth, a child of Mr. William Palfrey 3
21.	Joseph P. Lamprell Typhus Fever 23
Oct. 7.	Mrs. Fanny Hammatt 50
8.	Miss Ellen Dickinson 19
10.	An infant child of Mr. Batcheldor 4 mos.

Oct. 12.	Mr. Joseph Eustis		79
13.	Deacon John Wells, chosen deacon in Mar. 1812 68 ys.		
24.	Mr. Benjamin Tuttle		33
29.	Mrs. Sarah Fracker	Lung-Fever	76
Nov. 1.	+ Mrs. Hannah Proctor		85
8.	+ Elizabeth Tucker, daughter of Mr. J. Priest Brattle Street		6
11.	+ Mrs. Mary, widow of Mr. S[amuel]. Prince 59		
30.	+ Capt. John Howe (Mr. Emersons)		55
Dec. X.	Mrs. Elizabeth Vernon		72
__ 13.	+ Mrs. Nancy, wife of Mr. Gurdon Steele		54
17.	Mrs. Elizabeth Richardson [Johnson written above the line] 72		

Total 36. 11 not of the Society.
Of the 25 of the Society, 18 were adults (7 over 70) & 7 children

{DEATHS, p. 487}
1833

Jan. 17.	+ An infant child of Mr. Edward H. Oliver		5 mos.
Mar. 20.	+ Mr. Samuel Rogers	apoplexy (Brattle St.)	57
May 10.	+ Mrs. Susan Paine Wilson		
	(Dorchester but of New North Church)		92
__ 23.	+ Mrs. Susanna Howe (Second Church)		89
June 4.	+ Mr. Ephraim Pierce (Chelsea, Mr. Alger's)		20
__ 7.	+ An infant child of Mr. George Howe		
	(Brattle St. Church)		7 mos.
June 22.	Capt. Stephen Hall ++ Ju.		51 ys.
July 2.	Mr. Asa Holbrook	++ Ju.	63
__ 6.	Horace, only child of Mr. James Hooton		
	(suffocation in a privy)		2
July 11.	Miss Mary Brockus decay		
	[Dr. Lowell written above the line]		75
16.	+ Mrs. Margaret Barrett, English		75
July 22.	+ Miss Mary Proctor	2d Church	70
23.	Mrs. Martha Atkins See old Records Oct. 25th 1747 86		
July 30.	Mrs. Sarah-Ann,		
	wife of Mr. S. N. Dickinson consumption		22
__ __.	Also, their infant child		2 mos.
August 6.	Mr. Henry Atkins	consumption	25
__ 15.	Mrs. Eliza D. wife of Mr. Joseph Fenno consumption 31		
18.	+ An infant child of Mr. Thomas Lyford		1 mo.
19.	+ A child of Mr. Thomas Hutchinson		2 ys.
20.	+ Maria, a child of Mr. Ebenezer Scott		3 ys.
26.	Caroline P., a child of Mr. Warren Lincoln Scarlet Fever 4 ys.		
30.	+ Mr. John Dodd Typhus Fever		36
__ __.	+ Miss Hepzibah Moore Mr. Emerson's		78
Sept. 1.	Redford Webster Esq.		72

4.	An infant child of Mr. Caleb G. Loring	1 mo.
	+ A child of Mr. Peirce	
25.	An infant child of Mr. Jos. Andrews, Sexton (Mr. Streeter) 19 mos,	
27.	Mrs. Clarissa, wife of William A. Stone,	
	Esq. Prospect, Maine	27

{DEATHS, p. 488}

[noted at top of page:] Total of deaths in 20 years 543. 404 deaths from New-North in 20 years.

Oct. 15.	+ An infant child of Mr. T. Mitchell Mr. Young's	4 mos.
30.	+ An infant child of Mr. [blank] Josselyn Second Church	2 mos.
Nov. 4.	+ Mr. A. Chandler, father of Rev. Joshua Chandler, Oxford	73
11.	+ Mrs. Esther Haynes (St. Paul's Church)	48
Dec. 7.	Mr. Thomas Williams, Chelsea	63
10.	Harriet G., child of Mr. Daniel Denny	2 ½
14.	+ Mrs. Nancy Hewes, of Coopers-town, N. Y.	24
15.	Mrs. Margaret, 2d wife of Mr. N. Clark, married Ap. 4, 1833	24
22.	Mrs. Hannah, widow of Redford Webster	67

[The above nine entries on p. 488 are repeated, with some alterations, at the top of p. 490] Total 37. 19 not of my Society. 12 under 5 years, 8 over 70, of whom 2 exceeded 80 & 1 was 92. Total of deaths in the city for 1833, 1476. Old Age 57. 51 between 70 & 80, 19 between 80 & 90, 4 between 90 & 100.

1834

The following table, collected from official sources, indicates the suicides, deaths by intemperance & consumption for 24 years past.

	Consumption	Intemperance		Suicide	Total morality in the city
1813	193	0	0	786	
[18]14	153	0	1	727	
[18]15	190	0	6	854	
[18]16	180	3	4	904	
[18]17	231	0	3	907	
[18]18	138	2	4	971	
[18]19	174	11	4	1070	
[18]20	220	31	6	1103	
1821	192	30	2	1420	
[18]22	166	25	5	1203	
[18]23	183	10	3	1154	
[18]24	242	22	5	1297	
[18]25	220	23	4	1450	
[18]26	231	38	5	1254	
[18]27	278	25	4	1022	
[18]28	217	34	9	1223	
[18]29	203	30	5	1221	

1830	193	19	8	1125
[18]31	203	30	12	1224
[18]32	246	44	8	1761
[18]33	240	40	14	1476

{DEATHS, p. 489}
1834

Jan. 10.	Miss Mary E., daughter of Mr. N. Clark	17 ys.
	Vide [see] Dec. 15. 1833 & May 25, 1831	
	[written above the line]	
11.	+ Mr. Lewis Bailey by suicide (Brattle St.)	44

[These two entries are repeated at top of p. 491]

{DEATHS, p. 490}
[the nine entries on this page are a repetition of the nine entries on p. 488, with some alterations]

Oct. X.	+ An infant child of Mr. T. Mitchell Mr. Young's	4 mos.
30.	+ An infant child of Mr. [blank] Josselyn Mr. Robbin's	2 mos.
Nov. 4.	+ Mr. A. Chandler, Andover	73 years
11.	+ Mrs. Esther Haynes St. Paul's Church	48
Dec. 7.	Mr. Thomas Williams, Esq., Chelsea	63
10.	Harriet G., child of Mr. Daniel Denny	2 ½
14.	+ Mrs. Nancy Hewes, of Coopers-town, N. Y.	24
15.	Mrs. Margaret, wife of Mr. Nathaniel Clark	24
22.	Mrs. Hannah, widow of R.[edford] Webster Esq.	7

Total 37, 18 of my Society

12 under five, 8 over 70, of whom 2 exceeded 80, & 1 92.

Total of deaths in the City for 1833 - - - 1476, of whom 570 under 5 – 51 over 70, 19 over 80.

The following table of population, mortality and causes of deaths from the year 1811, is taken from official returns.

Population of Boston in <u>1810</u> 33,250; d[itt]o in <u>1820</u>, 43,298; in <u>1830</u>, 61,392. Present Population over 70,000.

Deaths in 1811, 742; in 1812, 677; 1813, 786; 1814, 727 (1 Suicide); 1815, 854 (6 Suicide); 1816, 904 (4); 1817, 907 (3); 1818, 971 (3); 1819, 1070 (4); 1820, 1103 (6 Suicide); 1821, 1420 (2); 1822, 1203 (5); 1823, 1154 (3); 1824, 1297 (5 S.); 1825, 1450 (5 Suicide); 1826, 1254 (4); 1827, 1022 (5); 1828, 1233 (9); 1829, 1221 (5 Suicide); 1830, 1125 (8 Suicide); 1831, 1422 (12 Suicide); 1832, <u>1761</u> (the census number) (8 Suicide); 1833, 1476 (14 Suicide); 1834.

Of the 1476 who died in 1833, 240 were of consumption, of avg. age 57: 40 were from intemperance, 53 from accidents, burns, &c, and 14 from Suicide.

For the last twenty years, the average number of deaths from intemperance were 21; For the last 10 years, Thirty-One.

{DEATHS, p. 491}
1834

[The first two entries repeat the entries from p. 489, with some alterations]

Jan. X.	Miss Mary E., daughter of Mr. N. Clark	17 ys.
	Vide [see] May 1831 and Dec. 1833 [written above the line]	
12.	+ Mr. Lewis Bailey Brattle St. suicide, poison	42
Jan. 15.	+ An infant child of Mrs. C. Esculent, English	9 mos.
Feb. 7.	Mrs. Elizabeth, wife of Mr. Owen Jones fever	59
16,	+ Mr. Calvin Colburn fever	61
Mar. 27.	+ Mr. Alexander Young, father of Rev. A. Young, New-South 65	
April 12.	A child of Mr. William Fracker	5
13.	+ A Mr. [blank] of Dorchester intemperance 57	
May 14.	+ Amasa Seaver consumption	
	(In morte formosissimus) [the most handsome in death] 14	
19.	+ A child of the widow Sparhawk (Marblehead) 4	
25.	Capt. Benjamin Smith fever	65
June 4.	+ Rev. George Chapman, Pastor of the Church in Framingham 25	
	ordained Nov. 7, 1834 [sic] (Vide [see] Records) & died of	
	consumption	
22.	An infant child of Mr. Henry Hutchinson	5 mos.

July 27.   Mem[orandum]: the heat for this Sunday & three or four preceding days excessive. Thermometer 92° to 99°

July 27.	Mrs. Sarah Thomas decay	65
Aug. 10.	Georgianna. daughter of Mr. E. Parks	4
Aug. 13.	+ Mr. Frederick Mellen of Portland son of Judge Mellen 24	
Sept. 14.	+ Mrs. Hannah Williams, Widow, Chelsea	76
__ __.	Jacob Gragg, a child of Mr. George Harris	6
Sept. 27.	+ Mr. Joel R. Lilly	33
Oct. 18.	Mr. Charles H. Hammatt (Typhus Fever	24
__ 19.	+ Mr. John Kendrick (Br. Barrett's)	49
Dec. 7.	Miss Sarah W., daughter of Mr. [Christopher] Gore 23	
9.	+ Mr. Thomas Bottomore	28

23 Total, 10 only of the Society, of whom 5 were adults, 5 children. Dec. 31. Whole number of Deaths in Boston for 1834, 1544.

{DEATHS, p. 492}
1835

Feb. 7.	Mrs. Mary, widow of Mr. Larabee Edes	87
	+ An infant child of Mr. B. of Brattle Street 10 mos.	
Mar. 14.	Jacob Astor, child of Mr. Martin Bates	2 ys.
21.	+ Mr. Henry Briggs Lung Fever + note (Mr. Barrett's) 29	
Ap. 12.	+ Mr. [blank] Smith consumption	35
	A child of Mr. David W. Hill	3
May 10.	+ Mrs. Susanna Drew (Brattle St.)	86

24.	Mrs. Elizabeth Oliver (formerly Prescott)	72
June 19.	+ Mrs. [blank], widow of Mr. Samuel Hunt Dr. Lowell's	68
20.	Miss Sarah Jenkins asthma	80
July 11.	Mrs. Sarah Simmons Dropsy	74
19.	+ A child of Mr. John Mellen (Br. Barrett's)	2
21.	Mrs. Sarah, mater mihi carissima [dearest mother to me], widow of Samuel Parkman	80
26.	Deacon John Fenno, chosen Deacon, March 1826 consumption	70
Sept. 3.	Edward H. son of Mr. William Baker Dropsy in brain	4
24.	An infant child of Mr. Stephen Rhoades 15 mos.	
Oct. 7.	+ A child of Mr. [blank] Whitman, croup Mr. Barrett's	5 ys.
9.	+ Miss Susan, daughter of Mr. T. Dodd	27
15.	An infant child of Mr. N.[oah] Harod 6 mos.	
16.	+ An infant child of Mr. Lincoln (Br. Robbins)	
17.	+ Charles G., a child of Mr. Collamore Br. Barretts 5 years	
23.	Philip Adams, child of H. R. Williams 9 mos.	
31.	A child of Mr. William Fracker 13 mos.	
Nov. 2.	Mrs. Sarah, wife of Mr. David W. Hill 33 ys.	
__ 18.	Hannah, daughter of Mr. T. Lillie 35 ys.	
23.	Lavinia, child of Mr. Henry Hutchinson 8 mos.	
Dec. 4.	An infant child of Mr. S. Young 5 mos.	
12.	Capt. Silas Atkins Vide [see] Records 1747, Oct. 88	

+ Note: March 21. An unusual number of sudden deaths, this among persons under forty, by Lung & other fevers. Of these, were within the last ten days, Mr. Pickman, President of the Senate, Mrs. Curtis of apoplexy, 31 – Mrs. Emmons [?] and my friend & classmate Rev. Winthrop Bailey.

{DEATHS, p. 493}

Dec. 22.	Mrs. Mary-Ann Shelton (suicide)	39

Total 29, 10 not of my Society. 8 over 70, 9 under 5 years. Of 98 over 70, 40 were over 80 ys, 10 over 90 in 22 years.

1836

Jan. 3.	An infant child of Mr. A. H. Robinson Lowell 17 mo.	
Jan. 6.	Capt. Henry Atkins	93
__ 10.	+ Caroline, a child of Rev. Alexander Young 3	
__ 21.	Charles Lincoln, child of Josiah Peirce 6	
26.	Mrs. Deborah, consumption wife of Mr. J. F. Payson 37	
Feb. 15.	Mrs. Elizabeth Harris (widow)	76
__ 25.	+ Mr. Elbridge Lakeman, Candidate for the Ministry 34	
Mar. 3.	Mrs. Hannah, wife of Ammi Cutter	56
__ 24.	Mr. George C. Barrett Pleurisy Fever	27
Ap. 5.	+ Mrs. [blank] Jones	40
May 10.	+ Mrs. [blank] Jarvis	45

June 10.	Mrs. Harriet A., wife of Mr. Henry Cutting		32
__ 20.	+ A child of Mr. Edmund Smith		5 mo.
July 10.	Miss Susan H. Hill	Apoplexy	46
July 14.	An infant child of Mr. H.[enry] Cutting		10 mos.
__ __.	+ Mrs. Mallen (Rev. Mr. Hague's)		65
__ 30.	+ Mr. Ephraim Skerry Intemperance, fell down dead		47
Aug. 9.	Mr. John P. Sumbardo	Typhus Fever	19
24.	Mrs. Mary Perry		52
Sept. 7.	An infant child of Mr. B.[enjamin] H. Greene		7 mos.
14.	An infant child of Mr. Beately		8 mos.
23.	Mrs. Abigail, widow of Joseph Eustis		75
Oct. 20.	+ Mr. [blank] Gibbs (King's Chapel)		37
__ 26.	+ Mr. Augustus Hildreth (Second Ch.)		42

{DEATHS, p. 494}

Nov. 20.	Mrs. Mary Trevett	consumption	54
Dec. 7.	Mrs. Sylvia Hall, of color MC		84
9.	Mrs. Mary Atkins, mother of Mrs. Trevett		88
	21 Adults. Five Aged between 75 & 93. Total 27.		
	Nine not of the Society		

1837

Jan. 8.	Mrs. Mary Lincoln (M. C.)		74
__ 10.	Mrs. Helen A., wife of T. A. Gerry		24
__ 21.	An infant child of Mrs. S. P. Barrett		5 mos.
Feb. 24.	Mr. William Baker	Consumption	45
Mar. 7.	Mrs. Mills, wife of Mr. J. Mills		75
Ap. 18.	Mr. John Lee	Lung-Fever	49
19.	Mrs. Sarah, wife of John Cruft Cancer		53
May 8.	An infant child of Mr. Robert Restieaux Pleurisy Fever		11 mos.
10.	Mr. Edward Cutter		57
24.	Mr. Thomas Everett		46
June 1.	+ Mrs. Prescott (King's Chapel)		84
10.	+ Mrs. [blank] Snelling old age		94
July 8.	An infant child of Mrs. S. Stevens		11 mos.
__ __.	Mr. David, son of Mr. S. Wilkinson,		
	died at Havannah, of Yellow-Fever		24 y.
27.	Mrs. Susanna, wife of Mr. Robert Restieaux		28
__ __.	An infant child of Mr. O. Munroe		16 mos.
Aug. 23.	Mr. William E. æt.[atis, aged] 19,		
	son of Mr. George Darracoat		19
27.	Mrs. Lucy, wife of Mr. J. Hudson		49
Sept. 14.	An infant child of Mr. C. H. Stearns		7 mos.
24.	Mr. Charles Thomas, son of Christopher Gore,		
	at New-Orleans, Yellow Fever		20 y

Oct. 7.   Miss Martha W., daughter of Dr. W. Spooner   30
Nov. 12.   Mrs. Rebecca Lillie   Bilious Fever   32
Dec. 10.   An infant child of Mr. Winsor   3
                 [entry repeated on first line of next page, with slight alteration]

{DEATHS, p. 495}

Dec. 10.   An infant child of Mr. Winsor   2 ½
                 [entry repeated from last line of previous page, with slight alteration]
                 Total 23, 21 of the Society. 4 over 70, 5 between 20 & 30, 5
                 Infants [repeated at top of p. 497]

1838
Jan 12.   + An infant child of Mr. [blank] Nickerson Brattle St. 15 mo.
Feb. 10.   + An infant child of Mr. [blank]   9 mo.
March   Mrs. Joanna Anderson   Pleurisy   62 ys.
April 10.   Miss Delia Williams   consumption   63
May 6.   + A son of Mr. Joseph Smith Mr. Robbins   8
__ 18.   + Mr. John Webb, Cambridge   56
June 26.   + Mrs. Harriet, wife of Rev. Edward B. Hall, of Providence,
                 Buried at Cambridge   36
July 31. No death in my Parish for now nearly four months, and though the
heat has been extreme on several days (viz. from 92° to 98°) the city is in health.
August   + Benjamin Franklin Mead, Killed by lightening,
                 Farm School   14
Sept. 4.   + An infant child of Mr. Smith's Br. Robbins 5 mos.
__ 13.   + An infant child of Mr. Ebenezer Scott's Br. Robbins 4 mos.
         [The ten entries of individuals on this page (excluding the note on the
weather) are repeated with some alterations on page 497]

{DEATHS, p. 497 [sic]}

[repeated from p. 495] Total number of deaths in 1837 - - 23. Of these 21 be-
longed to the Society. 4 over 70. 5 between 20 & 30, 5 Infants
1838
         [The first ten entries are repeated from p. 495, with some alterations]
Jan 12.   + An infant child of Mr. Nickerson   15 mo.
Feb. 10.   + An infant child of Mr. [blank]   9 - -
March   Mrs. Joanna Anderson   (Pleurisy)   62 ys.
April 10.   Miss Delia Williams   (consumption)   63
May 6.   + A son of Mr. Joseph Smith   8
__ 18.   + Mr. John Webb (Cambridge)   56
June 26.   + Mrs. Harriet, wife of Rev. E. B. Hall of Providence,
                 buried at Cambridge   36
August   + Benjamin Franklin Mead, Killed by lightening,
                 at the Farm School   14
Sept. 4.   + An infant child of Mr. Smith Br. Robbins 5 mos.
__ 13.   + D[itt]oD[itt]o of Mr. Ebenezer Scott Br. Robbins 4 - -

__ 18.	Mr. Samuel N. Cutter consumption	29	
Oct. 10.	+ Miss Charlotte Bray consumption	34	
21.	+ Mr. Nathaniel Saltonstall, at Salem	54	
23.	+ Miss Ruth Mackay (Dr. Channings)	66	
Dec. 13.	Mrs. Emily F. wife of Mr. T. Williams	24	
__ 14.	Mr. Robert Restieaux consumption	32	

Total 16, 5 only of New-North. Total number of deaths in Twenty-five years, viz., from Dec. 8, 1813 – 659 – of whom 476 belonged to N.[ew] N.[orth]. Of this number 216 were under 10 years.

55 were between 60 & 70

42 were between 70 & 80

Nearly one third under Ten, & between 1/4 & 1/5 over Sixty

46 were between 80 & 90

11 were between 90 & 100

154 Total over 60   F. Parkman

{DEATHS, p. 498}

1839

Jan.	Mrs. Elizabeth Sprague	44	
30.	Mrs. E. Campbell	75	
Feb. 22.	Mr. Josiah Peirce	49	
Mar. 20.	Mr. William M. Thompson	19	
31.	Mrs. Sally H. Gore, wife of [Christ]opher G.[ore]	45	
Ap. 3.	A child of Mr. George Darracott Jun	8 mos.	
12.	Mrs. Hannah J., wife of Mr. B.[enjamin] Fessenden	30 ys.	
May 27.	+ Ellen Tree, child of Mr. W. B. Oliver Mr. Robbins	8 mos.	
29.	+ Esther Parkman, of Mr. W. B. Oliver	3 ys.	
June 23.	+ Mr. Theodore Wright, at North-Hampton	51	
25.	Mrs. Margaret Goodwin, the oldest member of the Church	81	
July 2.	James Everett, son of Mr. Daniel Denny	3	
12.	+ Mrs. Adeline, wife of Mr. George H. Kilburn (Mr. Dean's)	28	
25.	+ A child of Mr. [blank] (Mr. Barrett's)	5	
Aug. 14.	+ Mr. John T. Reed (Mr. Gannett's)	54	
Sept. X.	+ Mrs. Mary, wife of Mr. [blank] Childs (Mr. Robbins}	41	
21.	+ Miss Mary Cooper, of Charleston, S. C.	19	
25.	Mrs. Rachel Faxon	82	
Oct. 14.	+ Capt. Isaiah Atkins (removed to Newbury-Port)	64	
18.	Mrs. Ann, widow of Mr. Edward Oliver	76	
Oct. 30.	Mrs. Sarah, widow of Mr. John Bray	74	
Nov.	Miss Harriet W., daughter of Mr. Robert Lash	21	
Dec. 21.	Miss Sarah Ann Cutter consumption	26	

Total 23. 15 of the Society. 5 over Seventy, of whom 2 over 80. 5 between eighteen & thirty, 4 children under five years.

{DEATHS, p. 499}

1840

Feb. VI.	Mrs. Ann, widow of the late pastor of the church, Dr. John Eliot. She died at Dorchester æt.[atis, aged] 76
VII.	An infant child of Mr. C. H. Stearns 18 mos.
27.	+ Mrs. S. Dana, daughter of the late President Willard of Cambridge & mother of Mrs. George Ripley, Æt.[atis, aged] 65
May 24.	+ Mr. [blank] son of Mr. John Hudson 21
June 30.	+ Mr. Joseph Lathrop East-Cambridge, died at N. York 42
July 20.	Mrs. Martha, widow of Deacon [John] Wells 74 [?]
Sept. 5.	Mr. Thomas Edes Æt.[atis, aged] 57
Oct. 13.	An infant child of Mr. A. Wiggin
Oct. 18.	+ An infant child of Mr. Otis Norcross of Mr. Barrett's 10 mos.
	9 +5 not of the Society

1841

Jan. 29.	Mary Elizabeth, of Henry A. & Sarah Andrews X
March 25.	+ Daniel Parkman, son of Samuel Parkman
	Rheumatic Fever 46
June X.	+ Ann, daughter of Mr. Nathaniel Francis 26
Aug. 13.	An infant child of Mr. Joel Foster 18 mos.
__ 27.	+ Mrs. Joanna, wife of Mr. J. Bradlee (Dr. Frothingham's) 59
Sept. 8.	+ Edward Blake, son of Daniel Parkman 23
Oct. 14.	+ Two patients at the Seamen's (U. States') Hospital, Chelsea
Dec. 26.	Caroline Louisa, daughter of Mrs. Sarah J. Winslow 17
	Total 8, only 3 of the Society

1842

March 6.	+ Mrs. [blank] wife of Dr. Smith, of the Navy 48
July 2.	An infant child of J. T. & Sarah Wells 9 mos.

{DEATHS, p. 500}

Aug. 18.	+ Mrs. Elizabeth S., wife of Mr. Samuel C. Gray (of the King's Chapel), Æt[atis, aged] 33
21.	+ An infant child of Mr. E. Stearns (Mr. Robbins) 18 mos.
27.	Mr. Joseph Hart 60 ys.
30.	An infant child of Mr. Tuttle 3 mos.
Sept. 30.	Mrs. Nancy, wife of Mr. H. Hudson 72
Oct. 24.	Mr. Joseph Kettell Lewis 30
	Belknap, a child of Mr. J. B. Smith 6
Dec. 21.	An infant child of Mr. Abner Smith (buried by Mr. A. Smith 2
30.	Mrs. Mehitable Hart (died at N. Ipswich) 77
	Total XI. 8 of the Society, 4 of whom were adults, 3 of other churches

1843

March 17.	Mrs. Elizabeth, widow of A. Sigourney 77
April 15.	+ Miss M. T. Gale, a domestic from the house of Mr. D. Denny 35
May 1.	Arthur Stanley, of Daniel & Harriet G. Denny 20 mos.

June 19.	+ Hon. William Simmons consumption	65
July 20.	Mrs. Agnes Swift (consumption)	
	Mr. Smith attended the funeral- æt.[atis, aged]	76
Aug. 26.	Mrs. Eliza T., wife of Mr. S. C. Bradshaw	51
Sept. 15.	Mrs. Sarah, wife of Mr. Thomas Lillie	57
Oct. 21.	An infant child of Mr. David Adams	2 ys.
Nov. 22.	+ An infant child of Mr. [blank] Jones	4 ys.
25.	Harriet W. Lash, child of Mr. J. Sawin	3 ys
	10 + 3 not of the Society	

1844

Jan. 14.	+ An infant child of Mr. [blank] Pierce	15
17.	A child of Mrs. E. M. Center [?]	4 years
23.	Mrs. Sarah Leach	68
Feb. 22.	Mrs. Jane D. Brooks Lung-Fever	42
Mar. 3.	An infant child of Mr. John Gragg	19 mos.

{DEATHS, p. 501}

Mar. 26.	+ Mrs. [blank] Coates (Br. Robbins)	73 yeaers
April 17.	+ Charles Bulfinch Esq. (King's Chapel)	81 d[itt]o
July 9.	+ Two children of Mr. W. D. Shortwell (Br. Gray's)	
	Scarlet Fever 1 y. & 3 ys.	
July 19.	+ James H. Ritchie	16 mos.
Sept. 14.	Ann Matilda Darracott	9 months
Oct. 12.	Mrs. Betsey, wife of Mr. Henry Gurney	51 ys.
Nov. 21.	+ Mr. Samuel A. Raymond (Mr. Ellis' [?])(Charlestown)	31
	Total 12 deaths, 6 of the Society	

1845

Mar. 5.	+ Mr. Shaw, of Maine, brother of Mr. R. G. S.[haw]	
__ 12.	+ Mr. Putnam, of Stirling, brother of Rev. G. Putnam	
__ 17.	Miss Susan Edes Æt.[atis, aged]	57
April 2.	+ Mrs. Hannah G. Newman (Bennett St)	Aged 68
July 11.	Mrs. Mary Francis	79 years
July 21.	Mary Abigail Hartt	15 years, 7 months
Sept. 8.	Helen Augusta Tewksbury	10 months
Nov. VI.	Miss Lydia Wilson consumption Æt.[atis, aged] 51	
Dec. 12.	+ Mrs. Goldthwait, sister of Mrs. J. Doak Æt.[atis, aged] 73	
	Total 9. + 4 not of the Society	

1846

Mar. 19.	An infant child of Mr. Joseph Nason	8 mos.
27.	Mr. Edward Chamberlin	70
Feb. 20.	Albert Gurney	22
Feb. 21	+ George Colln (a German)	34
April 15.	+ George Green	49

May 31.	+ George Henry Calder	17 m's.

{DEATHS, p. 502}

June 1st.	Mr. J. Basset, at Cincinnati, son of J. Bassett, Esq. 27	
__ 26.	+ Mr. Charles H. Perry consumption (E. Boston) 38	
July 24.	Mrs. Sophia H., wife of R. R. Herriott Mr. Smith attended	
	consumption	33
31.	Mrs. Jane, wife of Mr. David Adams Mr. S.[mith] attended 36	
Aug. 1.	Mr. Daniel Lillie, son of Thomas Lillie	48
__ 1.	Twin-children of Mr. [blank] Campbell	11 mo
June 21.	* Benjamin H. Bromade	3 m's
July 11.	* Robert Lyford	17 yrs
Sept. 1.	* Mary Elizabeth Burrows	4 m's
22.	Miss Elizabeth Cordwell	87
__ __.	+ Miss Anna Eliot, eldest daughter of the late	
	Rev. Dr. John Elliot, died in Milton	56
Oct. 3d.	Hannah A. Sargent	3 m's
Nov. 24.	Mrs. Sarah, widow of Mr. S. Hall	81 ys.
Dec. 16.	Maria Louisa, daughter of Mrs. B. Hartt	21
__ 28.	+ Mrs. Anna, wife of Rev. Ezra S. Gannett D. D. 34 ys	
	Total in 1846 - - 22. + Not of the Society 8.	

1847

Jan. 3.	Susanna Farrow (Mrs) (Mr. Smith attended) 59	
12.	Clarissa Skerry (Mrs) member of the church 55	
Feb. 1.	Jonathan Snelling (Instructor in Writing) 78	
Ap. X.	Sarah, widow of Edward Blake Funeral by Mr. Smith 71	
Mar. 9.	James Aiken, child of Mr. B. Leavitt by Mr. Smith 6	
June 6.	Alice B., wife of Mr. John Campbell consumption 34	
July 6.	Rebecca A. S., daughter of Joseph Lewis,	
	wife of Horace Cushing, Inflammation of Brain 23	
__ 27.	+ Lowell M. Stone Esq, cashier of M. Bank East-Cambridge 31	
29.	Joseph Austin Esq.	85
Sept. 10.	Mr. Stephen Winchester Mr. Smith attended (consumption) 42	

{DEATHS, p. 503}

Sept. 14.	William Benjamin A child of Mr. B. Fessenden	
	Mr. Smith attended	10
August 2d.	William P. Kemp	4 ½ yrs
__ 13th.	Belknap Smith	5 yrs.
Sept. 15th.	Charles W. B. Colbath	1 yr.
__ 21st.	Charlotte Augusta Hooper	6 yrs.
Nov. 14.	Mr. Henry Fowle dropsy	+ 54 ys.
	Total 16, 2 not of the Society	

1848

Jan. 25.	Mr. Thomas G. (Gilman) Wells consumption 25 y.	

Mar. 4.	Mr. Stephen Brown	84
June 9.	Miss Mary Hall	67
July X.	Mrs. Sibella Lee Luckis	78

Aux. X.   Mrs. Catharine M., wife of Mr. J. B. Smith
                 (and daughter of Mr. James Clark   29 ys.

August 27.   Charlotte Olivia Morse   2 yrs, 2 ms.

Nov. 4.   + Mrs. S. C. Colburn, Mass. Gen. Hospital   51
                 Total VII. + one not of the Society

1849

Jan. 3.   Hon. Peter C. Brooks, ætate venerabilis, virtute insignis
                 [venerable in age, distinguished in virtue]
                         Æt.[atis, aged] LXXXII

Jan. 13.   Mrs. Anna, wife of J. Cazneau and last surviving
                 child of Rev. William Symmes D. D. of North-Andover   81

Jan. 14.   Mrs. Betsey, wife of S. Wilkinson (of Mr. Barrett's Society) 66

Feb. 6.   Mrs. Elizabeth Gooding   76

Continued on next page by Joshua Young

{DEATHS, p. 504}

March 16.   Mr. Isaac Cazneau   84 yrs.
                 Three months after his wife, without whom life lost
                 its attractions and its charm.

April 9.   An infant – daughter of Mrs. Wiswall's sister
                 (Mrs. Smith)   10 months

__ 16.   Betsey Hart – in Roxbury   66 yrs.

[??] 20.   + Mr. John Green   48 yrs.

[??] 23.   Mrs. Harriet Hudson   59 yrs.
                 A worthy Church member 23 years

[illeg.]   Infant child of Mrs. Barnes. Bradley Tufts   14 mos.

[??] 25.   Martha Hall Leeds   2yr. 8 mos.

Sept. 18.   Samuel F. Gooding   3 ms. 3 days

__ 19.   Charles Augustus English   7 weeks

Nov. 23.   George Parkman M. D. (Murdered at Med[ical] College) 59 yrs
                 Total 10. + Two not of the Society

1850

Jan. 21.   Mary Ella Krogman   2 yrs. 3ms. 7 days

March 10.   Thomas Andrews, Sexton of N. N. C.

__ 13.   Mrs. Caroline F. Kruger   30 yrs.

April 6.   Benjamin Hannas [?]   84 ys 5 mos.

Aug. [?] 20.   + Isaiah King   67 yrs.

Aug. 30.   Professor John White Webster, of Harvard University.
                 Executed for murder of Dr. Parkman. Both once members
                 of the N. N. R. S.   57 ys. 10 mos.

Oct. 19.   Mrs. Susannah Parker   91 ys 10 ms 5 days

Dec. 14.   Mr. Philip Adams   78 yrs.

Total 7. + one not member

{DEATHS, p. 505}

Jan. 28.	x A. J. Dole	34 yrs.
Feb. 5.	x Laura O. Lash of Thomaston	17 yrs 7 ms.
__ 14.	x Charles Howe	38 yrs.
March 1st.	Mary Eliza Hayden, of T. T. & M. O. Hayden	4 ys 10 ms.
__ 20.	Sarah B. Smith	24 yrs 10 ms.
June 2.	Miss Martha Tuttle	60 yrs.
Sept. 4.	Alice Campbell, of T. T. & Mary O. Hayden	1 yr 10 ms [?]days
Oct. 3.	Abigail W. wife of Benson Leavitt Esq.	50 yrs.

Total 8. x not of the Parish

1852

Jan. 8th.	Joseph Bassett ("A good man")	67 yrs.
__ 15.	Annie Eleanor Pierce	11 ms.
Feb. 1.	Harriet Farrar French	41 yrs.
March 31.	Susan Blanchard	71 yrs.
May 13.	Sarah Austin	60 yrs.

Total 5.

Continued on next page by A. B. Fuller

{DEATHS, p. 506}

1853

| July 19th. | Mrs. Elizabeth Young | 42 yrs. |
| __ 20. | Edward Carnes | 72 " |

Mrs. Young was a daughter of Mr. Carnes. Both were well on Sunday & both were dead on Monday night at 12 o'clock.

Sept. 11th.	George H. Shaw, of Consumption	26 "
__ 12th.	Arthur Angelo Fuller, at Reading	5 mos.
Oct. 11th.	Elizabeth Beatley at Chelsea	74 years
__ 31.	Emery Goss	about 45 yrs
__ __.	Mr. [blank] Sholes old age	92 yrs 4 mos.
Nov. 1st.	[blank] Shaw, child of George H. Shaw	
__ 21.	Thomas G. Atkins dysentery	63 yrs.
Dec. 6.	At Nashua, N. H. Daniel Abbot	77 yrs.

1854

Jan. 20.	Daughter of Mr. & Mrs. Cutter Charter St.	10 yrs.
Jan. 21.	Walter, son of Mr. & Mrs. Eben D. Jordan	5 years
	Infant son of Dr. Jobic on Salem St.	
	Lucy Ella daughter of Edward & Lucy Briggs	9 yrs. 7 ms.
April 16.	Mrs. Hannah Locke – Funeral was attended by Rev. Mr. Huntington as Mrs. L had removed to South part of City & recently attended his church. She still continued however	

a member of New North & deeply attached to it tho age & distance kept her from its Sabbath worship. She was a most excellent

& exemplary woman full of almsgiving, good deeds & holy faith.

{DEATHS, p. 507}

June 13.	Herman R. Nash Dysentery	35 years 6 mos.
__ 16.	Child of Mrs. Margaret Lathrop	5 yrs
July 2d.	Mrs. Oliver	Aged 72 yrs.
__ 5th.	Mrs. Mary D. Dolliver Consumption	28 yrs.
15.	Mr. Hammatt (a grandson of Dea[con] J. B. Hammatt) 24 yrs.	
19.	Mr. Joseph Noyes	84 yrs-7 mos-18 days
24.	Mrs. Sarah Shaw Consumption	50 yrs.
Oct. 8th 1854	Mrs. Canterbury	

[1855]

Feb. 1855.	George Harris	Aged 46 Seaman
March 6, 1855	Mrs. Eliza Shaw	
__ 19 __.	Miss Emily Wells. Aged 36 – A sincere & consistent Christian – a devoted Sabbath School teacher – active in every good work.	
__ 26.	A child of Mr. & Mrs. [blank]	Aged 5 mos.
July 6th.	Miss Martha Adams	Aged 52 yrs.
Oct. 24.	Miss Knowles	23 "
Nov. 2.	Miss Fitch	24 "
__ .	Mr. Perry	Aged 71
Dec. 10.	Mr. Chandler	" 56
Dec. 27.	Joseph Parker [Meizner]	__ 4 yrs & 5 mos.

The first Sabbath School Scholar who has died in my parish since the commencement of my ministry A lovely Child of Mr. T. L. Meizner.

In 1853 I attended 10 funerals
" 1854 "   "   13   "
" 1855 "   "   10   "   B. Fuller

{DEATHS, p. 508}
1856

Jan.	Infant son of Mr. Ranstead [?]	
Jan.	Mr. Duff a parishioner of Mr. Winkley. We attended the funeral together & shared the services.	
Feb. 22.	Rice Dudley	33 yrs 4 mos

He was a former parishioner of mine while in Manchester, N. H. was united by me in marriage in that city. He died in Pembroke N. H. some 70 miles from here & I attended his funeral by his dying request.

Feb. 23.	A colored woman – servant of Mrs. Lakeman	
25.	Albert, infant son of Mr. & Mrs. Benford of Somerset in	

Pennsylvania. I had never seen the parents, they were stopping at a hotel in this city at the time of their bereavement.

March 4th 1856. Died of pleuritic fever following the birth of our little boy Mrs. Elizabeth G. Fuller. Aged 24 years 6 months & 23 days. Alas that a husband's hand must record this bereavement which leaves my heart so desolate. A life of more than earthy purity is ended here, a spirit of great sanctity is removed to its appropriate sphere in Heaven. I do not mourn on her account but in the best of wives is gone, the most gentle & yet judicious of mothers is taken; an example for my parish has left us & for myself, for my little children for my people & with them I do & must grieve. God forbid that I should murmur. Let me here record my gratitude {p. 509} for the deep sympathy expressed by my people both in word & deed. Their kindness to me at this trying hour is balm only exceeded by that found in Gilead which Christ the Great Physician affords to the wounded spirit. Arthur B. Fuller. March 13, 1856

{DEATHS, p. 509}

March 14, 1856 Attended the funeral of William T. Clarke – Aged about 30. He was a young man married by me about 18 months ago. He died of small pox leaving a wife & one little babe. Truly real life is full of sad tragedies. But I know it shall be well with them that fear God,

July 1856.	Mrs. Mair	Aged about 45
Aug. __.	Mr. Noah Lincoln	" " 83
Sept. 18, 1856	Child of Mr. Dole	
__ 3.	Mrs. Marsh	50
__ 2.	Child of Mr. & Mrs. Stanton	8 weeks
Sept. 21.	Mr. Davis	31 yrs.

[1857]

Jan 1857	Child of Mr. Nelson	2 yrs.
__ __.	Mrs. Hale	24 "
__ __.	Mrs. Burbank	30
Feb. 5.	Louis and Lawson	1 – 5 mos.
__ 19.	Mrs. Barnes	72 yrs.
May [?].	Mrs. Tilden	79
	Mr. Chandler	

{DEATHS, p. 510}

May 1857	Mr. Murry	Aged 56
Sept. __.	Mr. Anderson	" 7 yrs.
Nov. 3 1857	Child of Mr. Wilbur	" 19 mos.
__ 6th __.	Mrs. Bessy	70 yrs.
__ 15 __.	Mr. Parsons	17 "
__ 29.	Mrs. J. D. Mitchell	26 "
Dec.	Mr. Matthew Ellis	70 "

[1858]

Feb. 1858.	Mrs. Perry Gifford	40 "
__ __.	Mr. Foster	19 "
April 13 __.	Eliza Swift	19 "
	Mrs. Folsom	72 "

May 22d.	George Harris	70 "
June	Mr. Sheldon	36 "
—	Mrs. King	72 "
Sept. 10.	Susan, child of Mr. & Mrs. Grasse	3 "
__ 18.	Miss Dodd daughter of Mr. & Mrs. B. Dodd	38 yrs.
Id[em]	Mr. Charles Mason	31 yrs.
Nov.	Mr. George Nash	about 43

[1859]

Jan. 1859	Mr. Leonard Mizner	37
__ 26.	Mrs. E. M. Thacker	22
__ 23,	Mr. William Deblois	about 40
Feb. 13.	Miss Singleton	14
__ 17.	Josephine Smith	2
__ 24.	Mr. Wright	78
__ 25.	Mrs. Ames	37 [?]
__ 26.	Mrs. Goddard	75
March 13.	Miss Hewes	24
18.	Mrs. Beateley	51

{DEATHS, p. 511}

April 22.	Mrs. Rebecca Nash	Aged 76
__ 23.	Mr. Davis	" 67
__ 25.	Mr. Thaddeus Whipple	" 35
June	John McNemath	" 40
July 16.	William Poole Waterhouse	" 38
__ 27.	Margaret Bassett	" 50
__ __.	Child of Charles B. & Emma D. Leavitt	11 mos.
__ 31.	Mrs. Mehitable Hillman	Aged 95 yrs 3 mos 6 days

1863

March 24.	Mr. Joseph Veazie [?]	Aged 77

{DEATHS, p. 512}
1862

April 27th.	Rev. R. C. Waterston preached his funeral Sermon
May	
June 29.	Rev. F. [?] Holland preached – it [?] Communion in the

afternoon and proved to be the last Service held in the House, at the corner of Hannover & Clark Sts.

1863

March 7th.	Purchase of the Bulfinch St. Church

The
New North Church
Records
Volume the Third
Commencing with the Minist[ry]
of the
Rev.d Francis Parkma[n]
who was Ordained
December the 8.th 1813

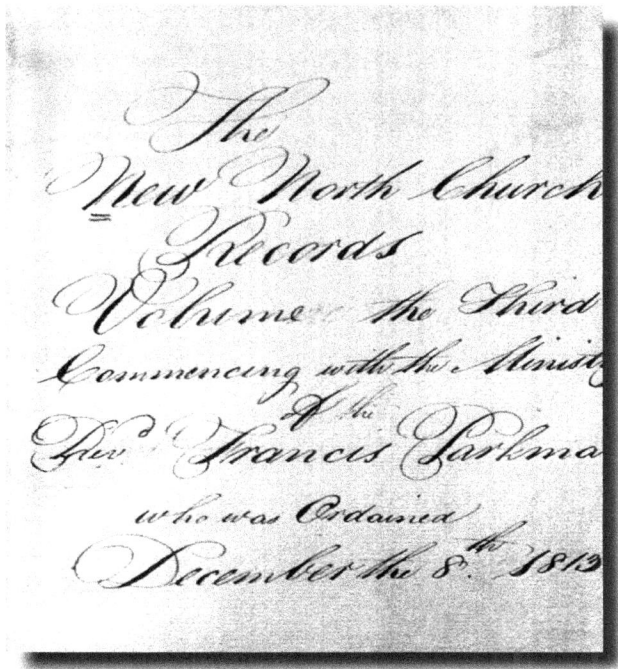

USING THIS INDEX

This Index is for the Records Section—Marriages, Births, Membership, and Deaths. Records listed in this book are an exact representation as they appear in the actual records. To use the Index, for example, find the person you are looking for and note the page. Go to that particular section—eg. *Births*, and then look at the **Bold Face** pages listing within that record section. You will find the person you are looking for in addition to other information as that event was recorded.

The record order is:
> Marriages (pages 151-181)
> Baptisms (pages 282-321)
> Members (pages 361-386 and pages 426-427)
> Deaths (pages 462-512).

INDEX OF NAMES IN THE RECORDS OF
MARRIAGES, MEMBERS & COVENANTERS,
BAPTISMS, AND DEATHS

A

Adams, - - -, married - - - Maclstarm?, p. 181

Abbot, Daniel, deaths, p. 506

Abbot, Esther, married Charles Gilbert Singleton, p. 159

Adams, infant child of David Adams, deaths, p. 500

Adams, Abigail H., married Henry R. Williams, p. 164

Adams, Charles, baptism, p. 303

Adams, Charles R., married Catharine S. Holbrook, p. 179

Adams, David, married Jane Perkins, p. 169

Adams, Delia Woodward, married Roswell Emerson Messenger, p. 167

Adams, Elizabeth, member, p. 361

Adams, Elizabeth, widow, deaths, p. 463

Adams, Elizabeth H., married Isaac Taylor, p. 172

Adams, George, baptism, p. 306

Adams, Hannah Elizabeth, child of Phillip Adams, baptism, p. 289

Adams, Henry, married Mary D. Fitzgerald, p. 161

Adams, Henry Quincy, child of Henry & Mary D. Adams, baptism, p. 300

Adams, Jane, wife of David Adams, deaths, p. 502

Adams, Joanna P., married Elbridge Lakeman, p. 163

Adams, Joanna, wife of P. Adams, deaths, p. 468

Adams, Martha, deaths, p. 507

Adams, Mary, member, p. 382

Adams, Miss Mary, member, p. 376

Adams, Mrs. Mary D., member, p. 383

Adams, Mary P., married Thomas A. Williams, p. 169

Adams, Mary Pearson, child of Phillip & Joanna Adams, baptism, p. 286

Adams, Mary T., married Horatio N. Allen, p. 184

Adams, Philip, deaths, p. 504

Adams, Sarah C., married Ebenezer F. Gay, p. 167

Ainslie, George, married Martha Whitcomb, p. 151

Albert, Mary, married Cornelius A. Kelley, p. 169

Albree, John, married Nancy Shepherd, p. 161

Alger, Horatio, married Olive Augusta Fenno, p. 165

Alger, Rev. Horatio Sr., pastor of Chelsea Unitarian Church 1829-1844, p. 487

Alger, Rev. William R., pp. 385-6

Allen, infant child, deaths, p. 481

Allen, Amherst A., married Georgina M. Cook, p. 177

Allen, Horatio N., married Mary T. Adams, p. 184

Allen, Phebe, married William Perkins, p. 158

Allen, Phineas, baptism, p. 304

Allen, William Henry, baptism, p. 295

Ames, Mrs., deaths, p. 510

Ames, Mrs. Sarah Ann, baptism, p. 322, member, p. 385

Anderson, Mr., deaths, p. 510

Anderson, Joanna, deaths, pp. 495, 497

Anderson, Margaret, member, p. 382

Andrews, child of Joseph E. Andrews, deaths, p. 468

Andrews, infant child of J.[oseph] E. Andrews, deaths, p. 474

Andrews, infant child of Thomas Andrews, deaths, p. 485

Andrews, infant child of Jos[eph] Andrews, deaths, p. 487

Andrews, Agnes McKean Austin, child of Henry & S.[arah] P. Andrews, baptism, p. 302

Andrews, Almira, child of Joseph Ellis & Sarah Andrews, baptism, p. 286

Andrews, Henrietta Richmond, child of Henry & S.[arah] P. Andrews, baptism, p. 308

Andrews, Henry, married Sarah Parker Hill, p. 163

Andrews, James Babson, child of Thomas & J.[erusha] Andrews, baptism, p. 307

Andrews, Joseph E., covenant, p. 426

Andrews, Joseph Ellis, child of Joseph Ellis & Sarah Andrews, baptism, p. 286

Andrews, Joseph Ellis, child of Joseph E. & Sarah Andrews, baptism, p. 289

Andrews, Joseph Ellis, baptism, p. 286

Andrews, Joseph Winslow, child of Thomas & J.[erusha] Andrews, baptism, p. 308

Andrews, Margaret A. Hill, child of Henry & Sarah P. Andrews, baptism, p. 308

Andrews, Marianne, child of Thomas & Jerusha Andrews, baptism, p. 306

Andrews, Mary Elizabeth, child of Henry & Sarah P. Andrews, baptism, p. 303; deaths, p. 499

Andrews, Sarah, baptism, p. 286

Andrews, Sarah, married John Ellms, p. 156

Andrews, Sarah, covenant, p. 426

Andrews, Sarah Grace, child of Henry & S.[arah] P. Andrews, baptism, p. 305

Andrews, Sarah-Ann, child of Joseph Ellis & Sarah Andrews, baptism, p. 286

Andrews, Thomas, deaths, p. 504

Andrews, Thomas Franklin, child of Thomas & Jerusha Andrews, baptism, p. 306

Appleton, Martha, widow, deaths, p. 481

Appleton, William C., married Mary A. L. Smith, p. 173

Archbald, George, married Mary-Ann Pratt, p. 157

Armstrong, John H., married Mrs. Ann Stevens, p. 155

Arnold, Abigail R., married Elisha Wales, p. 161

Arnold, Charles, married Elizabeth H. Whalan, p. 162

Arnold, Charles, covenant, p. 427

Arnold, Charles Frederick, child of Samuel Arnold, baptism, p. 305

Arnold, E.[lizabeth] H., covenant, p. 427

Arnold, Elizabeth Whalen, child of Charles & E. H. Arnold, baptism, p. 297

Arnold, Emeline Phipps, child of Charles & Elizabeth Arnold, baptism, p. 301

Aspinwall, Mrs. Atlanta Matilda, baptism, p. 314

Aspinwall, Atalanta M., member, p. 382

Aspinwall, Miss Helen Elizabeth (Gerry), baptism, p. 314

Aspinwall, Samuel, married Atlanta Hill, p. 154

Aspinwall, Samuel, member, p. 378, 382

Aspinwall, Mrs. Samuel, member, p. 378

Atkins, child, of Isaiah Atkins, Jun., deaths, p. 463

Atkins, child of Capt. Isaac Atkins, deaths, p. 471

Atkins, infant child of Capt. H. Atkins, deaths, p. 465

Atkins, Ann-Fitz, child of Isaac & Sally Atkins, baptism, p. 289

Atkins, Captain, grandfather of John Quincy, deaths, p. 465

Atkins, Eliza, married Jacob Stone, p. 164

Atkins, Eliza, member, p. 371

Atkins, Helen A., member, p. 374

Atkins, Helena Augusta, child of Isaiah & Mercy Atkins, baptism, p. 287

Atkins, Henry, deaths, p. 487

Atkins, Henry Jun., member, p. 371

Atkins, Henry Sen., member, p. 371

Atkins, Capt. Isaiah, deaths, p. 498

Atkins, Isaiah S., member, p. 368; deaths, p. 469

Atkins, John West, child of Isaiah & Mercy Atkins, baptism, p. 282

Atkins, Lucy Goodwin, child of Isaac & Sally Atkins, baptism, p. 283

Atkins, Marcy, member, p. 368

Atkins, Margaret, child of Isaac & Sally Atkins, baptism, p. 286

Atkins, Martha, deaths, p. 487

Atkins, Mary, member, p. 361

Atkins, Mary, mother of Mrs. Trevett, deaths, p. 494

Atkins, Mary G., member, p. 371

Atkins, Nathaniel Goodwin, child of Isaac & Sally Atkins, baptism, pp. 287, 297

Atkins, Nathaniel Goodwin, child of Capt. I[saac] Atkins, deaths, p. 474

Atkins, Sally Goodwin, member, p. 363

Atkins, Sarah G., married Wm. Read, p. 163

Atkins, Sarah Spear, child of Isaiah & Mercy Atkins, baptism, p. 284

Atkins, Capt. Silas, deaths, p. 492

Atkins, Thomas G., deaths, p. 506

Atkins, Winifred, member, p. 366

Atkinson, Emily, child of William P. & S.[arah] C. Atkinson, baptism, p. 313

Atkinson, Francis Charles, child of William P. & Sarah C. Atkinson, baptism, p. 312

Atkinson, William Parsons, married Sarah Cabot Parkman, p. 172

Austin, Agnes, member, p. 377

Austin, Elizabeth D., married Joshua B. Fowle, p. 157

Austin, Israel Rust, deaths, p. 480

Austin, Joseph, married Agnes McKean, p. 162

Austin, Joseph, deaths, p. 502

Austin, Lydia, member, p. 361

Austin, Lydia, Miss, daughter of Joseph Austin, deaths, p. 474

Austin, Lydia, Mrs., wife of Joseph Austin, deaths, p. 474

Austin, Mary-Ann, married Elisha Parks, p. 151

Austin, Nathaniel, deaths, p. 468

Austin, Richard, married Mary P. Harris, p. 156

Austin, Sarah, member, p. 369; deaths, p. 505

Austin, Sarah, Miss, daughter of Joseph Austin, deaths, p. 473

Austin, William B., son of Joseph Austin, deaths, p. 471

Austin, William Bowles, baptism, p. 295

Averill, child, deaths, p. 463

Avery, James E., deaths, p. 462

Ayres, infant child, deaths, p. 479

B

Babb, Sarah B., married Amassa T. Wild, p. 156

Babson, Betsey J., married William G. Clark, p. 170

Babson, George Frederic, baptism, p. 304

Babson, Mrs. Jane, married Levi Younger, p. 165

Baccoon, Anna, member, p. 368

Backus, Thomas, deaths, p. 486

Bacon, Dresser, married Mehitable Tuttle, p. 169

Bacon, Thomas, baptism, p. 293

Bailey, Elizabeth, member, p. 362

Bailey, James, married Catharine More, p. 168

Bailey, John Fenno, child of Lewis & Sally Bailey, baptism, p. 295

Bailey, Joshua Moore, child of Lewis & Sally Bailey, baptism, p. 302

Bailey, Lewis, deaths, p. 491

Bailey, Lewis J., married Sally Fenno, p. 155; covenant, p. 427

Bailey, Margaret Augusta Fenno, child of Lewis & Sally Bailey, baptism, p. 302

Bailey, Margaret N., married William Fenno, p. 163

Bailey, Nancy Noror-wood, child of Lewis & Sally Bailey, baptism, p. 302

Bailey, Sally, covenant, p. 427

Baker, Mrs. (widow), deaths, p. 481

Baker, Mrs. (widow), deaths, p. 469

Baker, infant child of William Baker, deaths, p. 480

Baker, Augustus Parker, child of William & Susan Baker, baptism, p. 306

Baker, Charles Bradbury, child of William & Mary Baker, baptism, p. 292

Baker, Edward, deaths, p. 464

Baker, Edward H., son of William Baker, deaths, p. 492

Baker, Edward Henry, child of William & Susan Baker, baptism, p. 303

Baker, Edward O., deaths, p. 478

Baker, Elizabeth, married William Pike, p. 158

Baker, Gilbert Stewart, child of William & Mary Baker, baptism, p. 296

Baker, Louisa, married Nathaniel Hayward, p. 170

Baker, Sarah Elizabeth, child of William & Susan Baker, baptism, p. 295

Baker, Susan, child of William & Susan Baker, baptism, p. 291

Baker, Susan, baptism, p. 289

Baker, Susan, member, p. 369; covenant, p. 426

Baker, William, child of William & Susan Baker, baptism, p. 289

Baker, William, baptism, p. 289; covenant, p. 426; deaths, p. 494

Baker, William, married Susan Wilson, p. 154

Baldwin, Mary B., married George W. Banker, p. 183

Ball, Martha, child of Samuel & Martha Ball, baptism, p. 282

Ball, Martha, deaths, p. 471

Ball, Samuel, child of Samuel & Martha Ball, baptism, p. 285

Ballough, Samuel, baptism, p. 295

Bangs, Eleanor, deaths, p. 468

Bangs, Harriet Groves, child of Thomas G. & Eleanor Bangs, baptism, p. 283

Bangs, Mary Chamberlain, child of Thomas G. & Eleanor Bangs, baptism, p. 285

Bangs, Thomas G., married Elizabeth Ann Tucker, p. 159; deaths, p. 478

Banker, George W., married Mary B. Baldwin, p. 183

Bannister, infant child of J. Bannister, deaths, p. 464

Baptist, Anthony married Martha Lock, p. 161

Barber, child of J. Barber, deaths, p. 464

Barber, Henry Hutchinson, baptism, p. 306

Barber, John Knoar, baptism, p. 283; covenant, p. 426

Barber, Mary, married Charles Melander, p. 155

Barber, Nancy, wife of John K. Barber, deaths, p. 464

Barber, Nancy Paine, child of John Knoar & Nancy Paine Barber, baptism, p. 283

Barber, Nancy Paine, baptism, p. 283; covenant, p. 426

Barber, Samuel, deaths, p. 470

Barber, Susan P., Miss, deaths, p. 478

Barcolm, Andrew married Harriet Kittredge, p. 151

Barker, Joshua Eaton, baptism, p. 290

Barnacoat, Lucy Ann, married Aaron R. Cloues, p. 169

Barnecoat, child of William Barnacoat, deaths, p. 473

Barnecott, William Warren, son of William Barnecott, deaths, p. 470

Barnicott, Lucy, baptism, p. 286

Barnard, Mrs., deaths, p. 478

Barnes, Mrs., deaths, p. 509

Barnes, Bradley Tufts, infant child of Mrs. Barnes, deaths, p. 504

Barnes, Christiana, member, p. 382

Barnes, Eliza, member, p. 369

Barnes, Elizabeth, deaths, p. 473

Barnes, Harvey, married Harriet Gragg, p. 164

Barnes, Isaac Freeman Rowe, child of Thomas B. & Christiana Barnes, baptism, p. 314

Barnes, Mary, married Joseph Clark, p. 154

Barnes, Ruth, member, p. 369

Barnes, William H., married Elizabeth C. Hartt, p. 173

Barnett, Josiah M., married Lydia H. Wiswall, p. 156

Barnicoat, Edward W., married Augusta F. Stearns, p. 173

Barnicott, Lucy, member, p. 368

Barrett, infant child of S.[usan] P. Barrett, deaths, p. 494

Barrett, George Campbell, child of George C. & S.[usan] P. Barrett, baptism, p. 307

Barrett, George C., married Susan P. Chamberlain, p. 167; deaths, p. 493

Barrett, Isabelle T., married James Hobbs, p. 171

Barrett, Margaret, deaths, p. 487

Barrett, Ruth, member, p. 362

Barrett, Ruth (widow), deaths, p. 472

Barrett, Rev. Samuel, D. D., pastor of Twelfth Congregational Church, pp. 482, 491, 492, 498, 499, 503

Barrett, Susan Rebecca, child of [George C. &] Susan P. Barrett, baptism, p. 307

Barrett, Mrs. Susanna Payn, member, p. 375

Barstow, son of Jacob Barstow, deaths, p. 470

Barstow, Jacob, deaths, p. 481

Barstow, Lucy Abby, child of Nathaniel & Abby R. Barstow, baptism, p. 313

Barstow, Mary Elizabeth, child of Nathaniel & Abby R. Barstow, baptism, p. 313

Barstow, Sarah Richardson, child of Nathaniel & Abby R. Barstow, baptism, p. 313

Barstow, Thomas Emery, child of Jacob & Sarah Barstow, baptism, p. 285

Barstow, Thomas-Emery, child of Jacob & Sarah Barstow, baptism, p. 286

Bartlett, Mrs., member, p. 361

Bartlett, Elizabeth, deaths, p. 465

Bartlett, Henry, married Mrs. Elizabeth Gilbert, p. 152; deaths, p. 479

Bartlett, Lucy F., married George M. Washburn, p. 183

Bartlett, Lucy Faxon, member, p. 382

Bass, Moses, deaths, p. 465

Bassett, Frances E., married John D. W. Joy, p. 177

Bassett, Joseph, deaths, p. 505

Bassett, Mr. J., son of J. Bassett, deaths, p. 502

Bassett, Mary R., married Nathaniel G. Eliot, p. 172

Bassett, Susan M., married Joseph L. Holton, p. 181

Bastow, Nathaniel, married Abby R. Hammatt, p. 170

Batcheldor, infant child, deaths, p. 486

Bates, Ann Matilda, child of Martin & Susan Bates, baptism, p. 312

Bates, Caleb Francis, child of Martin & Susan Bates, baptism, p. 312

Bates, Caroline, child of Martin & Susan Bates, baptism, p. 312

Bates, Catharine, child of Martin & Susan Bates, baptism, p. 312

Bates, Charles Sweetser, child of Martin & Susan Bates, baptism, p. 312

Bates, Georgianna, child of Martin & Susan Bates, baptism, p. 312

Bates, Hosea, married Mrs. Susan Hunstable, p. 161

Bates, Jacob Astor, child of Martin Bates, deaths, p. 492

Bates, Jesse D., married Mary Elizabeth Fowle, p. 173

Bates, John, child of Martin & Susan Bates, baptism, p. 312

Bates, Jonathan, child of Martin & Susan Bates, baptism, p. 312

Bates, Joseph Sweetsor, child of Martin &

Susan Bates, baptism, p. 312

Bates, Mrs. Martin, member, p. 377, 381

Bates, Martin, child of Martin & Susan Bates, baptism, p. 312

Bates, Sarah, child of Martin & Susan Bates, baptism, p. 312

Bates, Mrs. Sarah, baptism, p. 312, member, p. 375

Bates, Susan Elizabeth, child of Martin & Susan Bates, baptism, p. 312

Bates, Susan Elizabeth, married Royal S. Warren, M. D., p. 175

Batie, Jane, married George Hardy, p. 175

Baxter, Abigail Wild, member, p. 364

Baxter, Charles, deaths, p. 474

Baxter, Ebenezer, deaths, p. 472

Beach, Amasa Jr., married Mary Jane Shepherd, p. 175

Beal, Ruth, married Charles Jennison, p. 153

Beals, John W., married Julia Rumney, p. 151

Bean, child of Horace Bean, deaths, p. 474

Bean, Mary, member, p. 362

Beateley, Mrs., deaths, p. 510

Beately, infant child, deaths, p. 493

Beatley, Elizabeth, deaths, p. 506

Beecher, Dr. = Rev. Edward Beecher, D. D., pastor of Salem Street Church (Congregational), son of Rev. Lyman Beecher, brother of Harriet Beecher Stowe and Henry Ward Beecher. p. 378

Beers, William, baptism, p. 291

Beers, William, baptism, p. 297

Belcher, Mrs., deaths, p. 465

Belcher, David, married Nancy Tippen, p. 151

Bell, Margaret, married Nathaniel Clark, p. 167

Bell, Mary, married Edward King, p. 152

Bellamy, William, married Ann Maria Dodd, p. 173

Benford, Albert, infant son, deaths, p. 508

Bennett, child of Cotton Bennett, deaths, p. 481

Benson, Laben, married Rhoda Gibson, p. 155

Bentley, infant child, deaths, p. 464

Berry, Arthur, married Mary Parr Taylor, p. 172

Bessy, Mrs., deaths, p. 510
Betteley, Albert Cabot, child of Albert & Mary Betteley, baptism, p. 316
Betteley, Charles, child of Albert & Mary Betteley, baptism, p. 316
Betteley, Frank, child of George W. Betteley, baptism, p. 317
Betteley, George Blanchard, child of George W. Betteley, baptism, p. 317
Betteley, Mary Jane, child of Albert & Mary Betteley, baptism, p. 316
Bigelow, Emma, member, p. 367
Bigelow, Maria, member, p. 366
Bigelow, Nancy, member, p. 366
Bignall, Frances Elizabeth, child of Bernard & H. Bignall, baptism, p. 288
Bignall, Harriet, covenant, p. 426
Bingham, James, married Eliza Pickett, p. 160
Bingham, John James, child of James & Eliza Bingham, baptism, p. 296
Bird, John Andrew, child of Jesse & Hephzibah Bird, baptism, p. 284
Bissett, Margaret, deaths, p. 511
Blake, Mr., deaths, p. 465
Blake, infant child of Edward Blake, Jun, deaths, p. 462
Blake, infant child of Nathaniel Blake, deaths, p. 474
Blake, Bridget, member, pp. 370, 373; covenant, p. 426
Blake, Bridget Shelton, wife of N. Blake, deaths, p. 483
Blake, Edward, child of Edward Blake, Jun., deaths, p. 462
Blake, Edward, Jun., member, p. 366; deaths, p. 465
Blake, Elizabeth Willard, child of Edward Blake, Jun., deaths, p. 462
Blake, Ellis Gray, married Sarah Blake Wiswall, p. 154
Blake, Hannah Tuckerman, child of Edward Blake, Jun., deaths, p. 462
Blake, John Doak, child of Nathaniel & Bridget Blake, baptism, p. 294
Blake, John Parkman, child of Edward Blake, Jun, deaths, p. 462
Blake, Nathaniel, married Bridget Shelton, p. 159
Blake, Nathaniel, covenant, p. 426

Blake, Sarah, member, p. 366
Blake, Sarah, wife of Ellis G. Blake, deaths, p. 471
Blake, Sarah, widow of Edward Blake, deaths, p. 502
Blake, Sarah R., married Charles P. Dexter, p. 159
Blake, Sarah R., member, p. 369
Blake, Susan, member, p. 371
Blake, Susan P., married Richard Robins, p. 171
Blanchard, Capt. Andrew, married Lydia Stanwood, p. 153
Blanchard, Joseph T., deaths, p. 472
Blanchard, Susan, deaths, p. 505
Blaney, William, married Sally Leach, p. 152
Blinn, Richard D., married Harriet Gragg, p. 163
Blodget, Hannah, married Joseph G. Spear, p. 153
Boardman, John, married Lydia White, p. 153
Bodge, Lydia, married Adam C. Goldback, p. 153
Boardman, Thomas, deaths, p. 479
Bond, George William, married Sophia A. May, p. 167
Bottomore, Thomas, deaths, p. 491
Bourne, Mary, married Seth Webber, p. 156
Bowen, Lucy, married Thomas Cooper, p. 163
Bowen, Lucy T., married Cato Prince, p. 161
Bowker, Francis Edwin, child of Edwin Bowker, baptism, p. 317
Bowker, James, married Charlotte Nottage, p. 175
Boyd, James Lawrence, baptism, p. 291
Boynton, Susan, married Alexander Brown, p. 166
Bradford, Charles R., married Miss Olivia Fowle (Morse), p. 176
Bradlee, Joanna, wife of J. Bradlee, deaths, p. 499
Bradley, Edwin, married Mary Jane Hammatt, p. 166
Bradshaw, Ann Rebecca, child of Samuel & E.[liza] Bradshaw, baptism, p. 303

Bradshaw, Benjamin Tuttle, child of Samuel & Eliza Bradshaw, baptism, p. 297

Bradshaw, Benjamin T., married Abby W. Eastman, p. 174

Bradshaw, Eliza T., wife of S. C. Bradshaw, deaths, p. 500

Bradshaw, Mary C., married Charles Jordan, p. 174

Bradshaw, Samuel Cook, child of Samuel C. & R. Bradshaw, baptism, p. 311

Bradshaw, Samuel C., married Rebecca Harris, p. 170

Bradshaw, Susanna (Mrs Jedediah Parker), member, p. 362

Bradshaw, Turell Tuttle, child of Samuel & E.[liza] Bradshaw, baptism, p. 303

Bray, Charlotte, Miss, deaths, p. 497

Bray, John, deaths, p. 482

Bray, Louisa, member, p. 374

Bray, Sarah, member, p. 366

Bray, Sarah, widow of John Bray, deaths, p. 498

Brazer, Mary (widow), deaths, p. 464

Breck, Hannah, member, p. 362

Breck, Hannah (widow) deaths, p. 475

Brenting, Charles Adams, baptism, p. 304

Bridge, Eliza, married William Grubb, p. 153

Bridge, Henry May, son of S. Bridge, deaths, p. 482

Bridgham, Mrs., deaths, p. 469

Briggs, Henry, deaths, p. 492

Briggs, Lucy Ella, daughter of Edward & Lucy Briggs, deaths, p. 506

Brockus, Mary, Miss, deaths, p. 487

Bromade, Benjamin H., deaths, p. 502

Brooks, Isaac, married Jane D. Francis, p. 171

Brooks, Jane D., deaths, p. 500

Brooks, Peter C., deaths, p. 503

Brown, infant child of James Brown, deaths, p. 474

Brown, Miss, deaths, p. 471

Brown, Abbie F., married Charles W. Longley, p. 183

Brown, Abigail, married John Mitchell, p. 151

Brown, Abigail H., married Alfred Fisher, p. 182

Brown, Albert Henry, child of Stephen &

Eliza Brown, baptism, p. 283

Brown, Alexander, married Susan Boynton, p. 166

Brown, Alvan, baptism, p. 307

Brown, Anna Maria, child of James & Mary Brown, baptism, p. 293

Brown, Caroline, child of James & Mary Brown, baptism, p. 289

Brown, Caroline, married Archibald Foster, p. 168

Brown, Caroline Elizabeth, child of Stephen & Eliza Brown, baptism, p. 283

Brown, Cecilia, married Thomas Cooper, p. 166

Brown, Edward, child of James & Mary Brown, baptism, p. 297

Brown, Eliza, member, p. 366

Brown, Mrs. Eliza, member, p. 377

Brown, Elizabeth, married Joseph Gardner, p. 163

Brown, Frederic Augustus, child of Stephen & Eliza Brown, baptism, p. 284

Brown, George Henry, child of George & Frances Brown, baptism, p. 315

Brown, Hannah, married Phineas Sprague, p. 156

Brown, Henry, child of James & Mary Brown, baptism, p. 287

Brown, James Orman, baptism, p. 302

Brown, John, married Harriet Potter, p. 157

Brown, John, married Cornelia Romana Susana Little, p. 159

Brown, John, member, p. 361

Brown, John William, child of George & Frances Brown, baptism, p. 315

Brown, Mary, member, p. 361

Brown, Mary Ann, married Nathaniel Colesworthy, p. 162

Brown, Mary Jane, child of Stephen & Eliza Brown, baptism, p. 287

Brown, Mary Jane, married M. Johnson Mandell, p. 172

Brown, Mary Susan, child of George & Frances Brown, baptism, p. 315

Brown, Rowena?, married James D. Mitchell, p. 181

Brown, Stephen, deaths, p. 503

Brown, Vernon, child of Stephen & Eliza Brown, baptism, p. 283

Brown, Vernon, married Susan H. A. Nash, p. 166

Brown, William, child of James & Mary Brown, baptism, p. 283

Browning, James, baptism, p. 307

Bruce, Abigail, deaths, p. 483

Bruce, Mary Blake, baptism, p. 288; member, pp. 369, 370

Bruce, Mary B., married Lewis Lyman, p. 157

Bruce, Sarah Blake, baptism, p. 294

Bryant, Francis, deaths, p. 486

Bucknam (Buckman), Ann Maria, married William W. Cole[s]worthy, p. 159

Bucknam, Charles Warren, baptism, p. 291

Bulfinch, Charles, deaths, p. 501

Bullard, Stephen A. H., baptism, p. 295

Bullock, Ebenezer Parsons, baptism, p. 291

Burbank, Mrs., deaths, p. 509

Burbeck, Elizabeth, deaths, p. 463

Burbeck, Henry, married Susan P. Hiler, p. 162

Burbeck, Susan Powers, child of Henry & Susan P. Burbeck, baptism, p. 301

Burbeck, Mrs. Susan Powers, baptism, p. 301

Burrell, Martha, member, p. 371

Burroughs, Harriet, granddaughter of Deacon John Simpkins, baptism, p. 301

Burrows, Betsey Fullerton, member, p. 363

Burrows, Mary Elizabeth, deaths, p. 502

Burrows, Sarah F., married John B. Tremere, p. 155

Bush, Ira, deaths, p. 462

Butler, Henry, married Judith Flancy, p. 155

Buxton, infant child, deaths, p. 482

C

Cade, Catharine, married Thomas L. Hutchinson, p. 153

Cade, Eliza H., married John W. Tuttle, p. 159

Cades, Ruth, member, p. 362

Cæsar, Jane, married Jefferson Didea, p. 166

Calder, George Henry, deaths, p. 501

Call, Jane, married Anthony Lebert, p. 162

Campbell, twin children, deaths, p. 502

Campbell, Alice B., wife of John Campbell, deaths, p. 502

Campbell, E., Mrs., deaths, p. 498

Campbell, John D., baptism, p. 303

Campbell, Mary, married Donald McClaskey, p. 177

Canterbury, Mrs., deaths, p. 507

Capen, Cordelia R., member, p. 383

Capen, Charles Gustavus Wells, child of Thomas W. & R. Capen, baptism, p. 318

Capen, Stoddard, deaths, p. 462

Capen, Thomas Wells, child of Thomas W. & C. R. Capen, baptism, p. 311

Capon, Thomas W., married Cordelia R. Wells, p. 172

Card, Mary, deaths, p. 463

Carnes, Edward, deaths, p. 506

Carnes, Edward, father of Elizabeth Young, deaths, p. 506

Carpenter, Daniel, baptism, p. 306

Carnes, Elizabeth, married James Young, p. 174

Carnes, Elizabeth F., member, p. 381

Carroll, James, married Mary Ann McDonough, p. 176

Carter, Albert, married Margaret Munroe, p. 176

Cathcart, Mary (Mrs. Hammatt), member, p. 362

Caziarc, Arthur Wheeler, child of Stephen & Maria L. S. Caziarc, baptism, p. 318

Caziarc, Louis Vasmer, child of Stephen & Maria L. S. Caziarc, baptism, p. 318

Caziarc, Mrs. M. L. S., member, p. 383

Caziarc, Maria Louisa Lusetta, baptism, p. 319

Cazneau, child of Andrew Cazneau, deaths, p. 486

Cazneau, Anna, member, p. 362

Cazneau, Anna, wife of I. Cazneau, deaths, p. 503

Cazneau, Elizabeth, member, p. 362; deaths, p. 475

Cazneau, Isaac, member, p. 361, 376; deaths, p. 504

Center, child of Mrs. E. M. Center, deaths, p. 500

Center, Eben, married Emily M.
Dickinson, p. 162

Cerminati, John, baptism, p. 293

Chamberlain, Edward Jun., married Ann
M. Powers, p. 167

Chamberlain, Hannah, member, p. 368

Chamberlain, Josiah Wilson, child of
Thomas & Susan Chamberlain, baptism,
p. 308

Chamberlain, Susan Ellen, child of
Thomas & Susan Chamberlain, baptism,
p. 304

Chamberlain, Susan P., married George
C. Barrett, p. 167

Chamberlain, Thomas, married Susan
Young   Hill, p. 164

Chamberlain, Thomas Edward, child of
Thomas & Susan Chamberlain, baptism,
p. 306

Chamberlain, unnamed child of Thomas
& Susan Chamberlain, baptism, p. 311

Chamberlain, Wheelwright, child of
Thomas & Susan Chamberlain, baptism,
p. 312

Chamberlin, Edward, deaths, p. 501

Chamberlin, Rebecca Page, member, p.
375

Chandler, Mr., deaths, p. 507, 509

Chandler, A., father of Rev. Joshua
Chandler, deaths, p. 488

Chandler, A., Mr., deaths, p. 490

Chandler, Abigail (Mrs. Robinson),
member, p. 362

Chandler, Emily, married Henry D.
Wolcott, p. 162

Chandler, Lucretia, member, p. 362

Channing, Eugene Giovanni, child of
W.[illiam] E.[llery] & E.[llen] K.[ilshaw
Fuller] Channing, baptism, p. 319

Channing, Rev. William Ellery, D. D.,
pastor of Federal Street Church, p. 497

Chapman, Rev. George, deaths, p. 491

Chase, Enoch M., married Mary Jane
Dunlap, p. 174

Chase, John H., married Eunice M.
Schoff, p. 183

Cheever, Henrietta, married Winslow L.
Knowles, p. 183

Cheever, Joshua, married Harriet Cutter,
p. 151

Cheney, Willson, married Permelia
Malcomb, p. 168

Childs, Mary, deaths, p. 498

Clap, Mrs., deaths, p. 469

Clapp, Helena, married Ezra F. Tirrell, p.
178

Clarke, infant child of James Clarke,
deaths, p. 471

Clark, infant child of Nathaniel Clark,
deaths, p. 472

Clark, infant child of Nathaniel Clark,
deaths, p. 480

Clark, Abby Ann, child of Nathaniel &
Elizabeth Clark, baptism, p. 293

Clark, Ann M., married George
Darracott, Jun., p. 169

Clark, Benjamin Jun., married Theresa E.
Ingalls, p. 160

Clark, Caroline, married Samuel E.
Holbrook, p. 166

Clark, Dixwell Homer, child of Nathaniel
Clark, baptism, p. 303

Clark, Elizabeth, member, p. 362, 367, 375

Clark, Elizabeth, Miss, deaths, p. 465

Clark, Elizabeth, wife of Nathaniel Clark,
deaths, p. 484

Clark, Elizabeth R., married Dexter W.
Wiswall, p. 170

Clark, Enoch James, child of Nathaniel &
Elizabeth Clark, baptism, pp. 292, 296

Clark, Frances Mehitable, child of
Nathaniel & Elizabeth Clark, baptism,
p. 290

Clark, George, married Hannah
Holbrook, p. 166

Clark, George Darracott, baptism, p. 311

Clark, George D., member, p. 375

Clark, Granville Mears, child of Mr., J.
Clark, deaths, p. 483

Clark, Harriet Mehitable, child of Joseph
& Mary Clark, baptism, p. 294

Clark, Henry J., married Mary G.
Holbrook, p. 178

Clark, James Henry, child of Nathaniel &
Elizabeth Clark, baptism, p. 297

Clarke, Mrs. James, member, p. 377

Clark, James N., married Mehitable Ford,
p. 183

Clark, John Dixwell, child of Nathaniel &
Elizabeth Clark, baptism, p. 300

Clark, Joseph, married Mary Barnes, p. 154

Clark, Joseph, member, p. 369

Clark, Julia M., married Eben Jordan, p. 174

Clark, Julia Maria, baptism, p. 311

Clark, Julia M., member, p. 375

Clark, Margaret, member, p. 373

Clark, Margaret, wife of N.[athaniel] Clark, deaths, p. 488, 490

Clark, Mary, member, p. 369

Clark, Mary E., daughter of N.[athaniel] Clark, deaths, p. 491

Clark, Mary Elizabeth, child of Nathaniel & Elizabeth Clark, baptism, p. 286

Clark, Mary Elizabeth, child of Joseph & Mary Clark, baptism, p. 288

Clark, Mary E. S., married A. H. Robinson, p. 166

Clark, Mary Jane, married Edward G. Lynes, p. 171

Clarke, Mehitable (Mrs. Hart), member, p. 362

Clarke, Nancy, deaths, p. 483

Clark, Nathaniel, married Margaret Bell, p. 167

Clark, Nathaniel, married Abigail Lane, p. 168

Clark, Nathaniel, member, p. 371

Clarke, Nathaniel Hill, child of Nathaniel & Elizabeth Clarke, baptism, p. 282

Clark, Sally, married Peter Seaver, p. 151

Clark, Sarah, married Oren Johnson, p. 166

Clark, Sarah, widow of Capt. J. Clark, deaths, p. 471

Clark, Sarah Daracott, child of Nathaniel & Elizabeth Clark, baptism, p. 288

Clark, Tabitha, member, p. 382

Clark, Thomas, married Mary Evens, p. 158

Clark, William A., married Mary A. Harris, p. 178

Clark, William D., married Eliza S. Mead, p. 170

Clarke, William Daracott, child of Nathaniel & Elizabeth Clarke, baptism, p. 284

Clark, William G., married Betsey J. Babson, p. 170

Clarke, William J., deaths, p. 509

Clark, William T., married Sarah A. Robinson, p. 178

Clinton, Henry W., married Susan B. Newell, p. 177

Cloase [*Clause], John, married Sarah Tatman, p. 165

Cloues, Aaron R., married Lucy Ann Barnacoat, p. 169

Clough, Moses, married Rhoda Jones, p. 151

Clough, Rebecca C., deaths, p. 469

Coates, Mrs., deaths, p. 501

Coates, Mr. J., deaths, p. 464

Cobb, Enos, married Eliza Weld, p. 152

Cobb, William D., married Hannah B. Hutchinson, p. 157

Coffin, Sarah Elizabeth, married Rev. Nathaniel Hall, p. 170

Cogswell, John, member, p. 361; deaths, p. 468

Cogswell, Sarah, deaths, p. 483

Cogswell, Sarah Lovering, Sarah, member, p. 362

Colbath, Charles W. B., deaths, p. 503

Colburn, Calvin, deaths, p. 491

Colburn, Mary, wife of Capt. James Colburn, deaths, p. 478

Colburn, Nancy, married Perry Cole, p. 157

Colburn, Mrs. S. C., deaths, p. 503

Cole, Mary-Ann, married Henry Thacker, p. 157

Cole, Perry, married Nancy Colburn, p. 157

Colesworthy, Ann Maria, baptism, p. 294

Colesworthy, Ann Maria, child of William W. & A[nn] M[aria] Colesworthy, baptism, p. 294

Colesworthy, A.[nn Maria], covenant, p. 427

Colesworthy, Anna M., wife of W. Colesworthy, deaths, p. 483

Colesworthy, Maria Penniman, child of Nathaniel & Mary-Ann Colesworthy, baptism, p. 300

Colesworthy, M.[ary Ann], covenant, p. 427

Colesworthy, Mary P., married William Knight, p. 157

Colesworthy, Nathaniel, married Mary Ann Brown, p. 162

Colesworthy, N.[athaniel], covenant, p. 427

Cole[s]worthy, William W., married Ann Maria Bucknam [Buckman], p. 159

Colesworthy, William W., covenant, p. 427

Colger, James, married Mary Ellen Fennelly, p. 172

Collamore, Charles G., child, p. 492

Collingridge, Sophia, married William Michael Cooper, p. 167

Collins, Ann, married John Lawless, p. 179

Colln, George, deaths, p. 501

Comey, Benjamin, married Nancy Howe, p. 165

Comey, Hannah, member, p. 366

Comey, Hannah, wife of Benjamin Comey, deaths, p. 482

Comey, Hannah Watts, child of Benjamin & Nancy Comey, baptism, p. 307

Comey, Harriet W., member, p. 378

Comey, Isabella Harris, child of Benjamin & Nancy Comey, baptism, p. 305

Comey, Isabel H., member, p. 378

Conant, Miss Mary, member, p. 362

Conant, Mrs. Mary, member, p. 362

Condon, Samuel, p. 386

Conery, John Quincy Adams, baptism, p. 291

Connor, Henry, married Elizabeth Lowe, p. 183

Converse, Alfred C., married Julia A. Woods   p. 180

Cook, Georgina M., married Amherst A. Allen, p. 177

Cook, Sarah Lizzie, baptism, p. 322

Cooke, McLaurin F., married Mary E. Moore, p. 179

Cooper, Mary, deaths, p. 498

Cooper, Thomas, married Lucy Bowen, p. 163

Cooper, Thomas, married Cecilia Brown, p. 166

Cooper, William Michael, married Sophia Collingridge, p. 167

Copeland, Emeline, married Henry Roaf, p. 159

Cordwell, Elizabeth, deaths, p. 502

Cordwell, Hannah, member, p. 362

Corlew, E., wife of E. J. S. Corlew, deaths, p. 481

Corlew, Elijah J. S., married Evelina Trott, p. 161

Cormier, Arthur Henry, child of Joseph H. & Eliza Cormier, baptism, p. 315

Corrigan, Andrew, married Elizabeth O'Dare, p. 173

Cosby, Alice Gray, child of Fortunatus & Ellen M. J. Cosby, baptism, p. 304

Cosby, Ellen Eliza, child of Fortunatus & Ellen M. J. Cosby, baptism, p. 304

Cosby, George Blake, child of Fortunatus & Ellen M. J. Cosby, baptism, p. 304

Cosby, Robert Todd, child of Fortunatus & Ellen M. J. Cosby, baptism, p. 304

Cotting, Amos, baptism, p. 294; covenant, p. 427

Cotting, Amos, married Harriet Tuttle, p. 160

Cotting, David Sears, child of Amos & Harriet Cotting, baptism, p. 297

Cotting, Ebenezer Francis, child of Amos & Harriet Cotting, baptism, p. 294

Cotting, Harriet, covenant, p. 427

Cutting, Henry, covenant, p. 427

Cotting, Mary-Ann Hammatt, child of William & A . S. Cotting, baptism, p. 305

Cotting, William, married Ann Sigourney Hammatt, p. 165

Cox, Susan S., married William P. Main, p. 155

Crane, Albert, married Abigail Maynard, p. 170

Crawford, Mary Jane, married John Gragg, p. 170

Crawley, Andrew Thomas, child of William & Mary E. Crawley, baptism, p. 317

Crawley, Catharine Louisa, child of William & Mary E. Crawley, baptism, p. 317

Crawley, Miss Elizabeth J., member, p. 384

Crawley, John Edward, child of William & Mary E. Crawley, baptism, p. 317

Crawley, William Henry, child of William & Mary E. Crawley, baptism, p. 317

Creamer, Ellen, married Joseph Francis, p. 162

Crocker, Ann B., covenant, p. 426;

Crocker, Ann B., wife of Thomas Crocker, deaths, p. 483

Crocker, Matthias, child of Thomas & Ann B. Crocker, baptism, p. 293

Crocker, Thomas, married Ann Boylston Trott, p. 158

Crosby, Mrs. Judith, married Henry Hutchinson, p. 166

Crosby, Otis, baptism, p. 296

Crosley, Heman, of Manchester, N. H., married Eveline Hill, of Newton, Mass., p. 171

Cross, Lois, married Peter Spiwood, p. 157

Cruft, infant child, deaths, p. 470

Cruft, Elizabeth, member, p. 370

Cruft, Hannah, member, p. 366; deaths, p. 480

Cruft, Sarah, wife of John Cruft, deaths, p. 494

Cummings, Mrs. Helen D., member, p. 382

Cummings, Thomas, married Rebecca J. Williston, p. 171

Curow, Jane, married James Gordon, p. 168

Curtis, Abigail Soal, married William Mills Jun., p. 151

Curtis, Eliza, married Thomas D. Francis, p. 159

Curtis, Francis, p. 386

Curtis, Margaret, married John Jones, p. 153

Curtis, Mary, widow of T. Curtis, deaths, p. 481

Curtis, Mary-Ann, married William Parsons Shelton, p. 153

Curtis, Sarah, deaths, p. 471

Curtis, Thomas, deaths, p. 468

Cushing, Abigail, deaths, p. 474

Cushing, Ann Eliza, married Ralph Webster, p. 158

Cushing, Bela, Mr., deaths, p. 462

Cushing, Elizabeth Margaret, married Isaac Hall, p. 167

Cushing, Ellison Baylies, child of Samuel A. & Caroline S. W. Cushing, baptism, p. 314

Cushing, Horace, married Rebecca A. S. Lewis, p. 174

Cushing, Mary (widow), deaths, p. 471

Cushing, Rebecca A. S., wife of Horace Cushing, deaths, p. 502

Cushing, Mrs. Samuel, member, p. 378

Cushing, Samuel Andrews, child of Samuel A. & Caroline S. W. Cushing, baptism, p. 314

Cushing, Sarah, married John G. Hall, p. 173

Cushing, Sarah B., wife of T.[homas] P.[arkman] Cushing, deaths, p. 475

Cushing, Thomas, baptism, p. 291

Cushing, Thomas Parkman, married Sarah B. Sigourney, p. 161

Cushing, Thomas Parkman, married Martha-Ann Sigourney, p. 165

Cushman, Mary-Ann, married Thomas Hendy, p. 155

Cutler, Mary, married George Geyer, p. 154

Cutter, daughter of Mr. & Mrs. Cutter, deaths, p. 506

Cutter, infant child of A. Cutter, Jun., deaths, p. 471

Cutter, Ammi Windship, child of Ammi & Hannah Cutter, baptism, p. 285

Cutter, Caroline, member, p. 370

Cutter, Caroline, Miss, [child of] A. Cutter, deaths, p. 483

Cutter, Charles Shaw, child of Edward & Ruth Cutter, baptism, p. 300

Cutter, Cordelia, child of Ammi & Hannah Cutter, baptism, p. 282

Cutter, Cornelia Torrey, child of Edward & Ruth Cutter, baptism, p. 287

Cutter, Edward, deaths, p. 494

Cutter, Esther L., married George B. Jones, p. 171

Cutter, Esther Lombard, child of Edward & Ruth Cutter, baptism, p. 292

Cutter, Eunice, member, p. 368; deaths, p. 464

Cutter, George Francis, child of Edward & Ruth Cutter, baptism, p. 289

Cutter, Hannah, member, p. 369

Cutter, Hannah, wife of Ammi Cutter, deaths, p. 493

Cutter, Harriet, married Joshua Cheever, p. 151

Cutter, John Adams Bates, child of Edward & Ruth Cutter, baptism, p. 296

Cutter, Samuel Nichels, child of Edward & Eunice Cutter, baptism, p. 285

Cutter, Samuel N., deaths, p. 497

Cutter, Sarah Ann, child of Edward & Eunice Cutter, baptism, p. 282

Cutter, Sarah Ann, member, p. 374

Cutter, Sarah Ann, Miss, deaths, p. 498

Cutter, Sidney Ammi, child of Hannah Cutter, baptism, p. 291

Cutter, Susan, married John Vannevar, p. 158

Cutter, Sydney, child of Ammi Cutter, deaths, p. 474

Cutting, infant child of Henry Cutting, deaths, p. 485

Cutting, infant child of H.[enry] Cutting, deaths, p. 493

Cutting, Harriet A., wife of Henry Cutting, deaths, p. 493

Cutting, Henry, married Harriet Ardelia Fenno, p. 163

Cutting, Henry Fenno, child of Henry & Harriet A. Cutting, baptism, p. 302

D

Dabney, Charles D., child of John & Sarah H. Dabney, baptism, p. 314

Dabney, John R., married Sarah H. Webster, p. 173

Dalton, Frances Elizabeth, child of H. L. & Mary Dalton, baptism, p. 318

Dalton, Mary Sophia, child of Henry L. & Mary Dalton, baptism, p. 321

Dana, Dexter, married Mary P. Eustis, p. 151

Danforth, Abigail, married Nathaniel S. Magoon, p. 152

Danforth, Hannah T., married Simon W. Robinson, p. 153

Daniels, infant child, deaths, p. 480

Darby, Ralph H., married Irene P. Harris, p. 178

Daricott, child of George Daricott, deaths, p. 462

Darracott, child of George Darracott, Jun., deaths, p. 498

Darracott, Ann Matilda, deaths, p. 501

Darracott, Elizabeth Clark, married Benjamin H. Greene, p. 165

Daracott, Frances Mehitable, child of George & Sarah Daracott, baptism, p. 286

Darracott, Frances Mehitable, child of George & Sarah Darracott, baptism, p. 304

Daracott, Franklin, child of George & Sarah Daracott, baptism, p. 290

Darracott, George, child of George, Jr. & Ann Matilda Darracott, baptism, p. 312

Daracott, George Jun., married Ann M. Clark, p. 169

Darracott, James Clark, child of George & Sally Daracott, baptism, p. 292

Darracott, James Clark, child of George Darracott, deaths, p. 475

Darracott, James Risdon, child of George & Sally Darracott, baptism, p. 297

Darracott, Lowell Blake, child of George & Sarah Darracott, baptism, p. 301; deaths, p. 482

Daracott, Mary Lowell, child of George & Sarah Daracott, baptism, p. 282

Darracott, Rebecca H., married Henry W. Fenno, p. 163

Daracott, Risdon, child of George & Sarah Daracott, baptism, p. 294

Darracott, Risdon, child of George Darracott, deaths, p. 475

Daracott, Rev. Risdon, p. 294

Darracott, Sally, member, p. 362

Darracott, Sarah C., married Joseph Nason, p. 172

Darracott, Sarah Clark, child of George & Sarah Darracott, baptism, p. 282

Darracott, Sarah Clark, child of George & Sarah Darracott, baptism, p. 284

Darracott, Sarah Nason, child of George, Jr. & Ann Matilda Darracott, baptism, p. 312

Daracott, William Earle, child of George & Sarah Daracott, baptism, p. 287

Darracoat, William E., son of George Darracoat, deaths, p. 494

Darby, Charles Franklin, child of Dr. Ralph Darby, baptism, p. 321

Darrow, Aaron L., married Ruthy Vinton, p. 151

Dodd, Julia, married Albert S. Pratt, p. 183

Dodd, Susan, daughter of T. Dodd, deaths, p. 492

Doddridge, Dr. Philip, p. 294

Dodge, Benjamin, married Rebecca Webb Howe, p. 167

Dodge, Henry U., married Eliza N. Jones, p. 168

Dole, child, deaths, p. 509

Dole, A. J., deaths, p. 505

Dolliver, James M., married Mary D. Gurney, p. 173

Dolliver, Mary D., deaths, p. 507

Dolliver, Thomas, baptism, p. 321; member, p. 384

Dolliver, Thomas H., married Maria B. Fenno, p. 164

Dominise, John, married Mary Jones, p. 161

Douglas, Sarah, member, p. 382

Downs, Mary H., member, p. 362

Draper, Edward, deaths, p. 484

Draper, Sarah L., deaths, p. 472

Drew, twin child of Sarah Drew (widow), deaths, p. 474

Drew, Merab Hutchins, child of John & Sarah Drew, baptism, p. 288

Drew, Sarah, member, p. 371

Drew, Sarah Snelling, child of John & Sarah Drew, baptism, p. 288

Drew, Sarah Snelling, member, p. 374

Drew, Susannah, member, p. 362; deaths, p. 492

Dudley, Rice, deaths, p. 508

Duff, Mr., deaths, p. 508

Duncan, James H., married Mary Willis, p. 162

Dunlap, Mary Jane, married Enoch M. Chase, p. 174

Dunkinsfield, William, married Nancy Guss, p. 152

Durant, Mary, married James Williams, p. 155

Dunham, E., Mr., deaths, p. 465

Dupee, Elizabeth, deaths, p. 463

Dutch, Henry Dawson, married Franscina M. Reed, p. 170

Dyer, Ruth, married Josiah Snow, p. 160

E

Eastman, Abby W., married Benjamin T. Bradshaw, p. 174

Eaton, Emily, married Leonard W. Spaulding, p. 161

Eaton, Prudence H., married Isaac Ward, p. 159

Eddy, Benjamin, child of Caleb Eddy, deaths, p. 472

Eddy, Mary Caroline, daughter of Caleb Eddy, deaths, p. 482

Edes, child of Capt. S. B. Edes, deaths, p. 462

Edes, Ann, child of Samuel & Mary S. Edes, baptism, p. 290

Edes, Betsey Green, member, p. 379, 381

Edes, Harriet Hill, child of Samuel B. & Elizabeth Edes, baptism, p. 282

Edes, John Eliot, child of Samuel & Mary S. Edes, baptism, p. 282

Edes, Larabee, member, p. 361

Edes, Larabbee, deaths, p. 472

Edes, Mary, member, p. 362

Edes, Mary S., member, p. 362

Edes, Mary, widow of Larabee Edes, deaths, p. 492

Edes, Sukey, member, p. 368

Edes, Susan, deaths, p. 501

Edes, Thomas, deaths, p. 499

Edgar, George Kirkpatrick, married Sally Nowell Jenks, p. 155

Edwards, infant child of E. P. Edwards, deaths, p. 485

Eliot, Rev. Andrew, D. D., p. 373

Eliot, Ann, member, p. 362

Eliot, Ann, widow of Dr. John Eliot, deaths, p. 499

Eliot, Anna, member, p. 362

Eliot, Anna, daughter of Rev. Dr. John Eliot, deaths, p. 502

Eliot, Charles Henry, child of George A. & Cordelia Eliot, baptism, p. 305

Eliot, Mrs. Cordelia, member, p. 372

Eliot, Elizabeth Langdon, member, p. 366

Eliot, Dr. Ephraim, son of Rev. Dr. A. Eliot, deaths, p. 480

Eliot, Elizabeth L., daughter of late, Rev. John Eliot, deaths, p. 483

Eliot, Rev. John, D. D., pp. 373, 469, 502

Eliot, George A., married Cordelia Howe, p. 163

Eliot, George Augustus, child of George A. & Cordelia Eliot, baptism, p. 303

Eliot, John Eliot, son of Rev. J. Eliot, deaths, p. 469

Eliot, Mary, member, p. 362

Eliot, Mary (Mrs. Joy), member, p. 362

Eliot, Mary, wife of Ephraim Eliot, deaths, p. 463

Eliot, Mary F., married Ezekiel Lincoln, p. 169

Eliot, Mary H., member, p. 374

Eliot, Nathaniel G., married Mary R. Bassett, p. 172

Eliot, Susanna (Mrs. Spooner), member, p. 362

Ellis, Miss Anna C., member, p. 384

Ellis, Rev. George Edward, D. D., pastor of Harvard Unitarian Church, Charlestown, p. 501

Ellis, Matthias, married Charlotte French, p. 166

Ellis, Matthew, deaths, p. 510

Ellis, Miss Sarah F., member, p. 384

Ellms, John, married Sarah Andrews, p. 156

Elroy, Matthew, married Bridget Feeney, p. 182

Emerson, infant child of William Emerson, deaths, p. 481

Emerson, Esther, child of Parker & Anna Emerson, baptism, p. 282

Emerson, George Walstein, child of George E. Emerson, baptism, p. 305

Emerson, Mary, child of Parker & Esther Emerson, baptism, p. 287

Emerson, Moses, married Eliza H. Pike, p. 153

Emerson, Rev. Ralph Waldo, pastor of the Second Church, pp. 164, 482, 483, 486, 487

Emerson, William, married Eliza Rogers Simpson, p. 158

Emery, Mrs. Mary, member, p. 377

Emery, Mary A., member, p. 381

Emery, Mary Adams, member, p. 370

Emery, Thomas K., deaths, p. 463

Emmons, Stephen, married Alice Silsby, p. 165

English, Charles Augustus, child of Nathaniel F. & Rebecca English, baptism, p. 314; deaths, p. 504

English, Charles Frederic, child of Nathaniel F. & Rebecca English, baptism, p. 315

Esculent, infant child of Mrs. C. Esculent, deaths, p. 491

Eunson ?, Caroline, only child of Mrs. Eunson, deaths, p. 471

Eunson, Mary (Mrs. Luce), member, p. 362

Eustis, Abigail, member, p. 366

Eustis, Abigail, widow of Joseph N. Eustis, deaths, p. 493

Eustis, Betsey, married Joseph Hart, p. 151

Eustis, Joseph, deaths, p. 486

Eustis, Mary P., married Dexter Dana, p. 151

Eustis, Sarah, married James Longley, p. 170

Evans, Eliza, married Titus Deetes, p. 161

Evens, Mary, married Thomas Clark, p. 158

Everett, Rufus H., married Susan J. Taft, p. 180

Everett, Thomas, deaths, p. 494

Ewer, James E., married Eliza Tilden, p. 166

F

Faguins, Adeline, married Daniel Low, p. 160

Falls, Maria A., married Otis Mann, p. 181

Farnsworth, child of Jacob & E.[lizabeth] Farnsworth, deaths, p. 465

Farnsworth, Abraham, baptism, p. 301

Farnsworth, Amos, M. D., married Mrs. Mary Webber, p. 160

Farnsworth, Amos, M.D., covenant, p. 427

Farnsworth, Amos Henry, child of Amos & Mary Farnsworth, baptism, p. 297

Farnsworth, Eliza West, child of Jacob & Elizabeth C. Farnsworth, baptism, p. 285

Farnsworth, Elizabeth C., covenant, p. 426

Farnsworth, Jacob, covenant, p. 426

Farnsworth, Mary Elizabeth, child of Amos & Mary Farnsworth, baptism, p. 294

Farnsworth, Sarah Riggs, child of Jacob & Elizabeth C. Farnsworth, baptism, p. 282

Farr, J., Miss, deaths, p. 471

Farrow, Susanna, deaths, p. 502

Farrow, William, married Susanna Stanton, p. 169

Faxon, Eunice, member, p. 366

Faxon, Eunice Maria, child of Nathaniel & Eunice Faxon, baptism, p. 282

Faxon, Francis Edwin, child of Nathaniel & Eunice Faxon, baptism, p. 282

Faxon, George Nathaniel, child of Nathaniel & Eunice Faxon, baptism, p. 282

Faxon, James Osmund, child of Nathaniel & Eunice Faxon, baptism, p. 282

Faxon, Nathaniel, member, p. 366

Faxon, Rachael, member, p. 371; deaths, p. 498

Feeney, Bridget, married Matthew Elroy, p. 182

Feeny, Mary, married Hans Peters, p. 182

Fennelly, Mary Ellen, married James Colger, p. 172

Fenno, Charlotte, member, p. 369

Fenno, Charlotte Augusta, child of John & Charlotte F. Fenno, baptism, p. 293

Fenno, Edward King, child of John & C.[harlotte] F. Fenno, baptism, p. 301

Fenno, Eliza, covenant, p. 427

Fenno, Eliza D., wife of Joseph Fenno, deaths, p. 487

Fenno, Emily Dommett, child of John & C.[harlotte] F. Fenno, baptism, p. 301

Fenno, Harriet Ardelia, married Henry Cutting, p. 163

Fenno, Harriet Cordelia, child of John & Charlotte Fenno, baptism, p. 295

Fenno, Henry W., married Rebecca H. Darracott, p. 163

Fenno, Henry W., member, p. 372

Fenno, John, member, p. 367

Fenno, Deacon John, deaths, p. 492

Fenno, John Jun., married Charlotte Frecker   p. 156

Fenno, John Jun., member, p. 369

Fenno, John Freeker, child of John & Charlotte Fenno, baptism, p. 291

Fenno, Joseph, covenant, p. 427

Fenno, Joseph Henry, child of Joseph & Eliza Fenno, baptism, p. 295

Fenno, Louisa Blake, child of Henry W. & R. H. Fenno, baptism, p. 303

Fenno, Maria B., married Thomas H. Dolliver, p. 164

Fenno, Martha, married Thomas Stowell, p. 167

Fenno, Olive, member, p. 367

Fenno, Olive Ann Catharine, child of John & C.[harlotte] F. Fenno, baptism, p. 301

Fenno, Olive Augusta, married Horatio Alger, p. 165

Fenno, Olive A., member, p. 372

Fenno, Rebecca H., member, p. 372

Fenno, Sally, married Lewis J. Bailey, p. 155

Fenno, Sarah Catharine, child of Mrs. Sybbel Fenno, baptism, p. 295

Fenno, Sarah Frances, child of Henry W. & R. H. Fenno, baptism, p. 302

Fenno, Sarah Matilda Jones, child of John & C.[harlotte] F. Fenno, baptism, p. 301

Fenno, William, married Margaret N. Bailey, p. 163

Fergus, William, married Frances A. Williams, p. 171

Ferguson, John, married Mary-Ann Wells, p. 169

Ferguson, Mrs. Mary A., member, p. 382

Ferrington, Nancy, married Henry Landerson, p. 163

Ferry, Hiram, married Mrs. Fannie G. Thompson, p. 182

Fessenden, Benjamin, member, p. 376, 380

Fessenden, Mrs. Benjamin, member, p. 376

Fessenden, Elizabeth Marietta, child of Benjamin & Elizabeth O. Fessenden, baptism, p. 313

Fessenden, Mrs. Elizabeth O., member, p. 381

Fessenden, Emily Frances, child of Benjamin & Elizabeth Orne Fessenden, baptism, p. 312

Fessenden, Hannah J., wife of B.[enjamin]

Fessenden, deaths, p. 498

Fessenden, Lucy Orne, child of Benjamin & Elizabeth Orne Fessenden, baptism, p. 313

Fessenden, William B., child of Benjamin & Hannah J. Fessenden, baptism, p. 308

Fessenden, William Benjamin, child of Mr. B. Fessenden, deaths, p. 503

Field, Ebenezer Hancock, child of Elisha & Meriam Field, baptism, p. 284

Field, Elisha, child of Elisha & Miriam Field, baptism, p. 287

Field, Miriam, deaths, p. 474

Fieldstad, Christian, married Emily C. French, p. 173

Fifield, Rebecca A., daughter of C. O. Fifield, deaths, p. 481

Fisher, Alfred, married Abigail H. Brown, p. 182

Fisher, Mrs. Emeline R., married William Parkman, p. 177

Fitch, Miss, deaths, p. 507

Fitzgerald, Mary D., married Henry Adams, p. 161

Flagg, Sophronia A., married Charles Partridge, p. 167

Flancy, Judith, married Henry Butler, p. 155

Floyd, Miss Eliza Frances, member, p. 385

Floyd, Elizabeth, member, p. 373

Floyd, Miss Elizabeth, member, p. 377

Floyd, Henry, member, p. 385

Floyd, Henry Augustus, baptism, p. 322

Floyd, Sarah (widow), deaths, p. 480

Floyd, Sarah A., married Gilbert F. Smith, p. 180

Ford, Mehitable, married James N. Clark, p. 183

Fosdick, Mrs., deaths, p. 468

Foss, Charlotte A., married John W. Hodges, p. 174

Foster, infant child of Joel Foster, deaths, p. 499

Foster, Dr., of Brighton, p. 478

Foster, Mr., deaths, p. 510

Foster, Ann Maria, married Francis W. Wetherbee, p. 177

Foster, Archibald, married Caroline Brown, p. 168

Foster, Charles, married Lydia Webb, p. 160

Foster, Deacon James, deaths, p. 479

Foster, James, deaths, p. 468

Foster, Sarah, child of Deacon J.[ames], Foster, deaths, p. 479

Fowle, Abby Frances, child of Henry & Mary Elizabeth Fowle, baptism, p. 313

Fowle, Abigail Bourne, child of William B. & M. A. Fowle, baptism, p. 293

Fowle, Charlotte Bray, child of Henry & Mary Elizabeth Fowle, baptism, p. 313

Fowle, Edward Gardiner, child of Henry & Mary Elizabeth Fowle, baptism, p. 313

Fowle, Eloisa Bourne, child of William B. & M[aria]-A. Fowle, baptism, p. 291

Fowle, Harriet Hunt, child of Henry & Mary Elizabeth Fowle, baptism, p. 313

Fowle, Henry, child of Henry & Mary Elizabeth Fowle, baptism, p. 292

Fowle, Henry, married Ruth Skimmer, p. 151

Fowle, Henry, deaths, p. 503

Fowle, Henry Jun., member, p. 367

Fowle, Joshua B., married Elizabeth D. Austin, p. 157

Fowle, Maria-Antoinette, child of William B. & Maria-A. Fowle, baptism, p. 289

Fowle, Mary, wife of Henry Fowle, deaths, p. 462

Fowle, Mary-Elizabeth, child of Henry & Mary Elizabeth Fowle, baptism, p. 289

Fowle, Mary Elizabeth, married Jesse D. Bates, p. 173

Fowle, Mary Elizabeth, member, p. 369

Fowle, Mary E., member, p. 377, 380

Fowle, Olivia, child of Henry & Mary Elizabeth Fowle, baptism, p. 295

Fowle, Olivia Kennedy, married Edward Winship Morse, p. 173

Fowle (Morse), Miss Olivia, married Charles R. Bradford, p. 176

Fowle, William Bentley, married Maria Antoinette Moulton p. 155

Fowle, William B., member, p. 367

Fracker, child of William Fracker, deaths, p. 491, 492

Fracker, George James Montgomery, child of George Fracker, baptism, p. 293

Fracker, George, member, p. 369

Fracker, John Tileston, married Nancy

Wood, p. 154

Fracker, Sarah, member, p. 363; deaths, p. 486

Fracker, Thomas, member, p. 361; deaths, p. 478

Francis, child of Nathaniel Francis, deaths, p. 465

Francis, Ann, child of Nathaniel & Eliza Francis, baptism, p. 289; deaths, p. 499

Francis, Charles, child of Nathaniel & Eliza Francis, baptism, p. 297

Francis, Eliza, child of Nathaniel & Eliza Francis, baptism, p. 289

Francis, Eliza, member, p. 370; covenant, p. 426 (twice)

Francis, Elizabeth U., married Levi Whitcomb, p. 154

Francis, George Hills, child of Nathaniel & E[liza] Francis, baptism, p. 291

Francis, Jane D., married Isaac Brooks, p. 171

Francis, John Wade, child of Thomas D. & Eliza Francis, baptism, p. 300

Francis, Joseph, married Ellen Creamer, p. 162

Francis, Mary, deaths, p. 501

Francis, Mary Jane, child of Thomas D. & Eliza Francis, baptism, p. 296

Francis, Mary Gendall, member, p. 363

Francis, Nathaniel, child of Nathaniel & Eliza Francis, baptism, p. 289

Francis, Nathaniel, member, p. 370; covenant, p. 426

Francis, Sarah Eliza Curtis, child of Thomas D. & Eliza Francis, baptism, p. 294

Francis, Tappan Eustis, child of Nathaniel & Eliza Francis, baptism, p. 294

Francis, Thomas D., married Eliza Curtis, p. 159

Francis, Thomas D., covenant, p. 426

Frecker, Charlotte, married John Fenno, Jun., p. 156

Frederickson, Adolph, married Sarah Russell, p. 158

Freeman, infant child of N.[athaniel] & C.[harlotte] Freeman, deaths, p. 471

Freeman, Miss [blank], deaths, p. 485

Freeman, Amasa Stetson, child of Nathaniel & Charlotte Freeman, baptism, p. 294

Freeman, Charlotte Rebecca, child of Nathaniel & Charlotte Freeman, baptism, p. 289

Freeman, Francis Parkman, child of Nathaniel & C.[harlotte] Freeman, baptism, p. 300

Freeman, Nathaniel Prentiss, child of Nathaniel & Charllotte Freeman, baptism, p. 287

French, Mr., deaths, p. 484

French, Adam, deaths, p. 472

French, Adam, Jun., deaths, p. 472

French, Benjamin, deaths, p. 471

French, Charlotte, married Matthias Ellis, p. 166

French, Dolly, married John F. Payson, p. 170

French, Dolly, widow of Adam French, deaths, p. 472

French, Emily C., married Christian Fieldstad, p. 173

French, Harriet Farrar, deaths, p. 505

French, Mary Allen, married William Howard, p. 159

Frost, Emeline, married William A. Kendrick, p. 176

Frost, E. R., p. 386

Frost, Walter Ingraham, child of Walter & Esther Frost, baptism, p. 297

Frothington, Mary Eliza, married Rev. Chandler Robbins, p. 167

Frothingham, Rev. Nathaniel L., D. D., pastor of First Congregational Church, pp. 289, 499

Frothingham, Nathaniel, deaths, p. 475

Fuller, Anna Cara, child of Eugene & Anna Eliza Fuller, baptism, p. 322

Fuller, Arthur Angelo, child of R.[ichard] F.[rederick] & S.[arah] K.[olloch] Fuller, baptism, p. 318;

Fuller, Arthur Angelo, deaths, p. 506

Fuller, Arthur B., member, p. 380

Fuller, Arthur Ossoli, child of A.[rthur] B.[uckminster] Fuller, baptism, p. 320

Fuller, Elizabeth G., wife of Arthur B. Fuller, deaths, p. 508

Fuller, Edith Davenport, child of A.[rthur] B.[uckminster] & E.[lizabeth] G. Fuller, baptism, p. 319

Fuller, Ellen Kilshaw, child of Eugene & Anna Eliza Fuller, baptism, p. 322

Fuller, Emily Rölker, child of William Henry & Frances E. Fuller, baptism, p. 322

Fuller, Julian, child of William Henry & Frances E. Fuller, baptism, p. 322

Fullerton, Betsey (Mrs. Burrows), member, p. 363

Fullerton, Mary Burrows, married William Thompson Jun, p. 152

Fulsom, Mrs., deaths, p. 510

G

Gale, Miss M. T., deaths, p. 500

Gannett, Anna, wife of Rev. Ezra S. Gannett, deaths, p. 502

Gannett, Rev. Ezra S., D. D., pastor of Federal Street Church, p. 498

Gardiner, George, deaths, p. 472

Gardiner, Sarah, widow of S. G. Gardiner, deaths, p. 473

Gardner, Hannah, married Benjamin Ticknor, p. 151

Gardner, Joseph, married Elizabeth Brown, p. 163

Garrett, J. Q. Adams, deaths, p. 485

Gassett, Catharine, married Andrew McMullen, p. 175

Gay, Ebenezer F., married Sarah C. Adams, p. 167

Gay, Frederick A., covenant, p. 426

Gay, Henry Bass, child of Frederick A. & Sarah A. E. Gay, baptism, p. 292

Gay, Sarah, covenant, p. 426

Gay, Sarah Ann, wife of Frederick A. Gay, deaths, p. 474

Gendall, Mary (Mrs. Francis), member, p. 363

Gerry, Helen A., wife of T. A. Gerry, deaths, p. 494

Gerry, Helen E., member, p. 378

Gerry, Hellen Elizabeth, married Samuel Smith, p. 177

Gerry, Samuel, married Sarah W. Newell, p. 154

Gerry, Sarah, baptism, p. 319

Geyer, Catharine Vannever, married Edward Tuttle, p. 152

Geyer, George, married Mary Cutler, p. 154

Gibson, Rhoda, married Laben Benson, p. 155

Gifford, Mrs. Perry, deaths, p. 510

Gilbert, Elizabeth, married Henry Bartlett, p. 152

Glossom, Agnes Eliza, baptism, p. 314

Gobleck, Robert Lyons, child of Adam & Ruth Gobleck, baptism, p. 283

Goddard, Mrs., deaths, p. 510

Goddard, Joseph, married Susan Snelling, p. 164

Godfrey, Nathaniel, deaths, p. 464

Goff, Eliza, deaths, p. 473

Golback, Adam, deaths, p. 465

Golbeck, Ruth, wife of Adam Golbeck, deaths, p. 462

Goldback, Adam C., married Lydia Bodge, p. 153

Goldthwait, Mrs., sister of Mrs. J. Doak, deaths, p. 501

Goodale, Julia E., married John F. Walker, p. 181

Gooding, Elizabeth, deaths, p. 503

Gooding, Elizabeth C., married Benjamin F. Snow, p. 170

Gooding, Samuel F., deaths, p. 504

Gooding, Thomas, deaths, p. 484

Goodman, James William, baptism, p. 296

Goodrich, child, deaths, p. 486

Goodspeed, Tabitha, married Sardine Stone, p. 168

Goodwin, Margaret, deaths, p. 498

Goodwin, Margarett Skillin, member, p. 364

Goodwin, Capt. Nathaniel, deaths, p. 465

Goodwin, Sally (Mrs. Isaac Atkins), member, p. 363

Goodwin, Thomas C., deaths, p. 473

Gookin, John M., married Lorinda C. Lash, p. 182

Gordon, James, married Mrs. Jane Curow, p. 168

Gordon, Joseph R., married Nancy Williams, p. 173

Gore, Ann-Maria, child of Christopher & Sally Gore, baptism, p. 292

Gore, Charles Thomas, child of Christopher & Sally Gore, baptism, p.

287; deaths, p. 494

Gore, Christopher, child of Christopher & Sally Gore, baptism, p. 284

Gore, Eliza Seaver, child of Christopher & Sally Gore, baptism, p. 289

Gore, Frances Hall, child of Christopher & Sally H. Gore, baptism, p. 295

Gore, John, deaths, p. 468

Gore, Mary-Ann Barker, child of Christopher & S[ally] Gore, baptism, p. 301

Gore, Sally H., wife of Christopher Gore, deaths, p. 498

Gore, Sarah W., daughter of Christopher Gore, deaths, p. 491

Gore, Theodore A., married Sarah A. Kiley, p. 170

Gorham, Mary, widow of N. Gorham, deaths, p. 479

Goss, Emery, deaths, p. 506

Goudy, Avery, baptism, p. 307

Gould, Jane A., married John Williams, p. 158

Gould, Lola Warren, baptism, p. 321

Gragg, infant child of John Gragg, deaths, p. 500

Gragg, Francis, son of Jacob Gragg, deaths, p. 482

Gragg, Harriet, married Harvey Barnes, p. 164

Gragg, Harriet, married Richard D. Blinn, p. 163

Gragg, Jacob, deaths, p. 473

Gragg, John, married Mary Jane Crawford, p. 170

Gragg, Mary-Ann, married David Townsend Jun, p. 168

Gragg, Sarah, married George Harris, p. 162

Gragg, Sarah, wife of Jacob Gragg, deaths, p. 480

Graham, Susanna Martha, married John Stockwell, p. 169

Grammar, Joseph, covenant, p. 426

Grammar, Nancy, covenant, p. 426

Grammar, Samuel Aspinwall, child of Joseph & Nancy Grammar, baptism, p. 295

Grammar, William Thomas, child of Joseph & Nancy Grammar, baptism, p. 292

Grammer, Rebecca, member, p. 363

Grasse, Susan, child, deaths, p. 510

Gray, child of J. Gray, deaths, p. 463

Gray, Elizabeth S., wife of Samuel C. Gray, deaths, p. 500

Gray, Rev. Frederick T., associated with Pitts Street Chapel, pp. 290, 501

Gray, Martha, member, p. 363

Gray, Peter, married Betsey Windship, p. 160

Green, George, married Mary Hiler, p. 172

Green, George, deaths, p. 501

Green, Mrs. J. W., member, p. 376

Green, John, deaths, p. 504

Greene, infant child of B.[enjamin] H. Greene, deaths, p. 493

Greene, Benjamin H., married Elizabeth Clark Darracott, p. 165

Greene, Benjamin H., member, p. 372

Greene, Benjamin Henderson, child of B.[enjamin] H. & E.[lizabeth] C. Greene, baptism, p. 307

Greene, David, deaths, p. 468

Greene, Elizabeth C., member, p. 372

Greene, George Francis, child of Benjamin H. & Elizabeth C. Greene, baptism, p. 305

Greene, John, married Mary Harvey, p. 163

Greene, Mary, deaths, p. 481

Greene, Mary L. Darrecott, child of Benjamin H. & E.[lizabeth] C. Greene, baptism, p. 308

Greene, Otis, married Sally Ann Hammatt, p. 171

Greene, Sarah, member, p. 363; deaths, p. 479

Greene, Sarah Elizabeth, child of Benjamin H. & Elizabeth C. Greene, baptism, p. 306

Greene, Rev. William B., married Anna B. Shaw, p. 173

Greenough, Jonathan, deaths, p. 484

Greenwood, Mr. [blank], deaths, p. 462

Greenwood, Charles, baptism, p. 291

Greenwood, Elizabeth, member, p. 366

Greenwood, Rev. Francis W. P., D. D. pastor of King's Chapel, p. 483

Greenwood, Frederick S., deaths, p. 471

Gregory, J., Mr., deaths, p. 464

Gregson, Isaac, married Nancy Nevers, p. 151

Grew, Henry, married Elizabeth P. Sturgis, p. 167

Gribbs, [blank], Mr., deaths, p. 493

Grover, Charles Shute, baptism, p. 291

Grubb, infant child of John Grubb, deaths, p. 484

Grubb, [blank], wife of William Grubb, deaths, p. 468

Grubb, Eliza, wife of William Grubb, Jun., deaths, p. 469

Grubb, John, married Adeline White, p. 160

Grubb, Sibbel, married Nathaniel H. Stevenson, p. 158

Grubb, William, married Eliza Bridge, p. 153

Grubb, William Francis, child of William & Sarah Grubb, baptism, p. 301

Grubb, William Jun., married Sarah Tuttle, p. 161

Grueby, Emma Frances, child of William H. Grueby, baptism, p. 317

Grueby, George Henry, child of William H. Grueby, baptism, p. 317

Gualt, Mary, married Samuel Lawrence, p. 162

Guliker, Jane, member, p. 363

Gulliker, Jane, deaths, p. 473

Gurney, Albert, married Sarah F. Dillaway, p. 173

Gurney, Albert, deaths, p. 501

Gurney, Betsey, wife of Henry Gurney, deaths, p. 501

Gurney, Catherine M., married George Savil, p. 174

Gurney, Eliza, Lewis Winde, p. 172

Gurney, Mary D., married James M. Dolliver, p. 173

Guss, Nancy, married William Dunkinsfield, p. 152

Gyles, Mercy, member, p. 363

H

Hague, Mr, perhaps Rev. William, pastor of First Baptist Church, p. 493

Hall, infant child of Jacob Hall, deaths, pp. 464, 480

Hale, Mrs., deaths, p. 509

Hall, Alonzo Ferdinand (Frederic), baptism, p. 304

Hall, Andrew Townsend, married Lydia Young Wells, p. 160

Hall, Ann, wife of Isaac Hall, deaths, p. 480

Hall, Caroline Wentworth, daughter of Jacob Hall, deaths, p. 484

Hall, Delia C., only child of E. F. Hall, deaths, p. 482

Hall, Eliza, member, p. 373

Hall, Eliza Tapley, married Robert Davis, p. 151

Hall, Miss Elizabeth W., member, p. 385

Hall, Harriet, wife of Rev. Edward B. Hall, deaths, p. 495, 497

Hall, Isaac, married Ann Payson, p. 161

Hall, Isaac, married Elizabeth Margaret Cushing, p. 167

Hall, Jacob, covenant, p. 426

Hall, Jacob, child of Jacob & Mary-Ann Hall, baptism, p. 288

Hall, Jacob, child of Jacob & Mary-Ann Hall, baptism, p. 291

Hall, John G., married Sarah Cushing, p. 173

Hall, John James, baptism, p. 295

Hall, John Webb, married Sarah Ann Priest, p. 167

Hall, Lizzie M., married John F. Payson Jr., p. 179

Hall, Maria S., married Gilbert Nurse, p. 161

Hall, Mary, member, p. 372

Hall, Miss Mary, deaths, p. 503

Hall, Mary, widow, deaths, p. 482

Hall, Mary-Ann, covenant, p. 426

Hall, Mary Elizabeth, child of Jacob & Mary-Ann Hall, baptism, p. 286

Hall, Mary Elizabeth, married Ephraim Lombard, p. 169

Hall, Mary Turner, deaths, p. 483

Hall, Rev. Nathaniel, married Sarah Elizabeth Coffin, p. 170

Hall, Samuel W., married Margaret B. Knowlton, p. 164

Hall, Sarah, widow of S. Hall, deaths, p. 502

Hall, Capt. Stephen, deaths, p. 487
Hall, Susanna, member, p. 363
Hall, Sylvia, deaths, p. 494
Hall, Timothy, member, p. 385
Ham, George Henry, baptism, p. 304
Hamilton, Amadella, baptism, p. 292;
covenant, p. 426
Hamilton, Clarissa Sherwood, child of
William Hamilton, baptism, p. 292
Hamilton, Mary, married William
Walkup, p. 170
Hamilton, William Robert Greer, child of
William Hamilton, baptism, p. 292
Hamilton, William, deaths, p. 472
Hamman, Hannah J., member, p. 367
Hammatt, child of William Hammatt,
deaths, p. 469
Hammatt, child of Mrs. J. Hammatt,
deaths, p. 471
Hammatt, Mr., grandson of Deacon J. B.
Hammatt, deaths, p. 507
Hammatt, Abby R., married Nathaniel
Bastow, p. 170
Hammatt, Abigail Parker, child of
William & Fanny Hammatt, baptism, p.
287
Hammatt, Abigail R., member, p. 373
Hammatt, Alfred, married Margaret S.
White, p. 171
Hammatt, Alfred, child of Charles &
Isabella Hammatt, baptism, p. 287
Hammatt, Andrew Sigourney, child of
Benjamin H. & M. Hammatt, baptism,
p. 306
Hammatt, Ann, member, p. 363
Hammatt, Ann Sigourney, married
William Cotting, p. 165
Hammatt, Augustus Francis, child of
Charles & Isabella Hammatt, baptism, p.
290
Hammatt, Benjamin, member, p. 365
Hammatt, Charles Edward, child of
Charles & Isabella Hammatt, baptism, p.
306
Hammatt, Charles H., deaths, p. 491
Hammatt, Edward Rumney, child of John
B. & Abigail Hammatt, baptism, p. 283
Hammatt, Edward Thornton, child of
Charles & Isabella Hammatt, baptism, p.
303; deaths, p. 486

Hammatt, Fanny, deaths, p. 486
Hammatt, George Frederick, child of
Charles & Is[abell]a Hammatt, baptism,
p. 301
Hammatt, Henry Hill, child of Charles &
Isabella Hammatt, baptism, p. 285
Hammatt, John B., member, p. 361, 380
Hammatt, Deacon J. B., p. 507
Hammatt, Joseph Thomas, child of
William & Fanny Hammatt, baptism, p.
282
Hammatt, Mary, member, p. 363
Hammatt, Mary Cathcart, member, p. 362
Hammatt, Mary Elizabeth, child of
Charles & Isabella Hammatt, baptism, p.
302; deaths, p. 486
Hammatt, Mary Jane, married Edwin
Bradley, p. 166
Hammatt, Nabby, member, pp. 363, 380
Hammatt, Sally Ann, married Otis
Greene, p. 171
Hammatt, Sally Ann, child of Charles &
Isabella Hammatt, baptism, p. 282
Hammatt, Samuel Parkman, child of
Charles & Isabella Hammatt, baptism, p.
292
Hammatt, Sarah, member, p. 363; deaths,
p. 463
Hammatt, Sarah A., married Lewis G.
Richardson, p. 172
Hammatt, William T., deaths, p. 469
Hammett, John B., member, p. 377
Hammett, Mrs. John B., member, p. 377
Hammond, Ann, married William
Spence, p. 169
Hammond, Hannah, married Scammell
Penniman, p. 161
Hannah, Charles, married Mrs Charlotte
Wilson, p. 167
Hannas?, Benjamin, deaths, p. 504
Hardy, George, married Jane Batie, p. 175
Harod, see Harrod
Harrington, Bowen, married Elizabeth P.
Ward, p. 167
Harrington, Charles Bowen, child of
Bowen & E.[lizabeth] P. Harrington,
baptism, p. 308
Harrington, Mary Ward, child of Bowen
& Elizabeth P. Harrington, baptism, p.
307

Heriott, Reuben R., married Sophia H. Howard, p. 171

Harris, infant child of Isaac Harris, deaths, p. 465

Harris, Anna, widow, deaths, p. 485

Harris, Charles Wellington, child of George & Phebe Harris, baptism, p. 317

Harris, Elizabeth, member, p. 363

Harris, Elizabeth, widow, deaths, p. 493

Harris, Elizabeth Kneeland, married Joseph N. Howe Jun, p. 159

Harris, George, married Sarah Gragg, p. 162

Harris, George, married Phebe A. Lyscom, p. 163

Harris, George, member, p. 382; deaths, pp. 507, 510

Harris, Mrs. George, member, p. 382

Harris, George Washington, child of George & P.[hebe] Harris, baptism, p. 304

Harris, Irene Putnam, baptism, p. 319

Harris, Irene P., married Ralph H. Darby, p. 178

Harris, Jacob Gragg, child of George & P.[hebe] Harris, baptism, p. 304; deaths, p. 491

Harris, Lucy A., married John P. Putnam, p. 174

Harris, Mary, deaths, p. 465

Harris, Mary Amanda, baptism, p. 319

Harris, Mary A., married William A. Clark, p. 178

Harris, Mary B., married Orramel H. Throop, p. 160

Harris, Mary P., married Richard Austin, p. 156

Harris, Mary Parker, member, p. 367

Harris, Rebecca, married Samuel C. Bradshaw, p. 170

Harris, Sarah, deaths, p. 474

Harris, Sarah, wife of George Harris, deaths, p. 481

Harris, Susanna, member, p. 366

Harris, Susanna K., baptism, p. 283

Harris, Major William, deaths, p. 475

Harod, infant child of N.[oah] Harod, deaths, p. 492

Harrod, Caroline Zoe, child of Noah & Zoe Harrod, baptism, p. 312

Harrod, Eliza R., married Samuel P. Oliver, p. 180

Harrod, Eliza Robinson, child of Noah & Zoe Harrod, baptism, p. 305

Harrod, Frances Eusebia, child of Noah & Zoe Harrod, baptism, p. 312

Harrod, George Henry, child of Noah & Zoe Harrod, baptism, p. 308

Harrod, Mary E., married Myron Shaw, p. 175

Harrod, Nancy S., married William A. Kruger, p. 175

Harrod, Noah, baptism, p. 316; member, p. 382

Harrod, Mrs. N.[oah], member, p. 382

Hart, child of Capt. J. Hart, deaths, pp. 469, 479

Hart, infant child of Joseph Hart, deaths, p. 465

Hart, Betsey, member, p. 367; deaths, p. 504

Hart, Elizabeth Clark, child of Joseph & Betsey Hart, baptism, pp. 284, 294

Hart, Harvey H., married Sophia Moore, p. 182

Hart, Joseph, married Betsey Eustis, p. 151

Hart, Joseph, deaths, p. 500

Hart, Joseph Clark, child of Joseph & Betsey Hart, baptism, p. 284

Hart, Maria Louisa, child of Joseph & Betsey Hart, baptism, p. 297

Hart, Mary Abigail, child of Joseph & Betsey Hart, baptism, p. 302

Hart, Mehitable Clarke, member, p. 362

Hart, Mehitable, deaths, p. 500

Hart, Sarah Ann, child of Joseph & Betsey Hart, baptism, p. 294

Hart, William, married Agnes Jones, p. 170

Hartshorn, Caleb, married Frances Hunt, p. 154

Hartt, Elizabeth C., married William H. Barnes, p. 173

Hartt, Mary Abigail, member, p. 375; deaths, p. 501

Hartt, Maria Louisa, daughter of Mrs. B. Hartt, deaths, p. 502

Hartwell, Eleazer D., married Eunice Woods, p. 169

Harvey, Mary, married John Greene, p. 163

Hastings, John M., baptism, p. 305

Haven, John, baptism, p. 295

Haven, Mrs. Percilla S., married Francis Stedman, p. 182

Hawkes, Lincoln Jun., married Sarah Webb, p. 157

Hayden, [unnamed], Mrs., deaths, p. 463

Hayden, child, deaths, p. 463

Hayden, infant child of Jos. Hayden, deaths, p. 483

Hayden, Alice Campbell, daughter of T. T. & Mary O., Hayden, deaths, p. 505

Hayden, John C., M. D., married Susan A. B. Williams, p. 169

Hayden, Mary Eliza, daughter of T. T. & M. O., Hayden, deaths, p. 505

Haydon, Alice Campbell, child of Thomas T. & Mary O. Haydon, baptism, p. 314

Hayes, John S., married Mrs. Augusta P. Nichols, p. 178

Haynes, Esther, deaths, pp. 488, 490

Hayward, Nathaniel, married Louisa Baker, p. 170

Hayward, Patty, widow, deaths, p. 471

Haywood, Abigail, member, p. 363

Haywood, Martha, member, p. 363

Hemmenway, William Henry, baptism, p. 295

Henderson, Edward, deaths, p. 462

Hendy, Thomas, married Mary-Ann Cushman, p. 155

Henry, Mrs., deaths, p. 478

Herriott, Sophia, wife of R. R. Herriott, deaths, p. 502

Hewes, Miss, deaths, p. 510

Hewes, Nancy, deaths, pp. 488, 490

Hewes, Mrs. Susan, baptism, p. 321; member, p. 384

Heywood, Reuben, married Dolly B. Wood, p. 156

Hildreth, Augustus, deaths, p. 493

Hildreth, Caroline, deaths, p. 478

Hiler, Mary, married George Green, p. 172

Hiler, Susan P., married Henry Burbeck, p. 162

Hill, child of David W. Hill, deaths, p. 492

Hill, Atlanta, married Samuel Aspinwall, p. 154

Hill, Eveline, of Newton, Mass,, married

Heman Crosley, of Manchester, N. H., p. 171

Hill, Grace, deaths, p. 479

Hill, Grace A., member, p. 368

Hill, Rebecca, member, p. 363; deaths, p. 463

Hill, Sarah, wife of Capt. Hill, deaths, p. 484

Hill, Sarah, wife of David W. Hill, deaths, p. 492

Hill, Sarah Parker, married Henry Andrews, p. 163

Hill, Sarah Parker, member, p. 369

Hill, Susan H., deaths, p. 493

Hill, Susan Young, married Thomas Chamberlain, p. 164

Hillman, Mehitable, deaths, p. 511

Hinckley, Edward David, p. 318; member, p. 382

Hobbes, Elizabeth, member, p. 375

Hobbes, Mrs. Elizabeth, member, p. 376

Hobbs, James, married Isabell T. Barrett, p. 171

Hodges, John W., married Charlotte A. Foss, p. 174

Hoffman, infant child of John Hoffman, deaths, p. 474

Hoffman, Harriet, wife of John B. Hoffman, baptism, p. 289

Hoffman, Harriet, covenant, p. 426

Hoffman, Harriet Malvina, child of John B. & Harriet Hoffman, baptism, p. 289

Hoffman, John B., covenant, p. 426

Holbrook, daughter of Mr. A. Holbrook, deaths, p. 468

Holbrook, infant child of S. Holbrook, deaths, p. 480

Holbrook, Asa, Mr., deaths, p. 487

Holbrook, Catharine S., married Charles R. Adams, p. 179

Holbrook, Catharine Smith, child of Jesse Holbrook, baptism, p. 319

Holbrook, Charles, married Nancy Oakman, p. 157

Holbrook, Charles Benjamin, child of Jesse Holbrook, baptism, p. 319

Holbrook, Miss Flora A., member, p. 384

Holbrook, Flora Alabama, child of Jesse Holbrook, baptism, p. 319

Holbrook, Frances Henrietta, child of

Jesse Holbrook, baptism, p. 319

Holbrook, Hannah, married George Clark, p. 166

Holbrook, Mary G., married Henry J. Clark, p. 178

Holbrook, Mary Young, child of Jesse Holbrook, baptism, p. 319

Holbrook, Samuel E., married Caroline Clark, p. 166

Holbrook, Sarah D., married Henry F. Spencer, p. 182

Holbrook, Sarah Dyer, child of Jesse Holbrook, baptism, p. 319

Holland, Rev. Frederick West, pastor of Third Congregational Society, East Cambridge, p. 512

Hollis, George Washington, p. 295

Holmes, Miss Martha Elizabeth, baptism, p. 321

Holmes, Miss Martha E., member, p. 384

Holt, Ann M., wife of Robert W. Holt, deaths, p. 486

Holt, Robert W., married Ann M. S. Jones, p. 164

Holt, William Proctor, baptism, p. 300

Holton, Joseph L., married Susan M. Bassett, p. 181

Hooper, Charlotte Augusta, deaths, p. 503

Hooper, Priscilla G., member, p. 382

Hooper, Priscilla Greenwood, member, p. 377

Hooton, Horace, only child of James Hooton, deaths, p. 487

Hopkins, Charles Haynes, baptism, p. 304

Hopkins, Joanna, covenant, p. 426

Hopkins, Joanna Cades, child of Nathaniel & Joanna Hopkins, baptism, p. 297

Hopkins, Nathaniel, covenant, p. 426

Hopkins, Nathaniel, child of Nathaniel & Joanna Hopkins, baptism, p. 294

Hopkins, Sterling Haynes, baptism, p. 304

Hosea, Mrs., [Mrs. Simpson?] deaths, p. 484

Hosea, Simpson B. [Hosea B. Simpson?], deaths, p. 474

Houghton, Warren, married Lydia Ann McKenney, p. 175

House, infant child, deaths, p. 482

House, Frederick Dacon, baptism, p. 306

Howard, Dorcas, married Henry Rasmasson, p. 151

Howard, Hannah, married Adam S. Ray, p. 162

Howard, Lucy, married James Madison Moore, p. 171

Howard, Mary, married Lawrence B. Johnson, p. 165

Howard, Mary Caroline, child of William Phillips & Caroline C. Howard, baptism, p. 316

Howard, Richard, married Hannah Waters, p. 158

Howard, Sophia H., married Reuben R. Herriott, p. 171

Howard, William Phillips, baptism, p. 316

Howard, William, married Mary Allen French, p. 159

Howard, William, deaths, p. 480

Howard, William Swift, child of William Phillips & Caroline C. Howard, baptism, p. 316

Howe, child of George Howe, deaths, pp. 480, 487

Howe, infant child of Isaac Howe, deaths, p. 463

Howe, infant child of Robert Howe, deaths, p. 485

Howe, Ann, member, p. 382

Howe, Ann Maria, child of Samuel & Eunice Howe, baptism, p. 291

Howe, Caroline, daughter of Samuel Howe, deaths, p. 472

Howe, Charles, deaths, p. 505

Howe, Cordelia, married George A. Eliot, p. 163

Howe, D. Sarah, daughter of William Howe, deaths, p. 482

Howe, Elizabeth K., covenant, p. 426

Howe, Elizabeth K., wife of Jos[eph] N. Howe, deaths, p. 482

Howe, Eunice Harriet, child of Samuel & Eunice Howe, baptism, p. 285

Howe, George Gustavus, child of William & Mary Howe, baptism, p. 285

Howe, Isaac Jun., member, p. 366

Howe, Isaac Cornelius, child of Isaac & Lydia B. Howe, baptism, p. 283

Howe, Isaac Gustavus, child of Isaac & Lydia B. Howe, baptism, p. 285

Howe, John, deaths, p. 481
Howe, Capt. John, deaths, p. 486
Howe, Jonathan, child of Samuel &
Eunice Howe, baptism, p. 282
Howe, Joseph N., covenant, p. 426
Howe, Joseph N. Jun., married Elizabeth
Kneeland Harris, p. 159
Howe, Lydia B., member, p. 366
Howe, Maria, married Alexander D.
McKinzie, p. 167
Howe, Martha Elizabeth, child of Joseph
N. & Elizabeth K. Howe, baptism, p. 294
Howe, Martha Lee, child of Samuel &
Eunice Howe, baptism, p. 303
Howe, Mary, member, p. 366
Howe, Nancy, married Benjamin Comey,
p. 165
Howe, Rebecca Webb, married Benjamin
Dodge, p. 167
Howe, Samuel, member, p. 361
Howe, Sarah Elizabeth, child of Samuel
& Eunice Howe, baptism, p. 288
Howe, Sarah T., married Horace P.
Moore, p. 161
Howe, Susanna, deaths, p. 487
Howe, William H., son of William Howe,
deaths, p. 481
Hudson, [blank], son of John Hudson,
deaths, p. 499
Hudson, Mrs. Benjamin, member, p. 376
Hudson, Eliza, daughter of John Hudson,
deaths, p. 485
Hudson, Elizabeth, member, p. 363;
deaths, p. 470
Hudson, Harriet, member, p. 371; deaths,
p. 504
Hudson, Lucy, wife of J.[ohn] Hudson,
deaths, p. 494
Hudson, Mary, child of John & Lucy
Hudson, baptism, p. 283
Hudson, Nancy, wife of H. Hudson,
deaths, p. 500
Hulin, Abram, married Joanna Ryan, p.
175
Hunstable, Nancy, married Manasseh
Knight, p. 164
Hunstable, Mrs Susan, married Hosea
Bates, p. 161
Huntstable, Susanna, member, p. 370
Hunstable, Thomas, deaths, p. 472

Hunt, [blank], widow of Samuel Hunt,
deaths, p. 492
Hunt, Frances, married Caleb Hartshorn,
p. 154
Hunter, Lucy, married John C. Neal, p.
174
Hunting, William Henry, child of Richard
& Margaret Hunting, baptism, p. 283
Huntington, Rev. Frederick D., pastor of
South Congregational Church, p. 506
Hurd, Jeremiah, married Mary McMellin,
p. 162
Hutchinson, infant child of Henry
Hutchinson, deaths, p. 491
Hutchinson, child of Thomas Hutchinson,
deaths, pp. 481, 487
Hutchinson, Catharine, member, p. 370;
covenant, p. 426
Hutchinson, Catharine Elizabeth, child
of Thomas L. & Catharine Hutchinson,
baptism, p. 292
Hutchinson, Charles Bright, child of
Thomas L. & Catharine Hutchinson,
baptism, p. 292
Hutchinson, Ebenezer, deaths, p. 479
Hutchinson, Emeline N., married
Abraham L. Stevens Jun, p. 165
Hutchinson, Hannah B., married William
D. Cobb, p. 157
Hutchinson, Henry, baptism, p. 282;
member, p. 366
Hutchinson, Henry, married Mrs. Judith
Crosby, p. 166
Hutchinson, Henry Jun., married Lavinia
Stevens, p. 164
Hutchinson, Henry-Blakely, child of
Thomas L. & Catharine Hutchinson,
baptism, p. 292
Hutchinson, Henry Bright, son of
T.[homas] L. Hutchinson, deaths, p. 480
Hutchinson, Isabella Maria, child of
Thomas L. & Catharine Hutchinson,
baptism, p. 295
Hutchinson, Lavinia, child of Henry
Hutchinson, deaths, p. 492
Hutchinson, Sarah Penniman, child of
Thomas & C.[atharine] Hutchinson,
baptism, p. 297
Hutchinson, Thomas, covenant, p. 426
Hutchinson, Thomas L., member, p. 371

Hutchinson, Thomas Albert Leach, child of T.[homas] L. & C.[atharine] Hutchinson, baptism, p. 301
Hutchinson, Thomas L., married Catharine Cade, p. 153

I

Ingalls, Theresa E., married Benjamin Clark Jun, p. 160
Ingals, Abigail, married Walter Miles, p. 163

J

Jacobs, George, married Rebecca L. Jones, p. 161
James, infant child of John James, deaths, p. 462
Jarvis, [blank], Mrs., deaths, p. 493
Jenkins, Sarah, deaths, p. 492
Jenkins, Susan, married Thomas Lyford, p. 166
Jenks, Sally Nowell, married George Kirkpatrick Edgar, p. 155
Jennings, Mrs. Martha, baptism, p. 321; member, p. 384
Jennison, Charles, married Ruth Beal, p. 153
Jepson, Mary, member, p. 367; deaths, p. 468
Jobic, infant son of Dr. Jobic, deaths, p. 506
Johnson, Isabella, member, p. 368
Johnson, Lawrence B., married Mary Howard, p. 165
Johnson, Joseph, married Sarah Palmer, p. 152
Johnson, Oren, married Sarah Clark, p. 166
Johnson, William, deaths, p. 481
Jones, [blank] Mrs., deaths, p. 493
Jones, infant child, deaths, p. 500
Jones, Agnes, child of Owen & Elizabeth Jones, baptism, p. 284
Jones, Agnes, married William Hart, p. 170
Jones, Ann M. S., married Robert W. Holt, p. 164
Jones, Benjamin C., baptism, p. 303

Jones, Catharine P., married Levi Younger, p. 153
Jones, Daniel, deaths, p. 484
Jones, Eliza N., married Henry U. Dodge, p. 168
Jones, Elizabeth, married George Lewis, p. 152
Jones, Elizabeth, wife of Owen Jones, deaths, p. 491
Jones, George B., married Esther L. Cutter, p. 171
Jones, Hans, married Elizabeth Doble, p. 165
Jones, John, married Margaret Curtis, p. 153
Jones, John Eliot, child of Owen & Elizabeth Jones, baptism, p. 282; deaths, p. 462
Jones, Robert, married Margaret Owens, p. 172
Jones, Sally D., married Enoch H. Snelling, p. 152
Jones, Thomas L., deaths, p. 485
Jordan, Charles, married Mary C. Bradshaw, p. 174
Jordan, Eben, married Julia M. Clark, p. 174
Jordan, Ellen, married John Tompson, p. 175
Jordan, James Clark, child of Eben D. & Julia M. Jordan, baptism, p. 317
Jordan, Mrs. Julia, member, p. 377
Jordan, Julia M., member, p. 381
Jordan, Walter, child of Eben D. & Julia M. Jordan, baptism, p. 317; deaths, p. 506
Josselyn, infant child, deaths, p. 488, 490
Joy, John D. W., married Frances E. Bassett, p. 177
Joy, Mary Eliot, member, p. 362

K

Kahler, Jeremiah, deaths, p. 481
Keen, Lewis, married Caroline E. Tuttle, p. 171
Keith, Martha Elizabeth, child of M. E. Keith, baptism, p. 323
Keith, Mrs. Sarah E., member, p. 385
Kell, Elizabeth James, child of John & Mary Kell, baptism, p. 317

Kell, Mary Elizabeth, child of John &
Mary Kell, baptism, p. 317
Kelley, Cornelius A., married Mary
Albert, p. 169
Kellogg, Richard K., married Caroline A.
Leach, p. 162
Kelton, Elisha, baptism, p. 307
Kemp, infant child, deaths, p. 484
Kemp, William, married Nancy Atwood
Rider, p. 158
Kemp, William P., deaths, p. 503
Kendall, Thomas, married Lydia H.
Singleton, p. 154
Kendrick, John, deaths, p. 491
Kendrick, William A., married Emeline
Frost, p. 176
Kettell, infant child, deaths, p. 479
Kettell, Charlotte, member, p. 367
Kettell, James, married Sarah Payne, p.
151
Kettell, Deacon Joseph, member, p. 361;
deaths, p. 463
Kettell, Maria, member, p. 367
Kettell, Rebecca, member, p. 363; deaths,
p. 475
Kilburn, Adeline, wife of George H.,
Kilburn, deaths, p. 498
Kiley, Sarah A., married Theodore A.
Gore, p. 170
King, Mrs., deaths, p. 510
King, Edward, married Mary Bell, p. 152
King, Isaiah, deaths, p. 504
King, Lydia, deaths, p. 472
Kittredge, Harriet, married Andrew
Barcolm, p. 151
Knight, child, deaths, p. 475
Knight, Charles, deaths, p. 483
Knight, Manasseh, married Nancy
Hunstable, p. 164
Knight, William, married Mary P.
Colesworthy, p. 157
Knowles, Miss, deaths, p. 507
Knowles, Winslow L., married Henrietta
Cheever, p. 183
Knoulton, Margarett, member, p. 363
Knowlton, John, married Sally Adams
Knowlton, p. 156
Knowlton, Margaret B., married Samuel
W. Hall, p. 164
Knowlton, Sally Adams, married John

Knowlton, p. 156
Knox, Mary, member, p. 363
Krogman, Mary Ella, deaths, p. 504
Kruger, Austain Hewes, baptism, p. 314
Kruger, Caroline, deaths, p. 504
Kruger, William A., married Nancy S.
Harrod, p. 175
Krugman, Frank Walter, child of S. R. &
Mary Ann Krugman, baptism, p. 318
Krugman, George Albert, child of S. R. &
Mary Ann Krugman, baptism, p. 318
Krugman, Mary Ann, baptism, p. 318

L

Lakeman, Elbridge, married Joanna P.
Adams, p. 163
Lakeman, Elbridge, deaths, p. 493
Lakeman, Mrs. Joanna, member, p. 376,
382
Lambard, Hannah, member, p. 368
Lambert, Abigail, member, p. 370
Lambert, Charles S., married Sophia A.
Lambert, p. 178
Lambert, Eliza A., married George P.
Milne, p. 166
Lambert, Elizabeth, deaths, p. 485
Lambert, Hanna, deaths, p. 482
Lambert, Mary, member, p. 363
Lambert, Sophia A., married Charles S.
Lambert, p. 178
Lampec, Catharine M., married Grant
Learned Jr., p. 181
Lamprell, Joseph P., deaths, p. 486
Lamson, Benjamin, child of Benjamin &
Henrietta Lamson, baptism, p. 287
Lamson, Benjamin, member, p. 380;
covenant, p. 426
Lamson, Mrs. Benjamin, member, p. 377
Lamson, Henrietta, member, p. 368;
covenant, p. 426
Lamson, Mrs. Henrietta, baptism, p. 284
Lamson, Sarah, child of Benjamin &
Henrietta Lamson, baptism, p. 284
Lamson, Sarah, member, p. 373
Landerson, Henry, married Nancy
Ferrington, p. 163
Lane, Abigail, married Nathaniel Clark,
p. 168
Lane, Simon Peter Fish, son of T. Lane,
deaths, p. 483

Larson, deaths, p. 509

Lasell, William, married Sarah M. Peabody, p. 173

Lash, infant child of Robert Lash, deaths, p. 465

Lash, Charlotte, married John Sawin, p. 162

Lash, Eliza Wild, child of Robert & Susan C. Lash, baptism, p. 285

Lash, Harriet Wild, child of Robert & Susan C. Lash, baptism, p. 288

Lash, Harriet Wild, member, p. 374

Lash, Harriet W., daughter of Robert Lash, deaths, p. 498

Lash, Laura O., deaths, p. 505

Lash, Lorinda C., married John M. Gookin, p. 182

Lash, Mary, deaths, p. 464

Lash, Rebecca S., member, p. 372, 377

Lash, Robert, member, p. 377, 380

Lash, Robert Jr., member, p. 361

Lash, Susan C., member, p. 368, 380

Lash, Susan R., member, p. 372

Lash, Susan Rand, member, p. 377

Lathrop, child of Margaret Lathrop, deaths, p. 507

Lathrop, Rev. John, D. D., pastor of the Second Church, p. 462

Laughton, Mary, deaths, p. 462

Lawless, John, married Ann Collins, p. 179

Lawrence, Abbot, child of Abbot Lawrence, deaths, p. 479

Lawrence, Samuel, married Mary Gualt, p. 162

Lawson, deaths, p. 509

Lawson, Louisa Zeporah, baptism, p. 321

Lawson, unnamed child, baptism, p. 322

Leach, Caroline A., married Richard K. Kellogg, p. 162

Leach, Desire, wife of Thomas Leach, deaths, p. 472

Leach, Frederick W., member, p. 386

Leach, Phoebe, married Samuel Leach, p. 151

Leach, Sally, married William Blaney, p. 152

Leach, Samuel, married Phoebe Leach, p. 151

Leach, Sarah, baptism, p. 305; member, p. 372; deaths, p. 500

Leach, Sophia Charlotte, married Elisha Webb, p. 156

Lear, Mrs. Margaret, married George Wistar, p. 183

Learned, Grant, Jr., married Catharine M. Lampec, p. 181

Leate, Mary, deaths, p. 471

Leate, William, deaths, p. 469

Leavitt, child of Charles B. & Emma D. Leavitt, deaths, p. 511

Leavitt, Abigail W., wife of Benson Leavitt, deaths, p. 505

Leavitt, Charles B., married Emma D. Stearns, p. 177

Leavitt, James Aiken, child of Mr. B. Leavitt, deaths, p. 502

Lebert, Anthony, married Jane Call, p. 162

Lee, John, married Laura W. Jones, p. 162; deaths, p. 494

Leeds, Daniel Davenport, child of Thomas & Sarah Leeds, baptism, p. 288

Leeds, Eliza Ann, married George H. Dodd, p. 179

Leeds, Henry Jr., married Melissa Amanda Nash, p. 184

Leeds, James B., married Helen R. Peters, p. 171

Leeds, James Blake, child of Thomas & Sarah Leeds, baptism, p. 288

Leeds, Lyman, baptism, p. 321

Leeds, Lyman, member, p. 384

Leeds, Martha Hall, deaths, p. 504

Leeds, Mary, member, p. 383

Leeds, Sarah Elizabeth, child of Thomas & Sarah Leeds, baptism, p. 288

Leeds, Thomas, child of Sally Leeds, baptism, p. 302

Leeds, Thomas, deaths, p. 483

Leseur, Joseph Addison, married Frances Wilkinson, p. 172

Levear, Hannah B., married John D. Silver, p. 162

Lewis, child of Joseph Lewis, deaths, p. 484

Lewis, infant child of Mr. J. Lewis, deaths, p. 468

Lewis, Elizabeth, covenant, p. 426

Lewis, George, covenant, p. 426

Lewis, George, married Elizabeth Jones, p. 152

Lewis, Hannah, married John Williams, p. 156

Lewis, John, deaths, p. 472

Lewis, Joseph, married Adeline Williams, p. 174

Lewis, Joseph Kettell, deaths, p. 500

Lewis, Josiah Quincy, child of Joseph & S. Lewis, baptism, p. 286

Lewis, Rebecca A. S., married Horace Cushing, p. 174

Lewis, Rebecca-Ann, child of George & Elizabeth Lewis, baptism, p. 286

Lewis, Sibellar, wife of Joseph Lewis, deaths, p. 464

Lewis, Silas, baptism, p. 291

Leynes, Catharine Clark, child of Edward & Mary Jane Leynes, baptism, p. 313

Lillie, [unnamed] wife of Daniel Lillie, deaths, p. 468

Lillie, child of Daniel Lillie, deaths, p. 484

Lillie, Abiah Page, married Samuel Low, p. 152

Lillie, Abigail Carnes, child of Thomas & Hannah Lillie, baptism, p. 285

Lillie, Daniel, son of Thomas Lillie, deaths, p. 502

Lillie, Daniel W., member, p. 378

Lillie, Mrs. Daniel W., member, p. 378

Lillie, Hannah, member, p. 363; deaths, p. 471

Lillie, Hannah, daughter of T.[homas ?] Lillie, deaths, p. 492

Lilly, Joel R., deaths, p. 491

Lillie, John Eliot, child of Thomas & Hannah Lillie, baptism, p. 283

Lillie, Rebecca, deaths, p. 494

Lillie, Sarah, wife of Thomas Lillie, deaths, p. 500

Lillie, Sarah, daughter of T.[homas?] Lillie, deaths, p. 475

Lillie, Susanna, member, p. 363; deaths, p. 464

Lillie, Theodore, baptism, p. 297

Lillie, Thomas, member, p. 367

Lillie, Thomas Page, child of Daniel & Nancy Lillie, baptism, p. 283

Lincoln, child of Noah Lincoln, deaths, p. 471

Lincoln, infant child, deaths, p. 492

Lincoln, Ann, wife of Warren Lincoln, baptism, p. 304

Lincoln, Ann, member, p. 372

Lincoln, Ann Maria, child of Warren & A[nn] Lincoln, baptism, p. 304

Lincoln, Augusta B., daughter of B. Lincoln, deaths, p. 481

Lincoln, Beza, member, p. 371, 380

Lincoln, Caroline Parker, child of Warren & A[nn] Lincoln, baptism, p. 304

Lincoln, Caroline P., child of Warren Lincoln, deaths, p. 487

Lincoln, Catharine Wild, child of Charles & Martha B. Lincoln, baptism, p. 303

Lincoln, Charles, member, p. 377;

Lincoln, Charles, covenant, p. 426

Lincoln, Mrs. Charles, member, p. 377, 381

Lincoln, Charles Nathaniel Minott, child of Charles & M. B. Lincoln, baptism, p. 293

Lincoln, Elijah, deaths, p. 475

Lincoln, Eliza, member, p. 371; covenant, p. 426

Lincoln, Evelina Barry, child of Warren & Ann Lincoln, baptism, p. 308

Lincoln, Ezekiel, married Mary F. Eliot, p. 169

Lincoln, Harriet Roby, child of Oliver & H.[arriet] R. Lincoln, baptism, p. 304

Lincoln, Harriet R., wife of Oliver Lincoln, deaths, p. 486

Lincoln, Henry Barry, child of Charles & Martha B. Lincoln, baptism, p. 303

Lincoln, Henry Nichols, child of Elijah & Mary Lincoln, baptism, p. 292

Lincoln, Henry N., child of E.[lijah] Lincoln, deaths, p. 474

Lincoln, Joshua, deaths, p. 479

Lincoln, M.[artha] B., covenant, p. 426

Lincoln, Martha Elizabeth, child of Charles & Martha B. Lincoln, baptism, p. 294

Lincoln, Mary, married Josiah Peirce, p. 152

Lincoln, Mary, member, pp. 367, 370; covenant, p. 426; deaths, p. 494

Lincoln, Mary, wife of Charles Lincoln, deaths, p. 485

Lincoln, Mary Eliza, child of Warren & Ann Lincoln, baptism, p. 311

Lincoln, Mary Elizabeth, child of Elijah & Mary Lincoln, baptism, p. 292

Lincoln, Mrs. Mary M., member, p. 371

Lincoln, Noah, deaths, p. 509

Lincoln, Oliver, member, p. 372

Lincoln, Oliver Fessenden, child of Oliver & Harriet R. Lincoln, baptism, p. 303

Lincoln, Sarah Minott, child of Charles & Martha B. Lincoln, baptism, p. 303

Lincoln, Sarah Winslow Copeland, child of Elijah & Mary Lincoln, baptism, p. 295

Lincoln, Susan Beals, child of Warren & Ann Lincoln, baptism, p. 308

Lincoln, Warren, married Nancy Parker, p. 163

Lincoln, Warren, member, p. 372, 376, 380

Lincoln, Mrs. Warren, member, p. 376, 381

Lincoln, Warren Parker, child of Warren & Ann Lincoln, baptism, p. 308

Lincoln, William, son of C.[harles] Lincoln, deaths, p. 475

Lincoln, William H., deaths, p. 465

Lincoln, William Oliver, child of Charles & Martha B. Lincoln, baptism, p. 303

Little, Cornelia Romana Susana, married John Brown, p. 159

Little, Henry A., married Margaretta A. Little, p. 164

Little, Margaretta A., married Henry A. Little, p. 164

Lock, Hannah, member, p. 370

Lock, Mrs. Hannah , member, p. 376

Locke, Hannah, deaths, p. 506

Lock, Martha, married Anthony Baptist, p. 161

Lombard, Miss, deaths, p. 468

Lombard, Ephraim, married Mary Elizabeth Hall, p. 169

Lombard, Esther, member, p. 367

Lombard, George, child of Nathaniel & Esther Lombard, baptism, p. 289

Lombard, Henry Chapman, child of Nathaniel & E.[sther] Lombard, baptism, p. 293

Lombard, Henry Chapman, child of N. K. Chapman, deaths, p. 474

Lombard, Mehitable, child of Nathaniel & Esther Lombard, baptism, p. 285

Long, Almira, married Samuel Sampson, p. 155

Long, William, baptism, p. 295

Longley, Charles W., married Abbie F. Brown, p. 183

Longley, Mr. James, married Sarah Eustis, p. 170

Lord, Robert, married Susanna Morse, p. 151

Loring, infant child of Caleb G. Loring, deaths, p. 487

Loring, Caleb G., married Harriet Tuttle, p. 154

Loring, Caleb G., covenant, p. 426

Loring, Charles Frederick, child of Charles G. & Harriet Loring, baptism, p. 288

Loring, Charles Gould, baptism, p. 288

Loring, Charles Gould, child of Charles G. & Harriet Loring, baptism, p. 290

Loring, Elizabeth, child of Caleb G. & Harriet Loring, baptism, p. 303

Loring, George, child of Caleb G. & Harriet Loring, baptism, p. 302

Loring, Harriet, covenant, p. 426

Loring, Mrs. Harriet, baptism, p. 296

Loring, Harriet, child of Charles G. & Harriet Loring, baptism, p. 293

Loring, Maria Louisa, child of Caleb G. & Harriet Loring, baptism, p. 300

Loring, Mary-Ann, child of Caleb G. & Harriet Loring, baptism, p. 296

Loring, William Henry, child of Caleb G. & Harriet Loring, baptism, p. 306

Lothrop, Joseph, deaths, p. 499

Lovering, Sarah (Mrs. John Cogswell), member, p. 362

Low, Charlotte, wife of John Low, deaths, p. 478

Low, Daniel, married Adeline Faguins, p. 160

Low, Lydia Oakes, child of Nathaniel & Rachael Low, baptism, p. 285

Low, Nathaniel, baptism, p. 295; deaths, p. 470

Low, Samuel, married Abiah Page Lillie, p. 152

Lowe, Elizabeth, married Henry Connor, p. 183

Lowell, Rev. Charles, D. D., pastor of the West Church, pp. 465, 482-484, 487, 492, 493

Lowell, Francis Cabot, deaths, p. 465

Luce, Mary Eunson, member, p. 362

Luckis, John Singleton, married Louisa Tippen, p. 160

Luckis, Sibellar, member, p. 366

Luckis, Sibella Lee, deaths, p. 503

Lyford, infant child of Thomas Lyford, deaths, p. 487

Lyford, Robert , deaths, p. 502

Lyford, Thomas, married Susan Jenkins, p. 166

Lyman, Lewis, married Mary B. Bruce, p. 157

Lyndes, George, married Catharine Robbins, p. 161

Lynes, Edward G., married Mary Jane Clark, p. 171

Lynes, Edward G., member, p. 375

Lynes, Edward Morton, child of Edward G. & Mary Jane Lynes, baptism, p. 312

Lynes, Mary J., member, p. 375

Lynes, Mary Jane, baptism, p. 311

Lynes, Mary Jane, child of Edward G. & Mary Jane Lynes, baptism, p. 312

Lynes, Raymond, child of Edward G. & Mary J. Lynes, baptism, p. 318

Lynes, Sidney, child of Edward G. & Mary J. Lynes, baptism, p. 318

Lyscom, Phebe A., married George Harris, p. 163

M

Maccomber, John Townsend, member, p. 384

Mackay, Ruth, deaths, p. 497

Maclstarm?, - - -, married - - - Adams, p. 181

Macoy, Abraham, married Elizabeth Williams, p. 164

Magee, Matthew, baptism, p. 305

Magee, Thomas, baptism, p. 305

Magoon, Abigail, covenant, p. 426

Magoon, Nathaniel S., married Abigail Danforth, p. 152

Magoon, Sarah-Ann, child of Nathaniel S. & Abigail Magoon, baptism, p. 286

Main, William P., married Susan S. Cox, p. 155

Mair, Mrs., deaths, p. 509

Malcom, Eliza C., married Freeman Reed, p. 168

Malcomb, Permelia, married Willson Cheney, p. 168

Mallen, Mrs., deaths, p. 493

Mandell, M. Johnson, married Mary Jane Brown, p. 172

Mann, Amos C., married Hannah T. Parsons, p. 163

Mann, Otis, married Maria A. Falls, p. 181

Mansir, William, baptism, p. 293

Mansur, John, baptism, p. 296

Marden, child of Mr. D. Marden, deaths, p. 481

Marsh, Mrs., deaths, p. 509

Marshall, Samuel, baptism, p. 306

Martin, George, baptism, p. 300

Mason, Mrs. Charles, deaths, p. 510

Matthews, John Shivers, baptism, p. 301

May, Sophia A., married George William Bond, p. 167

Maynard, Abigail, married Albert Crane, p. 170

McClaskey, Donald, married Mary Campbell, p. 177

McCleary, Mrs., wife of S.[amuel] F. McCleary, deaths, p. 469

McCleary, Hannah Parkman, deaths, p. 480

McCleary, Lynde Walter, child of Samuel F. & Maria L. McCleary, baptism, p. 294; deaths, p. 479

McCleary, Maria Louisa, child of S.[amuel] F. & M.[aria] L. McCleary, baptism, p. 297

McCleary, Maynard Walter, child of S.[amuel] F. & Maria L. McCleary, baptism, p. 301

McCleary, Samuel Foster, child of Samuel F. & M.[aria] L. McCleary, baptism, p. 292

McDonough, Mary Ann, married James Carroll, p. 176

McFarlane, James, baptism, p. 296

McGaw, Margaret, member, p. 366

McKean, Agnes, married Joseph Austin Esq., p. 162

McKean, Agnes, member, p. 363

McKean, Elizabeth M., member, p. 363

McKean, William, member, p. 361; deaths, p. 470

McKenney, Lydia Ann, married Warren Houghton, p. 175

McKinzie, Alexander D., married Maria Howe, p. 167

McKean, Agnes, married Joseph Austin Esq., p. 162

McKenney, Lydia Ann, married Warren Houghton, p. 175

McMullen, Andrew, married Catharine Gassett, p. 175

McNemath, John, deaths, p. 511

Mead, Benjamin Franklin, baptism, p. 306; deaths, pp. 495, 497

Mead, Eliza S., married William D. Clark, p. 170

Meizner, Joseph Parker, child of T. L. Meizner, deaths, p. 507

Meizner [Mizner], Martha Elizabeth, child of Thomas L. Meizner, baptism, p. 320

Meizner [Mizner], Thomas Leonard, child of Thomas L. Meizner, baptism, p. 320

Melander, Charles, married Mary Barber, p. 155

Mellen, child of John Mellen, deaths, p. 492

Mellen, Frederick, son of Judge Mellen, deaths, p. 491

Meprate, [blank], wife of Lewis Meprate, deaths, p. 464

Meriam ?, child of Mr. Meriam ?, deaths, p. 481

Meriam, Elisha, married Sarah Pike, p. 161

Merrifield, Thomas, deaths, p. 470

Merrill, James Freeman, deaths, p. 483

Merry, Jane, deaths, p. 478

Merry, Jonathan, deaths, p. 481

Messenger, Daniel, child of Daniel & Mary Ann Messenger, baptism, p. 291

Messenger, Daniel Jun., married Mary-Ann Smith, p. 156

Messenger, Mary Ann, wife of Daniel Messenger, baptism, p. 291

Messenger, Mary-Ann, covenant, p. 426

Messenger, Roswell Emerson, married Delia Woodward Adams, p. 167

Messenger, Susan Dorcas, child of Daniel & Mary-Ann Messenger, baptism, p. 305

Messenger, William Smith, child of Daniel & Mary-Ann Messenger, baptism, p. 305

Miles, Walter, married Abigail Ingals, p. 163

Millet, Abraham, married Abigail Smith, p. 159

Millett, William, married Martha H. Skerry, p. 170

Mills, infant child of William Mills, deaths, p. 471

Mills, infant child of William Mills, Jun., deaths, p. 473

Mills, Mrs., wife of J. Mills, deaths, p. 494

Mills, Abigail, child of William & Abigail S. Mills, baptism, p. 284

Mills, Abigail S., member, p. 368

Mills, George, child of William & Abigail S. Mills, baptism, p. 290

Mills, Henry, child of William & Abigail Mills, baptism, p. 292

Mills, John, baptism, p. 293

Mills, John, member, p. 370

Mills, Mary, member, p. 370

Mills, Mary Elizabeth, child of John & Mary Mills, baptism, p. 294

Mills, William, child of William & Abigail S. Mills, baptism, p. 287

Mills, William, child of John & Mary Mills, baptism, p. 297

Mills, William Jun, married Abigail Soal Curtis, p. 151; deaths, p. 473

Milne, George P., married Eliza A. Lambert, p. 166

Mitchell, infant child of T. Mitchell, deaths, pp. 488, 490

Mitchell, Elizabeth, deaths, p. 463

Mitchell, Mrs. J. D., deaths, p. 510

Mitchell, James D., married Rowena Brown?, p. 181

Mitchell, John, married Abigail Brown, p. 151

Mitchell, Thomas, baptism, p. 301

Mizner, Eliza Greene, baptism, p. 322

Mizner, Eliza Greene, married George P. Richardson, p. 184

Mizner, Eliza Greene, member, p. 385

Mizner [Meizner], Emma Eliza, child of T.[homas] L.[eonard] & E.[liza]

N

Oliver, Thomas, deaths, p. 468

Orcutt, David, married Dorcas W. Hall, p. 160

Orne, infant child of Henry Orne, deaths, p. 475

Orne, Frances B., wife of Judge Orne, deaths, p. 482

Osgood, John Hamilton, married Adeline Stevens, p. 168

Owens, Margaret, married Robert Jones, p. 172

P

Paddock, Peregrine, deaths, p. 483

Page, infant child of Mr. E. Page, deaths, p. 468

Page, infant child of Edward Page, deaths, pp. 474, 480

Page, Abigail Gooding, married Lewis Smith, p. 168

Page, Charles Marsh, child of Edward & Susan Page, baptism, p. 295

Page, Edward, covenant, p. 426

Page, Edward, child of Edward & Susan Page, baptism, pp. 286, 295

Page, Edward, son of Edward Page, deaths, p. 473

Page, Edward Francis, child of Edward & Susan Page, baptism, p. 287

Page, John, deaths, p. 478

Page, Sarah, widow of Thomas Page, deaths, p. 485

Page, Susan, covenant, p. 426

Page, Susan, child of Edward & Susan Page, baptism, p. 295

Page, Thomas, deaths, p. 485

Palfrey, Cazneau, member, p. 371

Palfrey, Elizabeth, member, p. 370

Palfrey, Elizabeth C., member, p. 381

Palfrey, Miss Elizabeth C., member, p. 376

Palfrey, Elizabeth Waterman, baptism, p. 302

Palfrey, Elizabeth W., member, p. 372, 381

Palfrey, Mrs. Elizabeth W., member, p. 376

Palfrey, Rev. John Gorham, D. D. pastor of Brattle Street Church, p. 480

Palfrey, Lydia, member, p. 364, 381

Palfrey. Mrs. Lydia, member, p. 376

Palfrey, Lydia Cazneau, child of William & E[lizabe]th W.[aterman] Palfrey, baptism, p. 306

Palfrey, Margaret S., member, p. 370, 381

Palfrey. Miss Margaret S., member, p. 376

Palfrey, Robert Bates, child of William & E.[lizabeth] W.[aterman] Palfrey, baptism, p. 311

Palfrey, Susan Elizabeth, child of William & E.[lizabeth] W.[aterman] Palfrey, baptism, p. 302; deaths, p. 486

Palfrey, William, member, p. 361, 372, 376; deaths, p. 470

Palfrey, William Waterman, child of William & E.[lizabeth] W.[aterman] Palfrey, baptism, p. 308

Palmer, Sarah, married Joseph Johnson, p. 152

Parker, Jedediah, member, p. 361; deaths, p. 479

Parker, Nancy, married Warren Lincoln, p. 163

Parker, Susannah, deaths, p. 504

Parker, Susanna Bradshaw, member, p. 362

Parker, Mrs. Susanna, member, p. 377

Parker, William, deaths, p. 471

Parkman, Alice, child of Rev. John & Susan S. Parkman, baptism, p. 312

Parkman, Caroline, member, p. 370

Parkman, Caroline Hall, child of Francis & Caroline Parkman, baptism, p. 296

Parkman, Charles McDonogh, child of Daniel & Mary G. Parkman, baptism, p. 300

Parkman, Daniel, member, p. 369

Parkman, Daniel, son of Samuel Parkman, deaths, p. 499

Parkman, Edward Blake, child of Daniel & Harriet Parkman, baptism, p. 288; deaths, p. 499

Parkman, Elias, baptism, p. 285

Parkman, Eliza Willard Shaw, child of Francis & C.[aroline] Parkman, baptism, p. 305

Parkman, Francis (pastor), member, p. 361; pp. 314, 373, 469

Parkman, Francis, child of Francis & Caroline Parkman, baptism, p. 294

Parkman, George, M. D., deaths, p. 504

Parkman, George Francis, child of George

& Eliza A. Parkman, baptism, pp. 286, 293

Parkman, George Francis, son of Dr. George Parkman, deaths, p. 469

Parkman, Harriet, wife of Daniel Parkman, deaths, p. 469

Parkman, Harriet Eliza, child of George & Eliza A. Parkman, baptism, p. 291

Parkman, Henry, child of Samuel & Mary B. Parkman, baptism, p. 287

Parkman, Rev. John Jun., married Susan P. Sturgiss, p. 169

Parkman, John Eliot, child of Francis & Caroline Parkman, baptism, p. 306

Parkman, Johnson, married Lucy Rogers, p. 168

Parkman, Mary-Agnes, child of Francis & Caroline Parkman, baptism, p. 300; deaths, p. 482

Parkman, Mary Brooks, child of Francis & Caroline Parkman, baptism, p. 303

Parkman, Mary B., member, p. 368; covenant, p. 426

Parkman, Mary-Harriet, child of Daniel & Mary Parkman, baptism, p. 300

Parkman, Powell Mason, child of Samuel & Mary B. Parkman, baptism, p. 289

Parkman, Samuel, father of Rev. Francis Parkman, deaths, p. 474

Parkman, Samuel, child of Samuel, Jun. & Mary B. Parkman, baptism, p. 285

Parkman, Samuel Jun., member, p. 368; covenant, p. 426

Parkman, Sarah, wife of Rev. Francis Parkman, deaths, p. 469

Parkman, Sarah, widow of Samuel Parkman, deaths, p. 492

Parkman, Sarah Cabot, child of Francis & Sarah Parkman, baptism, p. 288

Parkman, Sarah Cabot, married William Parsons Atkinson, p. 172

Parkman, Sarah Cabot, member, p. 374

Parkman, Sarah Rogers, baptism, p. 285

Parkman, William, married Mrs. Emeline R. Fisher, p. 177

Parks, Adeline Augusta, child of Elisha & Mary A.[nn] Parks, baptism, p. 305

Parks, Cornelia Eliza, child of Elisha & Mary-Ann Parks, baptism, p. 306

Parks, Elisha, married Mary-Ann Austin, p. 151

Parks, Emeline Foster, child of Elisha & Mary-Ann Parks, baptism, p. 301

Parks, Francis Parkman, child of Elisha & M.[ary Ann] Parks, baptism, p. 311

Parks, George Bradish, child of Elisha & Mary Ann Parks, baptism, p. 290

Parks, Georgianna, child of Elisha & Mary-Ann Parks, baptism, p. 302; deaths, p. 491

Parks, Harriet Austin, child of Elisha & Mary Ann Parks, baptism, p. 297

Parks, Maria Brown, child of Elisha & Mary Parks, baptism, p. 307

Parks, Mary-Ann, covenant, p. 426

Parks, Mary-Ann Austin, child of Elisha & Mary-Ann Parks, baptism, p. 295

Parks, Nathaniel Austin, child of Elisha & M.[ary Ann] Parks, baptism, p. 287

Parks, Samuel Augustus, child of Elisha & Mary-Ann Parks, baptism, p. 293

Parsons, Mr., deaths, p. 510

Parsons, Hannah T., married Amos C. Mann, p. 163

Partridge, Charles, married Sophronia A. Flagg, p. 167

Partridge, Sophronia A., baptism, p. 308

Partridge, unnamed infant child of Sophronia Partridge, baptism, p. 308

Payne, infant child of Thomas M. Payne, deaths, p. 463

Payne, Sarah, married James Kettell, p. 151

Payson, infant child of J.[ohn] F.[enno] Payson, deaths, p. 475

Payson, Ann, married Isaac Hall, p. 161

Payson, Deborah B., wife of J.[ohn] F.[enno] Payson, deaths, p. 493

Payson, Elizabeth B., wife of J.[ohn] F.[enno] Payson, deaths, p. 473

Payson, Harriet Elizabeth, child of John F.[enno] & Dolly Payson, baptism, p. 317

Payson, John Blandard, child of John Fenno Payson, baptism, p. 295

Payson, John F., married Dolly French, p. 170

Payson, John Fenno, Jr., baptism, p. 316

Payson, John F., Jr., married Lizzie M. Hall, p. 179

Payson, Olive F., married Samuel S. Stowers, p. 170

Peabody, Sarah M., married William Lasell, p. 173

Pearce, Parker H., married Hannah Withington, p. 154

Pearson, Abigail, widow, deaths, p. 473

Peirce, child, deaths, p. 487

Peirce, Dr. = Rev. John Pierce, D. D., pastor of the First Church in Brookline, p. 306

Peirce, Charles Lincoln, child of J.[osiah] & M.[ary] Peirce, baptism, p. 307; deaths, p. 493

Peirce, Eliza Lincoln, child of Josiah & Mary Peirce, baptism, p. 288

Peirce, Eliza Lincoln, member, p. 374

Peirce, Henrietta Lamson, child of Josiah & Mary Peirce, baptism, p. 292

Peirce, Henrietta Lamson, member, p. 374

Peirce, Josiah, married Mary Lincoln, p. 152

Peirce, Josiah, child of Josiah & Mary Peirce, baptism, p. 290

Peirce, Josiah, deaths, p. 498

Peirce, Mary-Ann, member, p. 373

Peirce, Mary-Ann Lincoln, child of Josiah & Mary Peirce, baptism, p. 285

Peirce, Sarah Roby, member, p. 374

Pendleton, Lillia L., married William G. Nichols, p. 181

Penniman, Scammell, married Hannah Hammond, p. 161

Pepper, Benjamin, married Margaret Vannah, p. 163

Perkins, Jane, married David Adams, p. 169

Perkins, Sarah, member, p. 364

Perkins, Sarah, widow, deaths, p. 465

Perkins, William, married Phebe Allen, p. 158

Perry, Mr., deaths, p. 507

Perry, Charles H., deaths, p. 502

Perry, Elizabeth, baptism, p. 318

Perry, Mrs. Elizabeth, member, p. 382

Perry, Francis Henry, child of George & Mary Perry, baptism, p. 284

Perry, George, deaths, p. 473

Perry, John Hammond, baptism, p. 293

Perry, Mary, member, p. 367; deaths, p. 493

Peters, Hans, married Mary Feeny, p. 182

Peters, Helen R., married James B. Leeds, p. 171

Peterson, John, baptism, p. 307

Pettes, Catharine A., member, p. 374, 381

Pettes, Miss Catharine A., member, p. 376

Pettes, Elizabeth F., member, p. 374, 381

Pettes, Miss Elizabeth F., member, p. 376

Pickett, Eliza, married James Bingham, p. 160

Pico, Abigail (Mrs. Prentiss), member, p. 364

Pierce, child, deaths, p. 468

Pierce, infant child of Josiah Pierce, deaths, p. 471

Pierce, infant child, deaths, p. 500

Pierce, Annie Eleanor, deaths, p. 505

Pierce, Augusta Maria, child of S. H. Pierce, baptism, p. 302

Pierce, Dorcas, widow, deaths, p. 469

Pierce, Ephraim, deaths, p. 487

Pierce [Peirce], Dr. = Rev. John Pierce, D. D., pastor of the First Church in Brookline, p. 306

Pierce, John Howard, child of S. H. Pierce, baptism, p. 302

Pierce, Lucy Maria, child of David & M. L. Pierce, baptism, p. 311

Pierce, Marianne Lincoln, married David Morgan, p. 171

Pierce, Mary Ann, married William Wooley, p. 175

Pierce, Sarah H., deaths, p. 483

Pierce, Sarah Roby, child of Josiah & Mary Pierce, baptism, p. 296

Pierpont, Elizabeth, deaths, p. 464

Pike, Eliza H., married Moses Emerson, p. 153

Pike, Mary, deaths, p. 483

Pike, Sarah, married Elisha Meriam, p. 161

Pike, William, married Elizabeth Baker, p. 158

Pitman, Mary-Ann, married Benjamin T. Wells, p. 164

Pitman, Nancy, member, p. 382

Pollard, Lucy, member, p. 364; deaths, p. 484

Pomeroy, William Henry, married Sibella Lukis, p. 163

Porter, child, deaths, p. 484

Porter, Mrs., member, p. 377

Potter, Harriet, married John Brown, p. 157

Powers, Ann M., married Edward Chamberlain Jun, p. 167

Pratt, Albert S., married Julia Dodd, p. 183

Pratt, Charles H., married Rachel M. Williams, p. 179

Pratt, Mary-Ann, married George Archbald, p. 157

Pratt, Susan A., member, p. 372

Prentiss, Abigail Pico, member, p. 364

Prescott, Mrs., deaths, p. 494

Priest, Elizabeth Tucker, daughter of Mr. J. Priest, deaths, p. 486

Priest, Sarah Ann, married John Webb Hall, p. 167

Prince, Cato, married Lucy T. Bowen, p. 161

Prince, Mary, widow of S.[amuel] Prince, deaths, p. 486

Prince, Samuel, deaths, p. 464

Proby, Joseph, member, p. 361

Proctor, Hannah, deaths, p. 486

Proctor, Mary, deaths, p. 487

Prout, Lydia, member, p. 364

Pulsifer, Capt. David, deaths, p. 465

Pulsifer, E., wife of Capt. Robert S. Pulsifer, deaths, p. 472

Pulsifer, Elizabeth Aspinwall, member, p. 374

Pulsifer, Elizabeth Aspinwall married Morrill Wyman, M. D., p. 171

Pulsifer, Elizabeth A., baptism, p. 307

Pulsifer, Sarah P., married Charles H. Stearns, p. 166

Putnam, Mr., brother of Rev. G. Putnam, deaths, p. 501

Putnam, Rev. George, D. D., pastor of First Church of Roxbury, p. 501

Putnam, John P., married Lucy A. Harris, p. 174

Q

Quincy, John, grandson of Capt. Atkins, deaths, p. 465

R

Rand, Abigail, deaths, p. 472

Randall, Daniel, baptism, p. 293

Ranlett, Seth A., married Mary Ann C.

Stevens, p. 167

Ranstead?, infant son, deaths, p. 508

Rasmasson, Henry, married Dorcas Howard, p. 151

Ray, Adam S., married Hannah Howard, p. 162

Raymond, Freeborn F., married Sarah E. Richardson, p. 179

Raymond, Samuel A., deaths, p. 501

Read, William, married Sarah G. Atkins, p. 163

Reed, [unnamed], deaths, p. 469

Reed, Franscina M., married Henry Dawson Dutch, p. 170

Reed, Freeman, married Eliza C. Malcom, p. 168

Reed, James Bartlett, baptism, p. 304

Reed, John T., deaths, p. 498

Renfield, Josiah Woodward, married Catharine Vanneever, p. 168

Restieaux, infant child of Robert Restieaux, deaths, p. 494

Restieaux, Edward B., child of Robert & Susanna B. Restieaux, baptism, p. 306

Restieaux, Robert, married Susanna Boylston Walker, p. 166; deaths, p. 497

Restieaux, Robert T., child of Robert & Susanna Restieaux, baptism, p. 308

Restieaux, Susanna B., member, p. 373; deaths, p. 494

Revere, Abigail, wife of George Revere, deaths, p. 471

Revere, George, married Abigail Tufts, p. 156

Rhoades, infant child of Stephen Rhoades, deaths, p. 492

Rhoades, son of Isaac Rhoades, deaths, p. 481

Rhoades, Mary Hatch, child of Stephen & Abby Rhoades, baptism, p. 304

Rhoades, Stephen, married Abigail B. Ward, p. 162

Rhoades, Stephen, child of Stephen & Abigail B. Rhoades, baptism, p. 306

Rhoades, William Ward, child of Stephen & Abby Rhoades, baptism, p. 301

Rich, Lemuel F., married Margaret Murray, p. 180

Richards, Mark, deaths, p. 479

Richardson, unnamed, member, p. 361

Richardson, Eliza, covenant, p. 426; deaths, p. 473

Richardson, Elizabeth, member, p. 368; deaths, pp. 482, 486

Richardson, George, deaths, p. 483

Richardson, George Partridge, baptism, p. 316

Richardson, George P., married Eliza Greene Mizner, p. 184

Richardson, George P., p. 386

Richardson, George P. Jr., member, p. 382

Richardson, George W., married Sarah W. Wilkins, p. 171

Richardson, Isaac, deaths, p. 463

Richardson, Mrs. Jane P., married Joseph S. Waterman, p. 154

Richardson, Joel Lyman, child of Joel & Elizabeth Richardson, baptism, p. 282

Richardson, Lewis G., married Sarah A. Hammatt, p. 172

Richardson, Mrs. Mary, member, p. 382

Richardson, Mary Elizabeth, child of George P. & Mary Richardson, baptism, p. 316

Richardson, Sarah E., married Freeborn F. Raymond, p. 179

Richardson, Theodore Mansfield, child of Joel & Elizabeth Richardson, baptism, p. 286

Richardson, William Henry, child of George P. & Mary Richardson, baptism, p. 316

Rider, Nancy Atwood, married William Kemp, p. 158

Ridgeway, Ann Sewell, child of Mrs. Ann Ridgeway, baptism, p. 290

Ridgeway, Anthony Brooks, child of Mrs. Ann Ridgeway, baptism, p. 290

Ridgeway, Edward Wolcott, child of Mrs. Ann Ridgeway, baptism, p. 290

Ridgeway, Henry Wolcott, child of Mrs. Ann Ridgeway, baptism, p. 290

Ridgeway, John West, child of Mrs. Ann Ridgeway, baptism, p. 290

Ridgeway, Philip Reynolds, child of Mrs. Ann Ridgeway, baptism, p. 290

Ridgeway, Samuel Sewell, child of Mrs. Ann Ridgeway, baptism, p. 290

Riggs, Abimilech, covenant, p. 426

Riggs, Sally F., covenant, p. 426

Riggs, William West, child of Abimelech & Sarah F. Riggs, baptism, p. 285

Ripley, S. Dana, daughter, Dr. Willard, deaths, p. 499

Ritchie, James H., deaths, p. 501

Ritchie?, William Henry Stuart, child of William & Isabella Ritchie?, baptism, p. 312

Roaf, Henry, married Emeline Copeland, p. 159

Robbins, Catharine, married George Lyndes, p. 161

Robbins, Rev. Chandler, pastor of the Second Church, married Mary Eliza Frothington, p. 167; pp. 376-377, 492, 495, 497-498, 500-501

Robins, Francis, deaths, p. 483

Robins, Richard, married Susan P. Blake, p. 171

Robinson, infant child of A. H. Robinson, deaths, p. 493

Robinson, A. H., married Mary E. S. Clark, p. 166

Robinson, Abigail Chandler, member, p. 362

Robinson, Elizabeth, member, p. 364; deaths, p. 473

Robinson, J., Mr., deaths, p. 463

Robinson, Jane, wife of Col. James Robinson, deaths, p. 475

Robinson, Sarah A., married William T. Clark, p. 178

Robinson, Simon W., married Hannah T. Danforth, p. 153

Rogers, Ann Phillips, child of Capt. T. Rogers, baptism, p. 300

Rogers, Edward Augustus, child of Capt. T. Rogers, baptism, p. 300

Rogers, Eliza, married Samuel N. Neat, p. 175

Rogers, Eliza, member, p. 367

Rogers, Emeline M., married Daniel C. Sampson, p. 162

Rogers, Hannah D., married John B. Thomas, p. 172

Rogers, Henry Derby, baptism, p. 319

Rogers, James Harvey, child of Capt. T. Rogers, baptism, p. 300

Rogers, Lucy, married Johnson Parkman, p. 168

S

Shaw, Elizabeth Willard, child of Robert G. & Elizabeth W. Shaw, baptism, p. 293; married Daniel A. Oliver, p. 173

Shaw, Francis G., married Sarah Blake Sturgis, p. 168

Shaw, Gardner Howland, child of Robert G. & Eliza Shaw, baptism, p. 289

Shaw, George H., deaths, p. 506

Shaw, Hannah [Anna] Blake, child of Robert G. & Eliza W. Shaw, baptism, p. 287

Shaw, Joseph Coolidge, child of Robert G. & Eliza Shaw, baptism, p. 291

Shaw, Mary Louisa, child of Robert & Mary L. Shaw, baptism, p. 313

Shaw, Mary-Ann, child of Robert G. & E.[liza] W. Shaw, baptism, p. 301

Shaw, Myron, married Mary E. Harrod, p. 175

Shaw, Quincy Adams, child of Robert G. & Eliza Shaw, baptism, p. 296

Shaw, Robert Gould, child of Robert G. & Eliza Shaw, baptism, p. 284

Shaw, Mrs. Sarah, deaths, p. 507

Shaw, Sarah Parkman, married George Robert Russell, p. 169

Shaw, Sarah P., member, p. 371

Shaw, William Henry, child of Robert G. & Eliza W. Shaw, baptism, p. 300; deaths, p. 480

Sheldon, Mr., deaths, p. 510

Sheldon, Francis, married Sarah Tremere, p. 175

Shelton, child, deaths, p. 479

Shelton, Bridget, married Nathaniel Blake, p. 159

Shelton, John Jones, child of William P. & Mary Ann Shelton, baptism, p. 288

Shelton, Mary-Ann, covenant, p. 426; deaths, p. 493

Shelton, Thomas Curtis, child of William P. & Mary-Ann Shelton, baptism, p. 291

Shelton, William Francis, child of William P. & Mary Ann Shelton, baptism, p. 286

Shelton, William Parsons, married Mary-Ann Curtis p. 153

Shelton, William P., covenant, p. 426; deaths, p. 473

Shepard [Shepherd], Lydia Reed, baptism,

p. 316

Shepard [Shepherd], Sarah Lavina, baptism, p. 316

Shepherd [Shepard], Lydia R., married William W. Woodbury, p. 177

Shepherd, Mary Jane, married Amasa Beach Jr., p. 175

Shepherd, Nancy, married John Albree, p. 161

Shipley, Mrs. Frances Spalding, baptism, p. 321; member, p. 384

Sholes, [blank] Mr., deaths, p. 506

Shortwell, 2 children of W. D. Shortwell, deaths, p. 501

Shute, unnamed, member, p. 383

Shute, Edwin, member, p. 383

Shute, Edwin Lincoln, child of Edwin Shute, baptism, p. 320

Sibley, Catharine, member, p. 373

Sigourney, Andrew, deaths, p. 470

Sigourney, Ann, member, p. 365; deaths, p. 468

Sigourney, Daniel, deaths, p. 468

Sigourney, Eliza Ann, married Joel Stone, p. 161

Sigourney, Elizabeth, member, p. 364

Sigourney, Elizabeth, widow of A. Sigourney, deaths, p. 500

Sigourney, Harriet Ardelia, child of Henry & H. Sigourney, baptism, p. 307

Sigourney, Harriet A., member, p. 372

Sigourney, Henry H. W., married Harriet A. Williams, p. 165

Sigourney, Henry H. W., member, p. 372

Sigourney, Henry H. Williams, child of Henry & H. Sigourney, baptism, p. 307

Sigourney, John Cathcart, deaths, p. 478

Sigourney, Martha, member, p. 364; deaths, p. 480

Sigourney, Martha-Ann, married Thomas Parkman Cushing, p. 165

Sigourney, Sarah B., married Thomas Parkman Cushing, p. 161

Silsbee, Mary, married Samuel Tuttle, p. 155

Silsby, child of Enoch Silsby, deaths, p. 462

Silsby, infant child of J. Silsby, deaths, p. 464

Silsby, Alice, married Stephen Emmons, p. 165

Silver, John D., married Hannah B. Levear, p. 162

232

Simmons, Sarah, member, p. 364; deaths, p. 482

Simmons, Hon. William, deaths, p. 500

Simpkins, Deacon John, member, p. 361; deaths, p. 484

Simpkins, M. T., Miss, daughter of Deacon Simpkins, deaths, p. 478

Simpkins, Mary, member, p. 364

Simpkins, Mehitable, wife of Deacon [John] Simpkins, deaths, p. 465

Simpson, Eliza Rogers, married William Emerson, p. 158

Simpson, Elizabeth Rogers, child of Henry & Mary Simpson, baptism, p. 285

Simpson, Mrs. Hosea?, [Mrs. Hosea], deaths, p. 484

Simpson, Hosea B.? [Simpson B. Hosea], deaths, p. 474

Simpson, Mary, child of Henry & Mary Simpson, baptism, p. 285

Simpson, Mary, married John Spear Jun, p. 157

Simpson, William Rogers, child of Henry & Mary Simpson, baptism, p. 285

Singleton, Miss, deaths, p. 510

Singleton, Charles Gilbert, married Esther Abbot, p. 159

Singleton, Lydia H., married Thomas Kendall, p. 154

Singleton, Mary, member, p. 364; deaths, p. 470

Skerry, infant child, deaths, p. 482

Skerry, Mrs. Clarissa, member, p. 372

Skerry, Clarissa, deaths, p. 502

Skerry, Clarissa, child of Clarissa Skerry, baptism, p. 302

Skerry, Ephraim, deaths, p. 493

Skerry, Ephraim, child of Clarissa Skerry, baptism, p. 302

Skerry, Francis Horace, child of Clarissa Skerry, baptism, p. 302

Skerry, Martha H., married William Millett, p. 170

Skillin, Margarett (Mrs. Nathaniel Goodwin), member, p. 364

Skimmer, Ruth, married Henry Fowle, p. 151

Sloan, Francis, baptism, p. 304

Slone, infant child, deaths, p. 465

Smith, [blank], Mr., deaths, p. 492

Smith, [blank], Mrs., wife of Dr. Smith, deaths, p. 499

Smith?, infant, deaths, p. 504

Smith, infant child, deaths, pp. 495, 497

Smith, infant child of Abner Smith, deaths, p. 500

Smith, child of Mrs. A. Smith, widow, deaths, p. 463

Smith, infant child of Capt. B. Smith, deaths, p. 480

Smith, child of Edmund Smith, deaths, p. 493

Smith, [unnamed], son of Joseph Smith, deaths, p. 495, 497

Smith, Abigail, married Abraham Millet, p. 159

Smith, Rev. Amos, junior pastor of New North Church, married Mary Elizabeth Williams, p. 173; member, p. 374; pp. 375, 500, 502-503

Smith, Ann, married Charles Mountfort, p. 153

Smith, Belknap, deaths, p. 503

Smith, Belknap, child of J. B. Smith, deaths, p. 500

Smith, Capt. Benjamin, deaths, p. 491

Smith, Benjamin Franklin, child of Franklin & J.[oanna] Smith, baptism, p. 306

Smith, Caroline, baptism, p. 287

Smith, Caroline, married Capt. William Smith, p. 151

Smith, Caroline, member, p. 374; covenant, p. 426

Smith, Caroline Dorcas, child of William & Caroline Smith, baptism, p. 287

Smith, Caroline Dorcas, member, p. 374

Smith, Caroline D., married Joseph Murdock, p. 172

Smith, Catharine Belknap, child of Joseph Belknap & Catharine Mears Smith, baptism, p. 313

Smith, Catherine M. Clark, wife of J. B., Smith, deaths, p. 503

Smith, Dorcas, wife of Capt. Benjamin Smith, deaths, p. 472

Smith, Elizabeth, baptism, p. 311; member, p. 375

Smith, Frances-Ann, child of Franklin & Joanna Smith, baptism, p. 304

Smith, Frank Langdon, child of Samuel &

Helen G. Smith, baptism, p. 323

Smith, Franklin, married Joanna Wells, p. 164

Smith, Gilbert F., married Sarah A. Floyd, p. 180

Smith, Josephine, deaths, p. 510

Smith, Josephine, child of G. F. & Sarah A. Smith, baptism, p. 322

Smith, Lewis, married Abigail Gooding Page, p. 168

Smith, Mary, wife of Benjamin Smith, baptism, p. 301

Smith, Mary A. L., married William C. Appleton, p. 173

Smith, Mary-Ann, married Daniel Messenger Jun., p. 156

Smith, Mary-Ann-Louisa, member, p. 374

Smith, Mary Ann F., married Francis P. Wells, p. 174

Smith, Mary-Ann Louisa, child of William & Caroline Smith, baptism, p. 289

Smith, Mary Elizabeth, child of Joseph Belknap & Catharine Mears Smith, baptism, p. 313

Smith, Morrill Aspinwall, child of Samuel & Helen E. Smith, baptism, p. 319

Smith, Rachel A., married James N. Wentworth, p. 181

Smith, Samuel, baptism, p. 319

Smith, Samuel, married Louiza Stockwell, p. 162

Smith, Samuel, married Hellen Elizabeth Gerry, p. 177

Smith, Sarah B., deaths, p. 505

Smith, Stephen W., married Sarah A. Taggard, p. 182

Smith, Thomas Beals, child of Benjamin & Mary Smith, baptism, p. 301

Smith, Capt. William, married Caroline Smith, p. 151; deaths, p. 473

Smith, William, baptism, p. 287; covenant, p. 426

Snelling, [blank], Mrs., deaths, p. 494

Snelling, child of Samuel G. Snelling, deaths, p. 462

Snelling, Enoch H., covenant, p. 426

Snelling, Enoch Howes, baptism, p. 285

Snelling, Enoch Howes, Jun, baptism, p. 285

Snelling, Enoch H., married Sally D. Jones, p. 152

Snelling, Jonathan, deaths, p. 502

Snelling, Josiah, child of Susan Snelling, baptism, p. 284

Snelling, Lydia, member, p. 364

Snelling, Samuel Greenwood, child of Susan Snelling, baptism, p. 284

Snelling, Samuel G., deaths, p. 463

Snelling, Susan, member, p. 368

Snelling, Sarah Anne, child of Enoch H. & Sarah Snelling, baptism, p. 288

Snelling, Sarah D., covenant, p. 426

Snelling, Susan, baptism, p. 284

Snelling, Susan, married Joseph Goddard Esq., p. 164

Snow, Benjamin F., married Elizabeth C. Gooding, p. 170

Snow, Josiah, married Ruth Dyer, p. 160

Sowther?, Caroline Blake, child of Edward & C. K.? Sowther?, baptism, p. 322

Sparhawk, child of Widow Sparhawk, deaths, p. 491

Spaulding, Leonard W., married Emily Eaton, p. 161

Spear, Benjamin, baptism, p. 304

Spear, John Jun., married Mary Simpson, p. 157

Spear, Joseph G., married Hannah Blodget, p. 153

Spear, Josiah, baptism, p. 307

Spear, Samuel, baptism, p. 307

Spear, William Arnold, child of Samuel A. & Mary Spear, baptism, p. 306

Spence, Martha, child of William & Ann Spence, baptism, p. 308

Spence, William, married Ann Hammond, p. 169

Spencer, Henry F., married Sarah D. Holbrook, p. 182

Spinney, Daniel, baptism, p. 319

Spinney, George R., married Sarah E. Stearns, p. 179

Spiwood, Peter, married Lois Cross, p. 157

Spooner, Elizabeth Willard, married Samuel W. Spooner, p. 168

Spooner, Martha W., daughter of Dr. W. Spooner, deaths, p. 494

Spooner, Samuel W., married Elizabeth Willard Spooner, p. 168

Spooner, Susanna Eliot, member, p. 362

Spooner, Theodore, child of William & Elizabeth Spooner, baptism, p. 286; deaths, p. 465

Sprague, Elizabeth, baptism, p. 307; member, p. 374; deaths, p. 498

Sprague, Phineas, married Hannah Brown, p. 156

Spurr, Henry C., married Martha Ann Stebbins, p. 165

Squire, Sarah, member, p. 364

Stablar, John, married Christiana F. Myers, p. 169

Stanton, child, deaths, p. 509

Stanton, George , deaths, p. 470

Stanton, Sarah A., deaths, p. 473

Stanton, Sarah-Ann, child of George & Susan Stanton, baptism, p. 289

Stanton, Susanna, married William Farrow, p. 169

Stanton, William, married Matilda P. Murray, p. 180

Stanwood, Lydia, married Capt. Andrew Blanchard, p. 153

Staples, Charles, baptism, p. 290

Stearns, infant child of C. H. Stearns, deaths, pp. 494, 499

Stearns, infant child of E. Stearns, deaths, p. 500

Stearns, Augusta F., married Edward W. Barnicoat, p. 173

Stearns, Charles H., married Sarah P. Pulsifer, p. 166

Stearns, Elijah, member, p. 376, 382

Stearns, Mrs. Elijah, member, p. 376

Stearns, Emma D., married Charles B. Leavitt, p. 177

Stearns, Mary, married Alfred Williams, p. 162

Stearns, Sarah B., member, p. 382

Stearns, Sarah Elizabeth, baptism, p. 318; member, p. 382

Stearns, Sarah E., married George R. Spinney, p. 179

Stebbins, Martha Ann, married Henry C. Spurr, p. 165

Stedman, Francis, married Mrs. Percilla S. Haven, p. 182

Steele, Nancy, wife of Gurdon Steele,
deaths, p. 486

Stevens, [blank] Mrs., widow, deaths, p. 475

Stevens, infant child of S. Stevens, deaths, p. 494

Stevens, Abraham L. Jun., married Emeline N. Hutchinson, p. 165

Stevens, Adeline, married John Hamilton Osgood, p. 168

Stevens, Mrs. Ann, married John H. Armstrong, p. 155

Stevens, John A., M. D., married Sarah Ann Dickinson, p. 168

Stevens, Lavinia, married Henry Hutchinson Jun, p. 164

Stevens, Mary Ann C., married Seth A. Ranlett, p. 167

Stevenson, Nathaniel H., married Sibbel Grubb, p. 158

Stockwell, John, married Susanna Martha Graham, p. 169

Stockwell, Louiza, married Samuel Smith, p. 162

Stone, Clarissa, wife of William A. Stone, deaths, p. 487

Stone, Eliza Ann, wife of Joel Stone, deaths, p. 474

Stone, Eliza Atkins, child of Jacob & Eliza Stone, baptism, p. 308

Stone, George F. Pearson, child of Jacob & Eliza Stone, baptism, p. 308

Stone, Goodwin Atkins, child of Jacob & Eliza Stone, baptism, p. 311

Stone, Jacob, married Eliza Atkins, p. 164

Stone, Joel, married Eliza Ann Sigourney, p. 161

Stone, Lois (Louisa) Parsons, child of Jacob & Eliza Stone, baptism, p. 308

Stone, Lowell M., deaths, p. 502

Stone, Sardine, married Tabitha Goodspeed, p. 168

Stone, William A., married Clarissa Dickinson, p. 164

Stowell, Thomas, married Martha Fenno, p. 167

Stowers, Samuel S., married Olive F. Payson, p. 170

Streeter, Rev. Sebastian, pastor of First Universalist Church, pp. 483, 487

Studley, Frances Lovell, child of George

& Mary Studley, baptism, p. 322

Studley, James Lovell, child of George & Mary Studley, baptism, p. 322

Studley, Stillman Simonds, child of George & Mary Studley, baptism, p. 322

Studley, William Henry, child of George & Mary Studley, baptism, p. 322

Sturgess, George, child of Nathaniel R. & Susan Sturgess, baptism, p. 286

Sturgis, Elizabeth P., married Henry Grew, p. 167

Sturgis, George, member, p. 374

Sturgis, Sarah Blake, married Francis G. Shaw, p. 168

Sturgiss, Susan P., married Rev. John Parkman Jun., p. 169

Stutson, Rebecca, member, p. 364

Sumbardo, Angelina, deaths, p. 484

Sumbardo, John P., deaths, p. 493

Swift, Agnes, deaths, p. 500

Swift, Elijah, deaths, p. 463

Swift, Eliza, deaths, p. 510

Swift, Sarah B., child of H. Swift, deaths, p. 478

Swift, William J., son of Widow Swift, deaths, p. 474

Sylvester, John May, baptism, p. 303

Symmes, Eliza, wife of Andrew E. Symmes, deaths, p. 464

Symms, Mary-Ann-Stevens, child of Andrew Eliot & Elizabeth Symms, baptism, p. 283

T

Taft, Susan J., married Rufus H. Everett, p. 180

Taggard, Sarah A., married Stephen W. Smith, p. 182

Tatman, Sarah, married John Cloase, p. 165

Taylor, Alphonso, child of Isaac & Elizabeth H. Taylor, baptism, p. 313

Taylor, Isaac, married Elizabeth H. Adams, p. 172

Taylor, Isaac Henry, child of Isaac & Elizabeth H. Taylor, baptism, p. 312

Taylor, Mary Parr, married Arthur Berry, p. 172

Taylor, Naomi, member, p. 370

Taylor, Seth, Jun., deaths, p. 482

Tewksbury, Helen Augusta, deaths, p. 501

Thacher, Mrs. E. M., deaths, p. 510

Thacher, Rev. Peter, p. 373

Thacker, Henry, married Mary-Ann Cole, p. 157

Thacker, Henry, married Deborah Westley, p. 163

Thacker, Henry James Walker, child of Henry & Mary A. Thacker, baptism, p. 292

Thacker, Mary Ann Webster, child of Henry & Mary A. Thacker, baptism, p. 293

Thacker, Rachel Matilda, child of Henry & Mary Thacker, baptism, p. 296

Thacker, Rachel M., married Charles Rose, p. 173

Thayer, John, deaths, p. 481

Thayer, Zeba, Mr., deaths, p. 483

Thomas, John B., married Hannah D. Rogers, p. 172

Thomas, Mary T., married Richard G. Wait, p. 168

Thomas, Sarah, deaths, p. 491

Thompson, child, deaths, p. 479

Thompson, Abby Louiza, child of William & Mary B. Thompson, baptism, p. 290

Thompson, Charles, child of William & Mary B. Thompson, baptism, p. 301

Thompson, David, baptism, p. 295

Thompson, Edward William Burrows, child of William & Mary B. Thompson, baptism, p. 305

Thompson, Elizabeth Burrows, child of William & M.[ary] Thompson, baptism, p. 288

Thompson, Mrs. Fannie G., married Hiram Ferry, p. 182

Thompson, Frances Mary, child of William & Mary B. Thompson, baptism, p. 296

Thompson, Henry, child of William & Mary B. Thompson, baptism, p. 300

Thompson, Margaret Cruft, child of William & Mary B. Thompson, baptism, p. 305

Thompson, Mary B., covenant, p. 426

Thompson, William, child of William & Mary B. Thompson, baptism, p. 293

Thompson, William Jun, married Mary Burrows Fullerton, p. 152

Thompson, William M., deaths, p. 498

Throop, Orramel H., married Mary B. Harris, p. 160

Ticknor, Benjamin, married Hannah Gardner, p. 151

Tilden, Mrs., deaths, p. 509

Tilden, Alfred, child of Benjamin & Mary Tilden, baptism, p. 290

Tilden, Benjamin, deaths, p. 482

Tilden, Edward, deaths, p. 474

Tilden, Eliza, married James E. Ewer, p. 166

Tilden, George M., son of B. Tilden, deaths, p. 483

Tilden, Marcy Little, child of Benjamin & Mary Tilden, baptism, p. 288

Tilden, Sarah, child of Benjamin & Mary Tilden, baptism, p. 283

Tileston, Master John, deaths, p. 479

Tileston, Lydia, widow of Master John Tileston, deaths, p. 484

Tippen, Louisa, married John Singleton Luckis, p. 160

Tippen, Nancy, married David Belcher, p. 151

Tirrell, Ezra F., married Helena Clapp, p. 178

Tisdale, Fred. Augustus, baptism, p. 317

Tompkins, John Shepherd, child of Abel & Mary Tompkins, baptism, p. 282

Tompson, John, married Ellen Jordan, p. 175

Torrey, infant child, deaths, p. 470

Torrey, Abby W., married James M. Weston, p. 179

Tower, Abigail, member, p. 368

Tower, Sarah Ellen, child of Abigail Tower, baptism, p. 284

Town, [unnamed], wife of Israel Town, deaths, p. 462

Townsend, David Jun., married Mary-Ann Gragg, p. 168

Trask, Nancy, married James Young, p. 161

Tremere, Benjamin Burrows, child of John B. & Sarah Tremere, baptism, p. 295

Tremere, Charles Frederick, child of John B. & S.[arah] F. Tremere, baptism, p. 303

Tremere, Eliza Burrows, child of John B.

& S.[arah] F. Tremere, baptism, p. 305

Tremere, Francis Henry, child of John B. & Sarah F. Tremere, baptism, p. 300

Tremere, Helen Maria, child of John B. & Sarah F. Tremere, baptism, p. 302

Tremere, John B., married Sarah F. Burrows, p. 155

Tremere, John B., covenant, p. 426

Tremere, John Sargent, child of John B. & Sarah F. Tremere, baptism, p. 292

Tremere, Sarah, married Francis Sheldon, p. 175

Tremere, Sarah, child of John B. & Sarah F. Tremere, baptism, p. 296

Tremere, Sarah, covenant, p. 426

Tremere, William Burrows, child of John B. & Sarah F. Tremere, baptism, p. 290

Trench, Hannah, member, p. 364

Trench, Nancy, deaths, p. 484

Trevett, Mrs, daughter of Mrs. Mary Atkins, deaths, p. 494

Trevett, Mary, deaths, p. 494

Trevett, Mary Russell, deaths, p. 475

Trevill, Mary, member, p. 364

Trott, Ann Boylston, married Thomas Crocker, p. 158

Trott, Evelina, married Elijah J. S. Corlew, p. 161

Truesdale, Artemas Ward, baptism, p. 302

Trull, John F., married Elizabeth Wilkinson, p. 163

Tucker, Elizabeth Ann, married Thomas G. Bangs, p. 159

Tuckerman, infant child of John Tuckerman, deaths, p. 483

Tuckerman, unnamed child of John & Catharine Tuckerman, baptism, p. 303

Tuckerman, Benjamin Curtis, baptism, p. 293

Tuckerman, Edward, child of Edward & Sophia Tuckerman, baptism, p. 287

Tuckerman, Edward, Jun., member, p. 367

Tuckerman, Frederick Goddard, child of Edward & S[ophia] Tuckerman, baptism, p. 291

Tuckerman, Hannah, wife of Edward Tuckerman, Jun., deaths, p. 462

Tuckerman, Hannah Parkman, member, p. 370

Tuckerman, John, married Catharine Tuttle, p. 162

Tuckerman, John Tuttle, child of John & Catharine Tuckerman, baptism, p. 303

Tuckerman, Rev. Joseph, D. D., pastor of Rumney Marsh (Chelsea), Pitts Street Chapel, p. 482

Tuckerman, Samuel Parkman, child of Edward & Sophia Tuckerman, baptism, p. 288

Tufts, infant child of T. Tufts, deaths, p. 479

Tufts, Abigail, married George Revere, p. 156

Tufts, Abigail, member, p. 367

Tufts, Ebenezer, child of Ephraim & Abigail Tufts, baptism, p. 283

Turner, Charles E., married Mary Ann Dazele, p. 175

Tuttle, child of Edward Tuttle, deaths, p. 478

Tuttle, child of Samuel Tuttle, deaths, p. 475

Tuttle, child of Turell Tuttle, Jun., deaths, p. 464

Tuttle, infant child, deaths, pp. 472, 500

Tuttle, Benjamin, deaths, p. 486

Tuttle, Caroline Elizabeth, child of Edward & Catherine V. Tuttle, baptism, p. 292

Tuttle, Caroline E., married Lewis Keen, p. 171

Tuttle, Catharine, married John Tuckerman, p. 162

Tuttle, Catharine V., covenant, p. 426

Tuttle, Charles Henry, child of Thomas & Catharine Tuttle, baptism, p. 317

Tuttle, Edward, married Catharine Vannever Geyer, p. 152

Tuttle, Edward, covenant, p. 426

Tuttle, Edward Wells, child of Edward & Catharine Tuttle, baptism, p. 286

Tuttle, Eliza, married Thomas Wells, p. 151

Tuttle, Eliza, member, p. 366

Tuttle, Mrs. Eliza, member, p. 376

Tuttle, Eliza Hopkins, baptism, p. 294

Tuttle, E.[liza] H., covenant, p. 427

Tuttle, Eliza H., member, p. 373

Tuttle, John, deaths, p. 480, 484

Tuttle, Harriet, married Caleb G. Loring, p. 154

Tuttle, Harriet, married Amos Cotting, p. 160

Tuttle, Harriet, member, p. 378

Tuttle, Harriet Caroline, child of John W. & Eliza H. Tuttle, baptism, p. 297 Tuttle, Miss Harriet E., member, p. 384

Tuttle, Henry Withington, child of Edward & Catharine Tuttle, baptism, p. 297

Tuttle, John Wells, child of John W. & Eliza H. Tuttle, baptism, p. 294

Tuttle, John Wells, child of Edward & C.[atharine] Tuttle, baptism, p. 304

Tuttle, John William, baptism, p. 302

Tuttle, John W., married Eliza H. Cade, p. 159

Tuttle, John W., covenant, p. 427

Tuttle, Martha, member, p. 375; deaths, p. 505

Tuttle, Miss Martha, member, p. 376

Tuttle, Martha-Ann, child of Edward & Catharine Tuttle, baptism, p. 301

Tuttle, Mrs. Mary, baptism, p. 296; member, p. 371

Tuttle, Mary, member, p. 364

Tuttle, Mary, wife of Samuel Tuttle, deaths, p. 478

Tuttle, Mary, wife of Turell Tuttle, deaths, p. 478

Tuttle, Mary-Ann, child of Edward & Catherine Tuttle, baptism, p. 302

Tuttle, Mehitable, married Dresser Bacon, p. 169

Tuttle, Ruth, wife of Samuel Tuttle, deaths, p. 465

Tuttle, Samuel, child of Edward & Catharine Tuttle, baptism, p. 306

Tuttle, Samuel, married Mary Silsbee, p. 155

Tuttle, Samuel, member, p. 371; deaths, p. 486

Tuttle, Sarah, married William Grubb Jun., p. 161

Tuttle, Sarah Elizabeth, child of William & Sarah Tuttle, baptism, p. 300

Tuttle, Sarah W. Gore, child of Eliza H. Tuttle, baptism, p. 307

Tuttle, Thomas Otis, child of Turell & Mary Tuttle, baptism, p. 283

Tuttle, Thomas Wells, child of Edward &

Catherine Tuttle, baptism, p. 290
Tuttle, Thomas Wells, child of Thomas &
Catharine Tuttle, baptism, p. 318
Tuttle, Turrell, member, p. 361
Tuttle, Turell, Sen., deaths, p. 484
Tyler, Abigail, member, p. 364

V

Vannah, Margaret, married Benjamin
Pepper, p. 163
Vanneever, infant child of A.[lexander]
Vanneever, deaths, p. 472
Vanneever, Catharine, married Josiah
Woodward Renfield, p. 168
Vanneever, Edmund Bowman, child of
Alexander & Betsey Vanneever, baptism,
p. 297
Vannevar, Evalina, child of Alexander &
Betsey Vannevar, baptism, p. 290
Vannevar, John, married Susan Cutter, p.
158
Vanneever, Lydia, child of Alexander &
Betsey Vanneever, baptism, p. 293
Vanneever, Lydia Fish, child of Alexander
& Betsey Vanneever, baptism, p. 294
Vanneever, Thomas, child of Alexander &
Betsey Vanneever, baptism, p. 301
Vanneever, William Ede, child of
Alexander & Betsy Vanneever, baptism,
p. 288
Vaughan, Elizabeth, deaths, p. 469
Vaughan, Samuel, deaths, p. 463
Veasey, J., member, p. 382
Veasey, R. J., member, p. 382
Veazie, Joseph, deaths, p. 511
Vernon, Elizabeth, member, p. 364;
deaths, p. 486
Veron, Abul, member, p. 364
Vincent, Joseph, baptism, p. 300
Vinton, Ruthy, married Aaron L. Darrow,
p. 151
Vose, Josiah, member, p. 361
Vose, Ruhamah, wife of Josiah Vose,
deaths, p. 462

W

Wade, Charles Freeman, baptism, p. 293
Wadsworth, George P., married Eliza

Webb, p. 168
Wait, Richard G., married Mary T.
Thomas, p. 168
Wales, Elisha, married Abigail R. Arnold,
p. 161
Walker, Charles Edwin, child of Charles
A. & Elizabeth M. Walker, baptism, p.
322
Walker, John F., married Julia E. Goodale,
p. 181
Walker, Marion Stimpson, child of
Charles A. & Elizabeth M. Walker,
baptism, p. 322
Walker, Mary, deaths, p. 482
Walker, Susanna Boylston, married
Robert Restieaux, p. 166
Walkup, William, married Mary
Hamilton, p. 170
Wallace, Francis Henry, baptism, p. 305
Wallace, William Ellis, baptism, p. 305
Ward, Abigail B., married Stephen
Rhoades, p. 162
Ward, Elizabeth P., married Bowen
Harrington, p. 167
Ward, Isaac, married Prudence H. Eaton,
p. 159
Ward, Mary, member, p. 370
Ward, Mrs. Mary, member, p. 376
Ward, Nahum, married Harriet Denny,
p. 174
Ward, William, deaths, p. 463
Ware, Elizabeth, wife of Rev. H. Ware,
deaths, p. 474
Ware, Rev. Henry Jr., pastor of the Second
Church, pp. 465, 468, 473-474, 478-479,
481-481
Ware, Henry, infant child of Rev. H.
Ware, deaths, p. 473
Warren, Royal S., M. D., married Susan
Elizabeth Bates, p. 175
Washburn, George M., married Lucy F.
Bartlett, p. 183
Washburn, Mary, member, p. 382
Waterman, Joseph S., married Mrs. Jane P.
Richardson, p. 154
Waterhouse, William Poole, deaths, p. 511
Waters, Hannah, married Richard
Howard, p. 158
Waterston, Rev. Richard Cassie, pastor of
Church of Our Saviour, pp. 184, 512

Watkins, Mr., of Charlestown, p. 479
Watson, David, deaths, p. 475
Watson, Elizabeth, deaths, p. 465
Watts, Caroline, baptism, p. 322; member, p. 385
Webb, infant child of Elisha Webb, deaths, p. 480
Webb, Charlotte S., child of Elisha Webb, deaths, p. 475
Webb, Elisha, married Sophia Charlotte Leach, p. 156
Webb, Eliza, married George P. Wadsworth, p. 168
Webb, John, deaths, pp. 495, 497
Webb, Rev. John, p. 373
Webb, Lydia, married Charles Foster, p. 160
Webb, Sarah, married Lincoln Hawkes Jun., p. 157
Webber, Mrs. K., deaths, p. 469
Webber. Mrs. Mary, married Amos Farnsworth, M. D., p. 160
Webber, Seth, married Mary Bourne, p. 156
Webster, Rev. C. H., p. 176
Webster, infant child of Dr. John Webster, deaths, p. 470
Webster, Hannah, member, p. 364
Webster, Hannah, widow of Redford Webster, deaths, pp. 488, 490
Webster, Harriet, member, p. 369
Webster, Harriet Wainwright, child of John W. & Harriet Webster, baptism, p. 292
Webster, John Redford, child of J.[ohn] W. & Harriet Webster, baptism, p. 288
Webster, Prof. John White, deaths, p. 504; p. 314
Webster, John W., member, p. 369
Webster, Mary-Ann White, child of John W. & Harriet Webster, baptism, p. 296
Webster, Ralph, married Ann Eliza Cushing, p. 158
Webster, Redford, deaths, p. 487
Webster, Sarah Hickling, child of John W. & Harriet Webster, baptism, p. 291
Webster, Sarah H., married John R. Dabney, p. 173
Welch, E., Mrs., deaths, p. 465
Weld, Eleanor, member, p. 367

Weld, Eliza, married Enos Cobb, p. 152
Weld, Helen Maria, child of James & Eleanor Weld, baptism, p. 283
Welles, Catharine Eustis, child of Benjamin & Sophia Welles, baptism, p. 284
Welles, Francis Edward, child of Benjamin & Sophia Welles, baptism, p. 284
Welles, Sophia Rumney, child of Benjamin & Sophia Welles, baptism, p. 284
Wells, child, deaths, p. 462
Wells, infant child of Benjamin T. Wells, deaths, p. 464
Wells, infant child of J. T. & Sarah Wells, deaths, p. 499
Wells, Benjamin T., married Mary-Ann Pitman, p. 164
Wells, Benjamin T., member, p. 366; deaths, p. 472
Wells, Caroline A., married James H. Morgan, p. 171
Wells, Charles Augustus, child of Benjamin T. & Lydia Wells, baptism, p. 285
Wells, Charles G., member, p. 380
Wells, Charles Gustavus, member, p. 379
Wells, Charles Gustavus, child of Benjamin T. & Lydia Wells, baptism, p. 286
Wells, Cordelia Rosanna, child of Benjamin T. & Lydia Wells, baptism, p. 286
Wells, Cordelia R., married Thomas W. Capon, p. 172
Wells, Emily, deaths, p. 507
Wells, Emily Frances, child of Benjamin T. & Lydia Wells, baptism, p. 289
Wells, Emily Frances, member, p. 374, 381
Wells, Francis Parkman, child of Benjamin T. & Lydia Wells, baptism, p. 282
Wells, Francis P., married Mary Ann F. Smith, p. 174
Wells, Joanna, married Franklin Smith, p. 164
Wells, Deacon John, member, p. 361; deaths, p. 486
Wells, Lydia, member, p. 366, 380
Wells, Mrs. Lydia, member, p. 376

Wells, Lydia Young, married Andrew Townsend Hall, p. 160

Wells, Martha, member, p. 364

Wells, Martha, widow of Deacon John Wells, deaths, p. 499

Wells, Mary-Ann, married John Ferguson, p. 169

Wells, Sophia, member, p. 368; deaths, p. 464

Wells, Thomas, married Eliza Tuttle, p. 151

Wells, Thomas, member, p. 366; deaths, p. 482

Wells, Thomas Eliot, child of Thomas & Eliza Wells, baptism, p. 289; deaths, p. 470

Wells, Thomas Gilman, child of Thomas & Eliza Wells, baptism, p. 292

Wells, Thomas G., member, p. 375; deaths, p. 503

Welsh, Mary, member, p. 366

Welsh, Sarah, member, p. 367

Wentworth, James N., married Rachel A. Smith, p. 181

Westley, Deborah, married Henry Thacker, p. 163

Weston, James M., married Abby W. Torrey, p. 179

Wetherbee, Francis W., married Ann Maria Foster, p. 177

Whalan, Elizabeth H., married Charles Arnold, p. 162

Whalan, James, deaths, p. 474

Whalan, Margery B., member, p. 372

Wheeler, Abigail, baptism, p. 282; member, p. 366

Wheeler, Abigail, married Eleazer Wheelock, p. 152

Wheelock, Eleazer, married Abigail Wheeler, p. 152

Whellen, Elizabeth, deaths, p. 464

Whitcomb, child of Lot Whitcomb, deaths, p. 464

Whitcomb, Dolly, covenant, p. 426

Whitcomb [Witcomb], Levi, married Elizabeth U. Francis, p. 154

Whitcomb, Lot, covenant, p. 426

Whitcomb [Witcomb], Lot, child of Lot & Dolly Whitcomb, baptism, p. 285

Whitcomb [Witcomb], Martha, married George Ainslie, p. 151

White, Adeline, married John Grubb, p. 160

White, Charles Walter, baptism, p. 295

White, Isaac, Jun., deaths, p. 464

White, Isaac, Sen., deaths, p. 464

White, Lydia, married John Boardman, p. 153

White, Margaret S., married Alfred Hammatt, p. 171

White, Mary, member, p. 369

White, Mary, widow, deaths, p. 479

Whitman, child, deaths, p. 492

Whitmarsh, Dorothy, member, p. 365

Whitmarsh, William, baptism, p. 291

Whittemore, Bernard, baptism, p. 287; covenant, p. 426

Whittemore, Bernard Bemis, child of B[ernard] & Jane Whittemore, baptism, p. 287

Whittemore, Jane, member, p. 368

Wiggin, infant child of Mr. A. Wiggin, deaths, p. 499

Wilbur, child, deaths, p. 510

Wild, Abigail (Mrs. Baxter), member, p. 364

Wild, Amassa T., married Sarah B. Babb, p. 156

Wild, Charles Tidd, child of Eben[ezar] & A.[bigail] B. Wild, baptism, p. 288

Wild, Eliza, member, p. 377

Wild, Miss Eliza, member, p. 371

Wild, Miss Elizabeth, member, p. 377

Wild, Harriet, child of Ebenezer & Abigail B. Wild, baptism, p. 284

Wiley, Henry Russell, baptism, p. 307

Wilkins, Sarah W., married George W. Richardson, p. 171

Wilkinson, Betsey, wife of S. Wilkinson, deaths, p. 503

Wilkinson, David, son of W. Wilkinson, deaths, p. 494

Wilkinson, Elizabeth, married John F. Trull, p. 163

Wilkinson, Frances, married Joseph Addison Leseur, p. 172

Wilkinson, John, deaths, p. 470

Willard, Dr., father of S. Dana Ripley, deaths, p. 499

Willard, Elizabeth, deaths, p. 463

Willard, Mrs. Elizabeth [Willard Parkman Shaw], sister of Samuel Parkman, baptism, p. 284

Williams, child of Thomas Williams, deaths, p. 463

Williams, child of Capt. Williams, deaths, p. 468

Williams, Adeline, married Joseph Lewis, p. 174

Williams, Alfred, married Mary Stearns, p. 162

Williams, Andrew Sigourney, child of Thomas & Emily F. Williams, baptism, p. 308

Williams, Miss Ardelia, member, p. 371

Williams, Catharine, member, p. 365

Williams, Delia, deaths, pp. 495, 497

Williams, Elizabeth, married Abraham Macoy, p. 164

Williams, Elizabeth, member, p. 365 (twice)

Williams, Elizabeth, widow of H. H. Williams, deaths, p. 470

Williams, Emily Foster, member, p. 374

Williams, Emily F., wife of T. Williams, deaths, p. 497

Williams, Frances A., married William Fergus, p. 171

Williams, Hannah, widow, deaths, p. 491

Williams, Harriet A., married Henry H. W. Sigourney, p. 165

Williams, Henry P. Adams, child of Henry R. & A.[bigail] H. Williams, baptism, p. 307

Williams, Henry R., married Abigail H. Adams, p. 164

Williams, James, married Mary Durant, p. 155

Williams, John, married Hannah Lewis, p. 156

Williams, John, married Jane A. Gould, p. 158

Williams, John, married Mary-Ann C. Derby, p. 168

Williams, Mary Elizabeth, married Rev. Amos Smith, p. 173

Williams, Mary E., member, p. 372

Williams, Nancy, child of Thomas & Elizabeth Williams, baptism, p. 283

Williams, Nancy, child of Thomas &

Elizabeth Williams, baptism, p. 289

Williams, Nancy, married Joseph R. Gordon, p. 173

Williams, Nancy, member, p. 372

Williams, Philip Adams, child of H.[enry ?] R. Williams, deaths, p. 492

Williams, Rachel M., married Charles H. Pratt, p. 179

Williams, Sarah, member, p. 369; deaths, p. 470

Williams, Susan A. B., married John C. Hayden, M. D., p. 169

Williams, Thomas, deaths, pp. 488, 490

Williams, Thomas A., married Mary P. Adams, p. 169

Williams, Thomas H., member, p. 372

Willis, Mary, married James H. Duncan, p. 162

Williston, Rebecca J., married Thomas Cummings, p. 171

Wilson, Mrs Charlotte, married Charles Hannah, p. 167

Wilson, Clarissa, baptism, p. 314

Wilson, Lydia, baptism, p. 287; member, p. 369

Wilson, Lydia, Mrs., deaths, p. 475

Wilson, Lydia, Miss, deaths, p. 501

Wilson, Sarah, member, p. 369

Wilson, Susan, married William Baker, p. 154

Wilson, Susan Paine, deaths, p. 487

Winchester, Stephen, deaths, p. 502

Winde, Lewis, married Eliza Gurney, p. 172

Windship, Betsey, married Peter Gray, p. 160

Windship, Lucy, deaths, p. 470

Winkley, Rev. Samuel H., pastor of Pitts Street Chapel, p. 508

Winslow, Caroline Louisa, daughter of Sarah J. Winslow, deaths, p. 499

Winslow, George Chapman, child of John & Sally S. Winslow, baptism, p. 290

Winslow, Horatio Bray, child of John & Sally S. Winslow, baptism, p. 290

Winsor, infant child, Mr., Winsor, deaths, pp. 494, 495

Wipple, Thaddeus, deaths, p. 511

Wise, Henry, married Catharine M. Younger, p. 169

Wistar, George, married Mrs. Margaret Lear, p. 183

Wiswall, Mr., deaths, p. 468

Wiswall, Dexter W., married Elizabeth R. Clark, p. 170; p. 313

Wiswall, Mrs. Elizabeth Raymond, wife of Dexter W. Wiswall, baptism, p. 313

Wiswall, Elizabeth Raymond, child of Dexter W.[ard] & Elizabeth R.[aymond] Wiswall, baptism, p. 323

Wiswall, George Clark, child of Dexter Ward & Elizabeth Raymond Wiswall, baptism, p. 313

Wiswall, Lydia H., married Josiah M. Barnett, p. 156

Wiswall, Mrs. Sarah, baptism, p. 316

Wiswall, Sarah Blake, married Ellis Gray Blake, p. 154

Wiswall, William Dexter, child of Dexter Ward & Elizabeth Raymond Wiswall, baptism, p. 313

Witcomb [Whitcomb], Susan Barber, child of Lot & Dolly Witcomb, baptism, p. 285

Withington, Hannah, married Parker H. Pearce, p. 154

Witton, child of Ezra Witton, deaths, p. 481

Wolcott, Henry D., married Emily Chandler, p. 162

Wood, Dolly B., married Reuben Heywood, p. 156

Wood, Nancy, married John Tileston Fracker, p. 154

Woodbury, William W., married Lydia R. Shepherd, p. 177

Woods, Eunice, married Eleazer D. Hartwell, p. 169

Woods, Julia A., married Alfred C. Converse, p. 180

Wooley, William, married Mary Ann Pierce, p. 175

Worcester, Alpheus, baptism, p. 297

Worcester, Rev. Noah, editor of *The Christian Disciple* and *The Friend of Peace*, p. 283

Wright, Mr., deaths, p. 510

Wright, Anna Jane, baptism, p. 314

Wright, Benjamin Stewart, baptism, p. 314

Wright, Daniel Gardner, baptism, p. 314

Wright, Emery Seaman, baptism, p. 314

Wright, Theodore, deaths, p. 498

Wyman, Morrill, M. D. married Elizabeth Aspinwall Pulsifer, p. 171

Y

Young, infant child of S. M. Young, deaths, p. 492

Young, Alexander, father of Rev. A. Young, deaths, p. 491

Young, Rev. Alexander, D. D., pastor of the New South Church, pp. 488, 490-491

Young, Caroline, child of Rev. Alexander Young, deaths, p. 493

Young, Elizabeth Carnes, daughter of Edward Carnes, deaths, p. 506

Young, Grace Desor, child of Joshua Young, baptism, p. 315

Young, James, married Nancy Trask, p. 161

Young, James, married Elizabeth Carnes, p. 174

Young, Joshua, member, p. 375

Young, Mary Elizabeth, child of Joshua & Mary Elizabeth S. Young, baptism, p. 314

Younger, infant child of Levi Younger, deaths, p. 481

Younger, son of Levi Younger, deaths, p. 480

Younger, C. P., covenant, p. 426

Younger, Catharine, child of Levi & Catharine P. Younger, baptism, p. 287

Younger, Catharine M., married Henry Wise, p. 169

Younger, Catharine P., deaths, p. 481

Younger, David Harris, child of Levi & Catharine Younger, baptism, p. 300

Younger, Esther Rowe, child of Levi & Catharine Younger, baptism, p. 300

Younger, Lawrence Curney, child of Levi & Catharine Younger, baptism, p. 296

Younger, Levi, married Catharine P. Jones, p. 153

Younger, Levi, married Mrs. Jane Babson, p. 165

Younger, Levi, covenant, p. 426

Younger, Levi, child of Levi & Catherine P. Younger, baptism, p. 290

ACKNOWLEDGEMENTS

Co-Author Steven Fanning, Ph.D., retired associate professor of Medieval History, University of Illinois at Chicago, for his authorship of Chapter 3 on Unitarianism and for his major effort in transcribing all Book III New North Church Records plus the detailed and useful index. We could not have completed this book without his major efforts.

Margaret (Peggy) Bendroth, director of Congregational Library, Boston for Chapter 4 excellent explanation of Covenant Relationship of Puritans and Congregationalists.

Erin Ryan Lordan, photographer, and Gerald F. Jordan, Boston native and director of Development for Fenwick High School, Oak Park, IL, for current photos in this book.

Andrea Cronin, asst. reference librarian, Massachusetts Historical Society, Boston; Kimberly Reynolds, curator of manuscripts, Boston Public Library; Leo W. Collins, 1st & 2nd Church historian, Boston, Church history diagram for Appendix II.

Sister Fidelma Conway, C.S.J., St. Stephen's Roman Catholic Church historian, Boston, for her work in 1995 on the current history since Near North Church left its church building; Mike Adaskaveg, staff photographer, The Boston Herald, Rose Kennedy 1995 funeral photos:. Laura V. Monti, Keeper of Rare Books & Manuscripts, Boston Public Library, for making Book III Records available in 1995; Harold Field Worthley, head librarian at Congregational Library; Shaune Diaz Cresman, Northeast Document Conservation Center, who diligently copied the original Book III; my cousin Rachael Lewellen, librarian at University of MA at Amherst, photography of Book III; Virginia Smith, reference librarian, MA Historical Society; and George Quintal Jr. of Worcester, MA, Revolutionary War lecturer and tour guide and author of *Patriots of Color at Bunker Hill* (2002), research of Boston newspapers on Parkman murder.

Selected Bibliography

I. Manuscript & Archival Materials

Boston Public Library, Rare Books Division

 New North Church Records, Volumes I, II & III (Microfilm at New England Historic Genealogical Society, Boston).

Massachusetts Historical Society, Boston

 Eliot Papers by Ephraim Eliot

II. Official & Semi-official Publications

Ancient & Honorable Artillery Company of Massachusetts, Vol. I & II: Alfred Mudge & Son, printers, Boston, 1897, compiled by Oliver Ayer Roberts.

Inventory of the Records of the particular (Congregational) Churches of Massachusetts Gathered 1620-1805, Harvard University Press, 1970, compiled by Harold Field Worthley, head librarian, The Congregational Library, Boston.

Memorial History of Boston (1630-1880), Vol. I & II, James R. Osgood & Company, Boston,1882, edited by Justin Winsor, librarian of Harvard University.

Record Commissioners, 10th Report, Doc. 150: Miscellaneous Papers: The Boston Directory of 1789 as printed and sold by John Norman at Oliver's Dock, Page 171. 1886, Published by City of Boston with Rockwell & Churchill, as City Printers.

Record Commissioners, 22nd Report, Doc. 92: 1798 List of Land, Lots & Buildings by Ward and Owner, Pages 1 – 441, *Boston Inhabitants,1790 Census.,* 1890, Published by City of Boston with Rockwell & Churchill, as City Printers.

The Quiet Philanthropy 1795 – 1995, Raymond J. Purdy, MA Charitable Mechanics Assn., Quincy, MA, 1995.

III. Other Published Primary Sources

Assessors' Taxing Books of the Town of Boston, 1780, Boston, Reprinted from the Bostonian Society's Publications, 1912.

Colesworthy, D. C., *John Tileston's School, Boston, 1778-1789, Diary 1761-1766,* (his students, teachers, and diary. Boston, Antiquarian Book Store, 1887.

Crawford, Mary Caroline, *St. Botolph's Town: An Account of Old Boston in Colonial Days,* Boston, L. C. Page & Company, 1908.

Drake, Samuel Adams, *Old Landmarks and Historic Personages of Boston,* Rutland, Vt., Charles E. Tuttle Company, Inc., 1971.

Eliot, Ephraim, *Historical Notices of the New North Religious Society in the Town of Boston with Notes about the Reverend Andrew and John Eliot,* Boston, Phelps & Farnham, 1822.

Hayward, John, *Boston Churches & Ministers from A Gazetteer of MA,* Boston, John P. Jewett & Co. 1849.

Kilmer, David H., *The Autobiography of Henry Fowle of Boston (1766-1837),* Bowie, Md., Heritage Books, 1991.

Reaman, G. Elmore, *The Trail of THE HUGUENOTS in Europe, the U.S., South Africa and Canada,* London, Frederick Miller LTD, 1963

Richardson, Peter Tufts, The Boston Religion, *Unitarianism in It's Capital City,* Rockland, ME, Red Barn Publishing 2003.

Thwing, Annie Haven, *Crooked and Narrow Streets of Boston,* Boston, Marshall Jones Company, 1920.

DEDICATION

This book is dedicated to my wife Suzanne Austin Wells, who has been an inspiration for this book since 1992 and who has kept me going in those dark times when it seemed impossible. She continues to be the bright light in my always unfolding world of history and publishing, designing this book from cover to cover. This is the 30th book she has designed for Chauncey Park Press and she continues to inspire us with new and interesting ideas and possibilities.

With deep love and sincere gratitude, I dedicate this book and remain her loving husband.

Charles Chauncey Wells,
September 8, 2014

Lineage of the Churches.

Old Church or 1st Ch 1630.

Old North or 2d Church 1649

1st Branch

2d Branch

North Bennett St Church 1741

New North Ch 1714

New Brick 1720

1779 Joined

Re-joined 1785.

Church

Joined

Bulfinch St. Church

Joined

1st church   2d church   New North

APPENDIX I
UPDATED DIAGRAM OF CHURCH HISTORIES
BY LEO W. COLLINS
FIRST/SECOND CHURCH, BOSTON

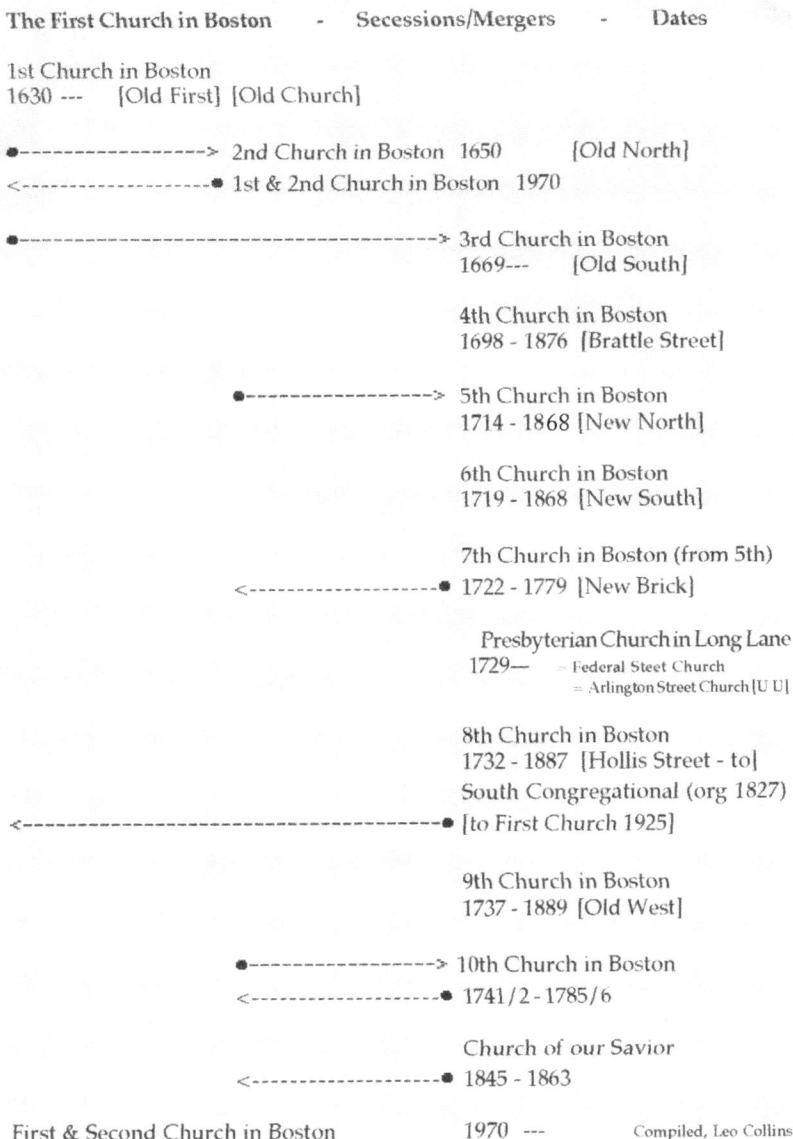

The First Church in Boston   -   Secessions/Mergers   -   Dates

1st Church in Boston
1630 ---   [Old First] [Old Church]

●------------------> 2nd Church in Boston   1650   [Old North]
<-------------------● 1st & 2nd Church in Boston   1970

●---> 3rd Church in Boston
                                     1669---   [Old South]

                                       4th Church in Boston
                                       1698 - 1876 [Brattle Street]

                ●------------------> 5th Church in Boston
                                       1714 - 1868 [New North]

                                       6th Church in Boston
                                       1719 - 1868 [New South]

                                       7th Church in Boston (from 5th)
                <-------------------● 1722 - 1779 [New Brick]

                                       Presbyterian Church in Long Lane
                                       1729—   = Federal Steet Church
                                                     = Arlington Street Church [U U]

                                       8th Church in Boston
                                       1732 - 1887 [Hollis Street - to]
                                       South Congregational (org 1827)
<--● [to First Church 1925]

                                       9th Church in Boston
                                       1737 - 1889 [Old West]

                ●------------------> 10th Church in Boston
                <-------------------● 1741/2 - 1785/6

                                       Church of our Savior
                <-------------------● 1845 - 1863

First & Second Church in Boston   1970 ---   Compiled, Leo Collins

"COMPLETION OF A CENTURY"
BY FRANCIS PARKMAN, NOVEMBER 27, 1814

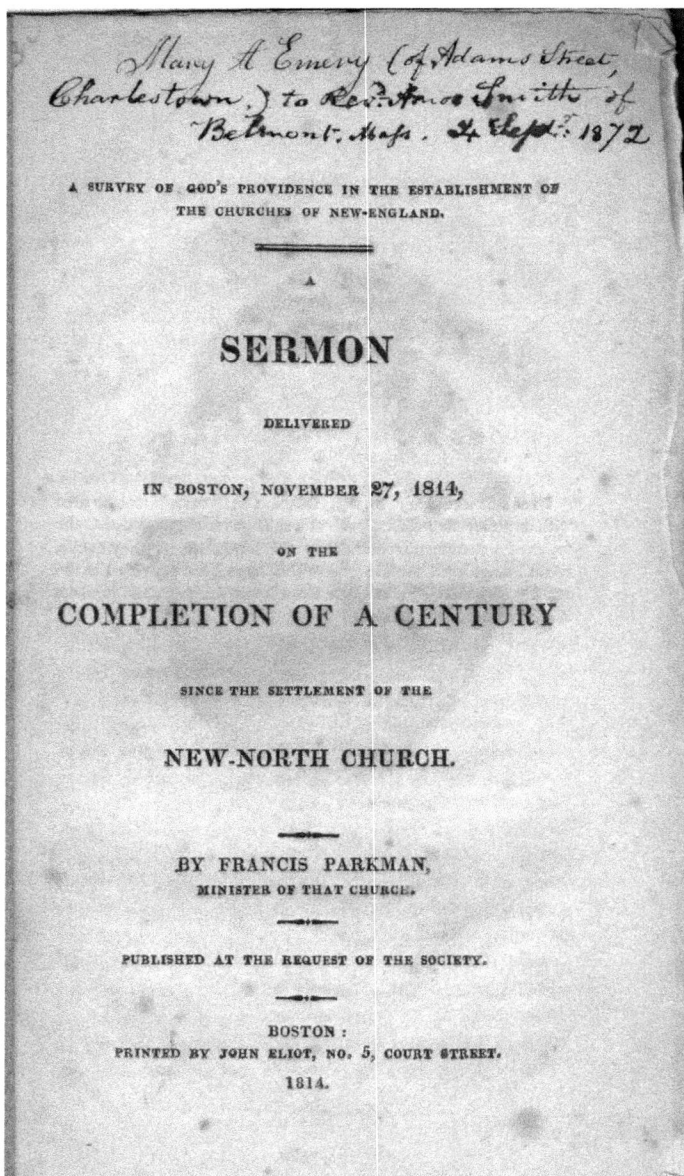

Mary A. Emery (of Adams Street, Charlestown,) to Rev. Mrs. Smith of Belmont. Mass. 24 Sept. 1872

A SURVEY OF GOD'S PROVIDENCE IN THE ESTABLISHMENT OF
THE CHURCHES OF NEW-ENGLAND.

A

SERMON

DELIVERED

IN BOSTON, NOVEMBER 27, 1814,

ON THE

COMPLETION OF A CENTURY

SINCE THE SETTLEMENT OF THE

NEW-NORTH CHURCH.

BY FRANCIS PARKMAN,
MINISTER OF THAT CHURCH.

PUBLISHED AT THE REQUEST OF THE SOCIETY.

BOSTON :
PRINTED BY JOHN ELIOT, NO. 5, COURT STREET.
1814.

Conclusion of Parkman Sermon:

another such remembrance can never return to us
again, or to any, who shall come after us, till we
have long been slumbering, and perhaps forgotten in
the dust. " Our fathers—where are *they* ?" Where
are they, who once filled the seats of your ancient
temple, and conducted your infant footsteps there?
They are passed away. They are numbered with
the vast congregation of the dead.—Your pastors—
where are *they?*—Their lips are sealed in silence;
they have rendered their account, and nothing now
remains of all, for which you loved them, but the remembrance of their instructions and the savour of
their lives. Where, let me ask, are now the fervent
prayers, that in the course of the long century, that
has past, ascended from the altars of your father's
hearts? What has become of all their sighs of peni-
tence, their holy resolutions, their works of love?
They have been marked and remembered by the
omniscient God, and, we trust, have been blest to
their soul's salvation. And what, let me ask, what
has been the fruit of all their cares and labors for us?
Be exhorted, my friends, solemnly to remember this
day "how ye have received and heard." Let us enquire what improvement we have made of all our
privileges; thus judging ourselves, that we be
not judged of the Lord. Let us work the work of
Him, that sent us, while it is day. Let us be prepared to follow our departed fathers to the world of
spirits ; and God of his mercy grant, that having inherited their privileges, and set down in the churches, they have formed on earth, we may be fellow-
heirs with them in that building of God, that house
not made with hands, eternal in the heavens.

SERMON EXCERPT

"HISTORICAL DISCOURSE"
ARTHUR B. FULLER, OCTOBER 1, 1854

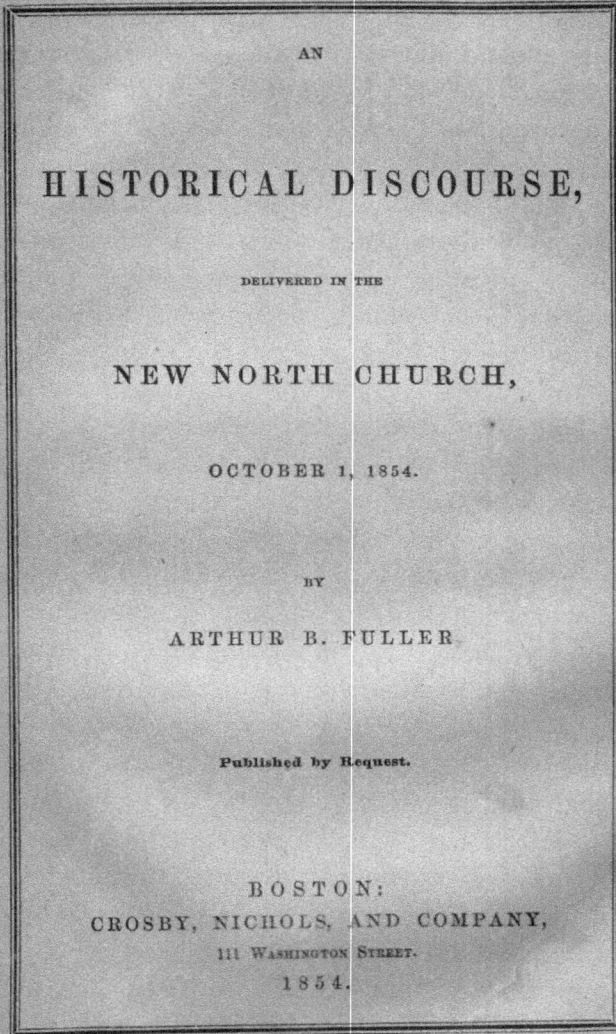

AN

HISTORICAL DISCOURSE,

DELIVERED IN THE

NEW NORTH CHURCH,

OCTOBER 1, 1854.

BY

ARTHUR B. FULLER

Published by Request.

BOSTON:
CROSBY, NICHOLS, AND COMPANY,
111 WASHINGTON STREET.
1854.

Conclusion of Fuller Sermon:

There is devout gratitude when we think of the providence which has watched over our fathers, and still watches over us. There is hope for the future when we rely upon the united and faithful labors of us all, with Heaven's blessing never withheld from those who diligently seek it. Yes, I dare use that word *hope*, though not without hesitation. For a series of years the native population has been gradually receding from some parts of the city, and this church, as well as others, has, from that and other causes, lost a large number of once active and devoted members. Nor should I dare to speak of hope, did I not feel a strong confidence that you will labor earnestly to maintain religious institutions in this house, both for yourselves and your children, and that you will strive that this society shall not be numbered with the things which have perished without much faithful endeavor on your part to keep alive the fire of incense upon this ancient altar. This cannot be done without your fidelity and zeal; without your readiness to make much sacrifice both of ease and of that money* which is so often, alas! preferred to religion. Above all, let us trust in God. Let us not put our trust and dependence upon mere beauty of architecture or earthly appliances, but on His grace and the reception to our hearts of the Gospel of His Son, — on the influences of that Holy Spirit freely imparted to those who ask it; and let our prayer to-day be in those words of sacred writ which formed the text for the discourse, when, a half-century ago, this church was dedicated: " The Lord our God be with us as he was with our fathers; let him never leave or forsake us."

SERMON EXCERPTS

COVER OF SERMONS BEFORE DESTRUCTION OF NEW BRICK CHURCH, THEN CALLED 2ND CHURCH MARCH 10, 1844.

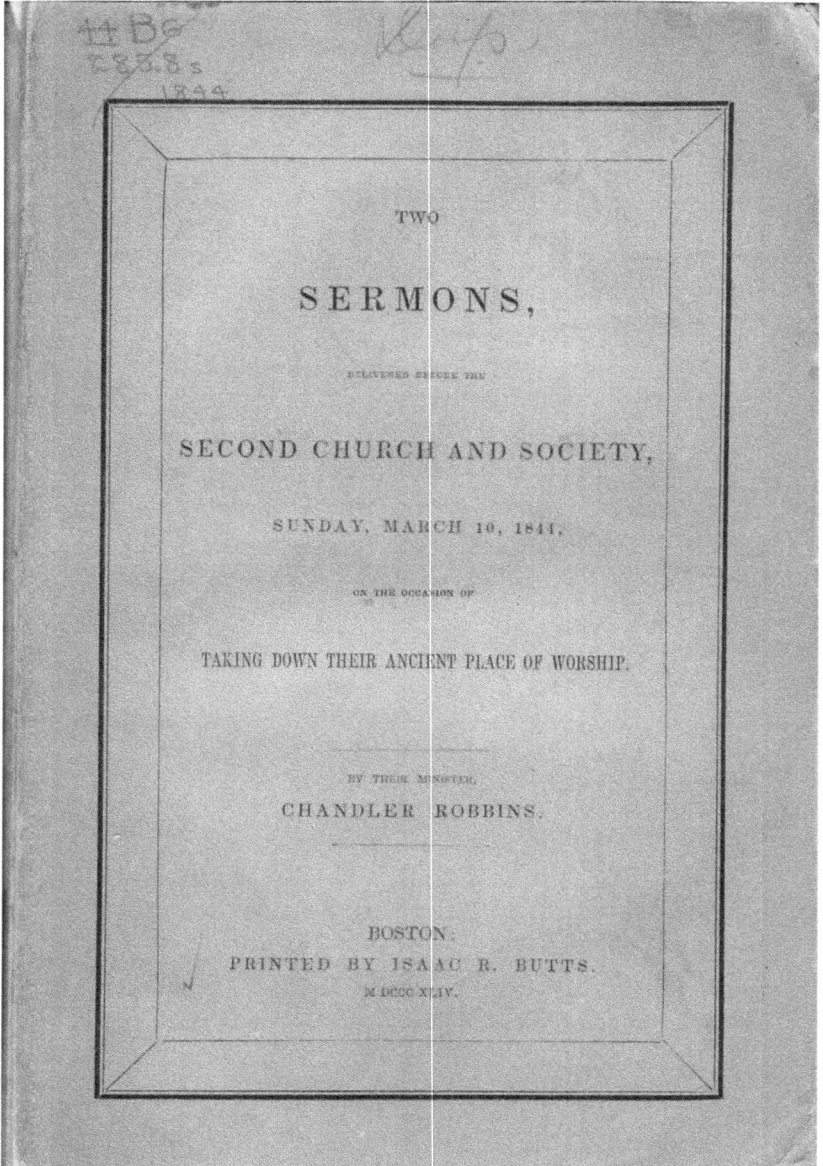

TWO

SERMONS,

DELIVERED BEFORE THE

SECOND CHURCH AND SOCIETY,

SUNDAY, MARCH 10, 1844,

ON THE OCCASION OF

TAKING DOWN THEIR ANCIENT PLACE OF WORSHIP.

BY THEIR MINISTER,

CHANDLER ROBBINS.

BOSTON:
PRINTED BY ISAAC R. BUTTS.
M DCCC XLIV.

Benj. Tuttle Wells son of John & Joanna Wells born on Friday March 17. 1775 of Boston was married to Lydia Appleton (born Feb 17. 1779) daughter of Thomas & Martha Appleton. on the 20th Oct. 1799. The births of their children are as follows.

Lydia Young Wells was born on Tuesday Dec 23. 1800 at half past 12 oclk now. baptized Sunday Jan 4. 1801 by Rev John Elliot D.D.

Mary Ann. born on Monday July 12. 1802. ¼ before 7 P.M. baptized Sunday July 25. 1802. by John Elliot D.D. (died Aug 1. 1853 5.30 PM)

Martha Appleton born on Friday June 1. 1804. quarter past 2 oclk a. m. baptized. Sunday June 10. 1804. Rev J. E.

Benjamin Tuttle jr. born Thursday Feb 27 1805. at half past 4 oclk a. m. baptized. Sun. March 23. 1806. J. E.

Joanna born Thursday Dec 17. 1807. 6 oclk a.m. bap—Sunday Dec 20. 1807. by J. E.

Caroline Augusta. born on Friday March 23. 1810 at 9 oclk P. M. baptized Sunday April 8. 1810. J. B.

John Thomas born on Wednesday March 18. 1812 quarter past 11 oclk P. M. bap. on Sun. April 12. 1812. by J. E.

Francis Parkman born Monday Jan 10. 1814 quarter past 2 oclk P. M. bap. Sun. Jan 23. 1814. by Rev F. Parkman

Charles Augustus born Monday July 15: 1816 half past 3 A. m. baptized Sun. August 18. 1816 by Rev F. Parkman.

Charles Gustavus & Cordelia Rosanna their children were born on Saturday, July 19. 1817 at half past 4 ock A. M. bap. on Sunday, August 3. 1817. by Rev Francis Parkman.

Emily Frances born Saturday Oct 9. 1819. 9 oclk P. M. baptized Sunday Oct 17. 1819 by Rev. F. P.

The Appleton-Wells Family Bible

Data from the Appleton Family Bible was given to Charles Chauncey Wells by Arthur K. Wells of Wellesley, MA, during a meeting in August, 1998. It holds important information from New North Church that has not been published before.

Benjamin Tuttle Wells, son of John and Joanna Wells of Boston, was born Friday, March 17, 1775. He was married Oct. 20, 1799, to:

Lydia Appleton, born Feb. 17, 1779, the daughter of Thomas and Martha Appleton (page 2).

Their 12 children:

Lydia Young Wells was born on Tuesday, Dec. 25, 1800 at half past 12 o'clock p.m. Baptized Sunday, Jan 4, 1801, by The Rev. John Eliot, D.D. (New North Church).

Mary Ann Wells, born on Thursday, July 12, 1802—1/4 before 7 p.m., baptized Sunday, July 25, 1802 by John Eliot, DD. (New North Church) Died Aug 1, 1885 at 5:30 p.m.

Martha Appleton Wells, born Friday, June 1, 1804, quarter past 2 o'clock a.m., baptized Sunday, June 10, 1804, Rev. J. E. (John Eliot, New North Church).

Benjamin Tuttle Wells Jr, born Thursday, Feb. 27, 1805 at half past 4 o'clock a.m., baptized Sunday, March 23, 1805, J. E. (John Eliot, New North Church).

Joanna Wells, born Thursday, Dec. 17, 1807, 6 o'clock a.m., baptized Sunday Dec. 20, 1807, by J. E. (John Eliot, New North Church).

Caroline Augusta, born on Friday, March 23, 1810 at 9 o'clock p.m., baptized Sunday, April 8, 1810, J. E. (John Eliot, New North Church).

John Thomas Wells, born Wed., March 18, 1812, quarter past 11 o'clock p.m., baptized on Sun., April 12, 1812, by J. E (John Eliot, New North Church).

Francis Parkman Wells, born Monday, Jan. 10, 1814, quarter past 2 o'clock p.m., baptized Sun., Jan. 23, 1814 by Rev. F. Parkman (New North Church)

Charles Augustus, born Mon., July 15, 1816, half past 3 a.m., baptized Sun., Aug. 18, 1816 by Rev. F. Parkman (New North).

Charles Gustavus & Cordelia Rosanna, twin children were born on Saturday, July 19, 1817 at half past 4 o'clock a.m., baptized on Sun., Aug. 3, 1817 by Rev Francis Parkman (New North).

Emily Frances Wells, born Sat., Oct. 9, 1819, 9 o'clock p.m., baptized Sunday Oct. 19, 1819 by Rev. F. P. (Francis Parkman of New North Church)

Vaccination against Small Pox: Lydia & Mary Ann vaccinated March 27, 1808, Martha & Benjamin, April 3, 1808, Joanna April 16, 1808. John Thomas, May 1812, Caroline & Francis May 14, 1815. Charles & Cordelia June 1819. Emily Frances June 13, 1820. all by Dr. Benjamin Shurtleff.

Appleton Family Data:

Thomas Appleton (father of Lydia Appleton Wells) was born March 15, 1744. He died Dec. 1, 1803, aged 59 years.

Martha Barnard Appleton (his wife) was born Dec. 17, 1747. They were married Dec. 15, 1766. Martha Appleton, mother of these children below, died very suddenly Jan 30, 1829, Aged 81 years.

Their 11 Children:

Samuel Appleton, born May 8, 1768, 12 o'clock p.m. He died Jan. 8, 1815, 47 years, 9 months.

Martha Appleton, born June 16, 1770. Martha Appleton Thayer died Oct. 7, 1848, aged 77 years, 4 months, of dysentery.

Thomas Russel Appleton, born June 12, 1772. Thomas Russel Appleton died at Haverhill, MA, April 6, 1863, aged 90 years, 10 months.

John Appleton, born Dec. 2, 2774, died 1868.

Benjamin Appleton, born Sept. 24, 1777, died March 15, 1778.

Lydia Appleton, born Feb. 17, 1779. Lydia Appleton Wells died at Boston March 22, 1872, aged 93 years 1 month, 5 days.

NOTE: She is the wife of Benjamin Tuttle Wells on the first page of these entries. Both were members of New North Church He bought the Wells-Adams House, 15 Back St and she occupied it for 50 years after he died in 1822.

Benjamin Barnard Appleton, born May 8, 1781. He died very suddenly April 23, 1844, aged 63 years.

Polly Appleton, born April 24, 1783, died Jan 5, 1792.

George Washington Appleton, Henry Knox Appleton, Joseph Warren Appleton were born June 6, 1786 (triplets). Joseph Warren Appleton died June 19, 1787. Henry Knox Appleton died Aug. 8, 1829, 45 years. George Washington Appleton died at Delevan, Illinois (prob. Wisconsin), March 28, 1850, 64 years.

Lydia Young, great grandmother of these children, died Sept. 27, 1793, Aged 88 years.

Mary Appleton, grandmother of these children, died Sept. 3, 1803, Aged 87 years.

Catharine Appleton died at Boston, Nov. 7, 1875, aged 85 years.

Andrew T. Hall died Nov. 22, 1875, Age 77 years, 3 months.

Marriages:

Lydia Young Wells married to Andrew T. Hall Nov. 30, 1823 by Rev. F. Parkman (Francis Parkman of New North Church)

Joanna Wells married to Franklin Smith Jan 21, 1830 by Rev. F. P. (Francis Parkman)

Benjamin Tuttle Wells Jr. to Mary Ann Pittman April 8, 1830 by Rev. F. P. (Francis Parkman)

Martha Appleton Wells to John A. Appleton Sept 8, 1839 by Rev. Waldo Emerson.

Mary Ann Wells to John Ferguson April 13, 1836 by Rev. F. P. (Francis Parkman)

Caroline Augusta Wells to James H. Morgan Nov. 5, 1839 by Rev. F. P. (Francis Parkman)

John Thomas Wells to Sarah Bartlett Dec. 19, 1839 by Rev. Chandler Robbins

Thomas W. Capen to Cordelia Rosanna Wells Sept. 12, 1841 by Rev. F. Parkman D.D.

Francis Parkman Wells to Mary Ann Smith Nov. 8, 1846 by Rev. F. Parkman

Charles Gustavus Wells to Jennie C. Woodside April 29, 1857 by Rev. Mr. Peters of N.Y.

Deaths:

Benjamin Tuttle Wells, Father of the above children died April 16, 1822, aged 47 years.

Charles Augustus died August 18, 1816

Benjamin Tuttle Wells Jr. died at New Orleans

Emily Frances Wells died March 19, 1855.

Joanna Wells Smith died at Brooklyn (N.Y.) May 1, 1864.

Cordelia Rosanna Wells Capen died at Dorchester Sept. 5, 1864.

Grandchildren: (All of Page 4)

Andrew T. Hall born Oct. 1, 1824, Died at St. Yago de Cuba Feb. 9, 1841, aged 16 yrs, 4 mos.

Mary Ann Hall August 19, 1829 Married to John Monroe, April 4, 1849.

Frances Ann Smith Sept. 6, 1831, April 16, 1857 married to Charles Fowler.

Benjamin T. Wells Dec. 13, 1831, married to Martha Wheeler Sept. 5, 1856, died March 18, 1899.

John A. Appleton March 22, 1834, married to Josephine Johns June 21, 1860.

Benjamin F. Smith Sept. 30, 1834 Married to Mary A. Hunt Feb. 11, 1858, died March 18, 1900.

Benjamin Ferguson March 19, 1837, died March 22, 1837.

Thomas A. Ferguson May 9, 1838, Died June 30, 1838.

Emily F. W. Appleton June 25, 1838.

William H. Ferguson Feb. 4, 1840, Died Feb. 25, 1841.

James H. Morgan Oct 17, 1840.

Andrew T Hall Wells Oct 8, 1841, Died June 29, 1842.

Caroline A. Morgan July 6, 1842.

Thomas W. Capen Sept. 25, 1842.

Sarah & John T. Wells (twins) born July 23, 1843.

Lydia W. Morgan Dec. 24, 1844.

Cordelia F. Capen June 6, 1845, died April 22, 2845

Charles G. Capen Dec. 15, 1846, Died Dec. 16, 1846.

Mary Ellen Wells July 4, 1847, died July 7, 1847.

Francis A. Wells Jan 6, 1849, died Jan 9, 1849.

Charles F. & Emily Cordelia Morgan (twins) April 29, 1848, Charles died Feb. 20, 1851.

Henry B. Wells Nov. 10, 1848 Died July 19, 1899

Sarah E. Capen Jan 9, 1849, died Jan 12, 1849.

Sarah Hersey Wells May 2, 1850, died July 1850.

Charles G. W. Capen July 9, 1851.

Frances E. Wells Oct. 13, 1852.

Cordelia R. Capen Sept. 13, 1854.

Helen L. Wells July 5, 1857.

Emily F. Wells Jan. 17, 1858.

Charles Gustavus Wells Jr. Oct. 21, 1863.

Nathaniel Clark Wells July11, 1857. (End of Page 4)

Great Grandchildren: (Bottom of Page 3)

Andrew T. Hall Munroe born Dec. 29, 1849 at Paris.

John W. Monroe Sept. 28, 1851

Alice Monroe Nov. 1, 1854, died June 22, 1856.

Nellie Wells June 5, 1857.

Frederick Monroe Jan 24, 1858.

Charles F. Fowler April 16, 1858, died Sept 1858.

Henry W. Monroe Dec. 4, 1859

Ellen B. Smith Dec 2, 1858

George K. Smith Oct. 30, 1860, died Jan 9, 1862.

Henry L Fowler born Dec. 1, 1860

Mary A. Smith Feb. 28, 1863, died March 4, 1863. Benjamin T. Wells Feb 1862.

George P. Monroe Oct 22, 1864.

INDEX TO CHAPTERS 1 – 8, HISTORY

NEWS ITEM: EARTHQUAKE OF 1755

EARTHQUAKE OF 1755.

I have alluded to the religious use made of the earthquake of 1727. The records of the " Associated Pastors of the Churches of Boston," contain an account of the proceedings of the clergy in relation to that of 1755, which, as it may be interesting to some readers, I here transcribe : —

" *November* 18, 1755. About twenty minutes after four, A. M., there was a very severe shock of an earthquake, which lasted about two minutes ; at first it came on moderately, preceded by a noise ; the shaking a little after abated something, and then came on a violent concussion. Great damage done to many buildings, but no life lost.

" At ten o'clock in the forenoon there was a religious exercise at the Old South. Mr. Prince prayed ; Dr. Sewall preached ; a full and serious assembly. A religious exercise at the same time at the New North ; Mr. Mather began with prayer ; then sung a psalm ; after this Mr. Pemberton preached ; after sermon Mr. Eliot prayed ; then sung ; after which Mr. Checkley, Jr. prayed ; a full and serious assembly.

266